RASTA *and* RESISTANCE

From Marcus Garvey to Walter Rodney

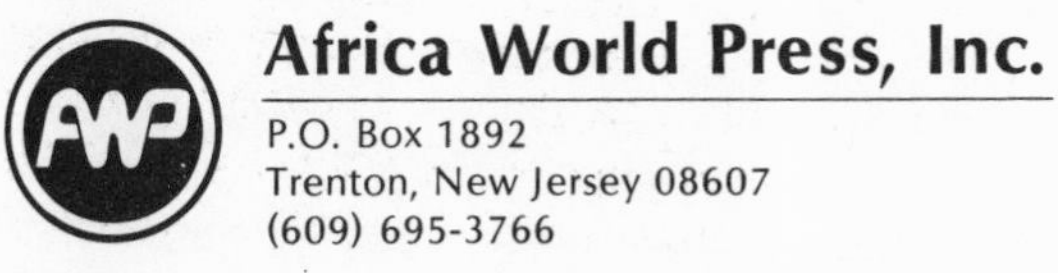

Africa World Press, Inc.
P.O. Box 1892
Trenton, New Jersey 08607
(609) 695-3766

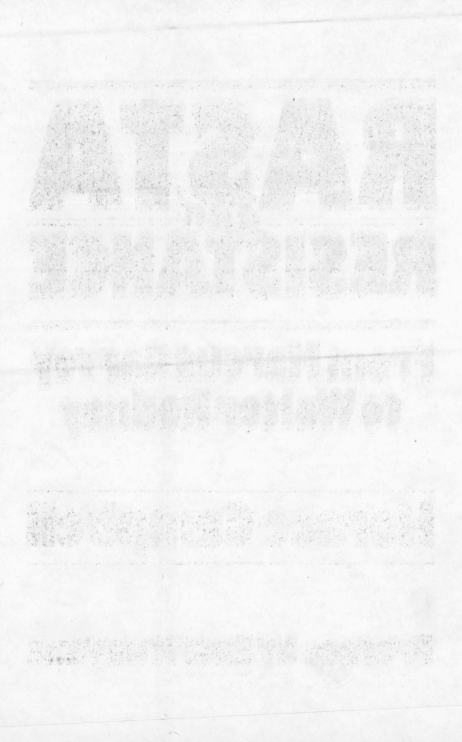

RASTA and RESISTANCE

From Marcus Garvey to Walter Rodney

Horace Campbell

Preface by Eusi Kwayana

Africa World Press, Inc.
P.O. Box 1892
Trenton, New Jersey 08607

First American Edition, 1987

Cover design by Adjoa Jackson-Burrowes

Library of Congress Catalog Card Number: 85-73332

ISBN: 0-86543-034-9 Cloth
0-86543-035-7 Paper

Dedicated to
My Late Father Ernest
My Mother Beatrice
and Bongo Clarissa
who has never wavered.

Acknowledgements

This study of the resistance of the Rastafari stemmed from a long period of active political and intellectual work among blacks and Rastafari in Jamaica, Canada, the Eastern Caribbean and the United Kingdom. In essence the study is a mirror of the Pan African traditions of the ex-slaves and this work was inspired by all those who urged me to merge my training in research and writing with the insights gained from living and struggling in the Pan African world.

It is impossible to name all those who gave active support in the actual process of the research. The research took me to the Eastern Caribbean, to the Library of Congress in Washington, to the old headquarters of the Ethiopian World Federation in New York, to Shashamane in Ethiopia, to the streets of Handsworth, Birmingham, in England, and the gullies of Jamaica. It is important to say that not a cent was contributed by any official state or philanthropic organisation. The actual process of writing and publishing this work reflects the upward struggle of the Rasta and dispersed African workers.

My wife, Makini Campbell, provided maximum support in many ways towards the completion of this work. David Johnson and Diane Powell read drafts of chapters and made useful suggestions. Vernella Fuller-Armah was very helpful in proof-reading. Thanks also to the staff at Hansib Publishing who were involved in the origination and production of the book.

Contents

Preface

Absence of a political enquiry into the Rastafari of the Caribbean has always been an uncomfortable gap in the record of the Caribbean revolution. Now Horace Campbell has made a big step towards the filling of that gap. This is not to suggest that Caribbean writers and thinkers (we should not confuse the two groups) have not done much investigation of the Rastafari way of life with all the clarity and depth which their areas of investigation permitted them; some have also ventured into the political dominion.

Campbell has many of the qualifications for the task he has undertaken. He has been struggling for some years to apply the scientific theory of society to the reality of African and Caribbean politics, and in the process has avoided the creation of false gods. When I first met him in Trinago in 1976, he said that he was a Marxist and that his mentors were Rodney, Fanon and Cabral. Readers of this work should welcome this attitude, because it is a clear indication of hostility to all forms of political and cultural dependence.

The formal emancipation of the African slaves in the Caribbean took place late in the first half of the 18th century. From that time there began a totalitarian assault on the African psyche, with similar aims to those of the various bondages imposed during the period of slavery. Some of the education was necessary to fit the African-Caribbean masses into the peculiar level of technology and the mode of production then ruling in the region.

The ignorance of the ruling classes, and their need for social control, produced a culture that filled the masses with self-contempt (Martin Carter). The splitting up of the free populations into classes more sharply divided than those of the slave period, and the introduction of immigrant labour from Asia, Africa and Europe robbed the masses in general of that self-confidence which is necessary before a people takes its destiny into its own hands. This is why the Caribbean has never resounded with anything similar to "Asia for the Asians" and "Africa for the Africans", regardless of the short-term nature of that nationalism.

Partly because of processes of this nature, and partly because of the uneven development of the integration process, the African presence has always had to find periodically a new mode of self-expression and self-proclamation from slavery until now. Experts in this area of study should review this claim. The need was not at all confined to African descendants. The Indian independence movement of the 1940s had a remarkable effect on the mass of the Indian population of the Caribbean. Movements with religious emphasis, or of religious reform, in India have also moved up the waters of the Caribbean.

What is it then that determines whether the dominant mode of expression argued above takes one form or another: bush negro villages, Maroons, liberated areas, Jordanites, Rastafari, Pocomania, Cumina, Spiritual Baptist, Islam? This is determined by the existing production relations and also by the place of the actors within those relations.

Campbell's book is thrice welcome because it deals with the historical, the political and the subjective levels of Rastafari. An individual crank here or there in any society can be ignored; a mass movement must be accounted for, as far as we are able to account for it.

The practising Rasta is a man of astonishing presence. In this country, Guyana, where the movement is perhaps weakest and most misrepresented, or in Trinago, the Rasta is typically male. He is a public figure, a picture of self-confidence and self-assurance. He is quick-witted and philosophical, flaunting his striking simplicity and peculiarity of dress in the face of cosmopolitan pretensions of Babylonian fashion. He exudes love. His conversation is lively verse. His replies are razor-sharp repartee. His world outlook is a duality of the material and the spiritual, the positive and the negative. His religious aspiration is total absorption into the being of Jah, to be achieved by contemplation and meditation.

The Rastafari faith, or even early liberation theology, has not escaped the dilemma which each of the great religions, especially Hinduism and Christianity, has set itself – the conflict between faith and works, contemplation and action. The fact that this very conflict now grips the soul of the Rastafari, in relation to politics, is not a sign of collapse but of maturity. So it is that there are differences of opinion among the Rasta, whether it is their work to storm the earthly kingdom and take it in order to change it; or to explain it, to enquire more deeply into the Maker and his mysteries; or to engage in both warfares.

The statement that the renaissance movements are determined in form by the production relations is not a mere phrase. Nor is the social need for rebirth an idle invention. Those who most consistently see it as an idle invention are precisely those whose education affords them the chance to learn the most about the slave experience.

Because the trampling of the sense of Africa was conducted with so much brutality during the course of slavery, and with so much ignorance, dishonesty and insensitivity after it, and because the institutions of propaganda which were raised up were so thorough and unrepresentative, every now and then Africans in the Diaspora have been gripped with the need to hold the old banner aloft. This need has been expressed in various forms and under the inspiration of various ideas.

At one period it is the "bush negro" movement or the Maroon version of the strategy of liberated areas, in which ideas of traditional religion and culture are mingled with ideas of state formation. Production relations at other times have taken the form of full-scale rebellion or revolution. At other times only pockets of conscious persons, with more interest in the spiritual than the physical, have been ready for the break with oppressive society. At later stages the main movement for self-expression has become more or less merged with the general movement of the whole population and no longer has race-worthiness as a major quest. As for the ideology of these movements, they have in various places, without comment on their quality, been inspired by traditional African religion, by Judaism and Christianity, by Islam, and they have produced the Jordanites, the Shakers, the Pocomania, the Cumina and the Rastafari.

The production relations determine the general form of the movement, because it is the social relations of production that will determine at any given moment the extent to which seizeable land is available, the extent to which it is possible to opt out of the market, set up a counter-market, and the extent to which formal schooling is an everyday need of the rebels.

Rastafari who wish to withdraw from the market and set up their own communities on the land are finding more and more that the modern state regards land not as a free gift of nature, but as an unfree grant of the state. This is what is meant by the statement that the forms of expression of the African presence are determined, at least in part, by the production relations of the day.

Campbell's concern is that many students of Rastafari see the movement as merely looking forward to a golden age. This is also the view of many in the ranks of the movement. In most of the great religions the majority of the faithful are content with the religious tenets of the faith, while an active group (often an influential minority) sees the social relations as an obstacle in the way of their dreams about a reformed humanity. Thus, while praying for all the necessary help, they work directly in the area of social relations. The two outlooks merge happily in the declaration of an early Christian saint, "I pray with my hands".

There are two problems facing the Rastafari community to which the public relations services of the movement and its allies need to give urgent attention. The first is the stubborn belief among sections of the public that the Rastaman is a criminal, and a violent one at that. Often this is a problem of the environment rather than of the Rasta themselves. Because Rasta is a dynamic lifestyle, and perhaps the only prestige-giving one within reach of the very poor, many of those already recruited into crime are attracted to it, just as daily in the courts of law we find accused offenders swearing on the holy books of Christianity, Islam and Hinduism, without casting the least slander on these religions. From the Rasta lifestyle, the poor wretches get attention and some esteem. They can use it as a weapon against any disparaging attack on a tainted past. Many offenders in prison may sincerely be converted: the brethren there may show others the light.

One case which slipped through the censors of the Guyana Broadcasting Corporation on a feature programme showed a clear link between crime and social policy. The programme featured a young offender who talked fluent Rasta language throughout the interview. He said that he had deserted his life of crime and hustle, and turned trader. However, the young woman Mayor of

Georgetown began to clear the pavements of traders in the interest of good order and a better Guyana. The offender said that because of this policy he was forced to stop trading and start hustling again.

Part of the problem is the other prospect offered to the Rasta by members of the establishment in various countries. These members are willing to let the Rastaman be; but only as a sort of agent and appendage to them as principals. The marijuana traffic, from the information at our disposal, is based on this kind of accommodation. The agent in the sub-culture is offered the prospect of earning money for his vital share in the traffic, but he must be prepared, at moments of public outcry, to "take a rap" and spend short periods in jail. At worst he comes out as a self-confessed recidivist, with ideas of earning money while he is out. At best he is able to step out of the ranks and join the ranks of a new petty bourgeoisie of the outcast in the slums.

The big question raised in this book is the role of the Rastafari in the Caribbean revolution. It is not an easy question. Yet it is a quest which is central to the movement against oppression in the Caribbean. It is so mainly because the Rastafari culture is perhaps the most influential cultural movement in the Caribbean today, in spite of the fact that many claiming to be Rastas in several places do all they can to discredit the movement. Wide cross-sections of the youth of various races are captivated by the style of the Rasta and in many cases by the bold thoughts and aspirations of the Rasta religion, by its thorough-going reclassification and redefinition of a life which wide sections of the society find unbearable and full of hyprocrisy.

The placing of the stamp of *Babylon* on the whole of official society and the wide acceptance of this description is one of the landmark achievements of the Caribbean revolution. The more it is seriously accepted, the more the culture divides into two poles of authority: a necessary forerunner to any long-term revolutionary objectives. Those members of the society who do not accept or embrace the dress, or need the religious ideas, accept the language; those who do not accept the language with the movement's redefinition of the order of things, accept the music. In fact, such is the power of art that Bob Marley's music has done more to popularise the real issues of the African liberation movement than several decades of backbreaking work of Pan-Africanists and international revolutionaries.

It is also relevant, as said before, that the mass of the practising Rastafari – as it was also with early Christianity – comes from among the most oppressed sections of the working population. The unemployed, the social outcasts from official society, and school drop-outs are all adrift. They see in Rasta life a way of being, a system or order, all giving dignity to the individual, not conformist dignity but an exciting anti-customary dignity.

It is no wonder that the style in whole or in part is assumed, sometimes internally, but often only externally, by wide sections of the oppressed and their allies in the Caribbean. Among these converts are included those who live by the hustle. They too yearn for dignity and they find it in Rasta. So it is that in many communities the people see Rasta as a criminal sect. It is this wide appeal, with due respect to the anti-Rastas in our midst, which makes the movement the formidable political force that it is, organised at the level of the sub-culture.

My own impression is that the Rastafari disdain to organise in the formal ways of a political party for political ends; that those Rastafari who become political activists are as effective as any other; that the Rastafari are not a party, that basically they shrink from the exercise of power over others, although many of them talk about a single power in the world. Yet it is the Rastafari who are most fitted to endure the trials and tribulations of a revolutionary process.

Perhaps the greatest single contribution of the Rastafari is at the level of consciousness, if I may use this term in the most common sense. By succeeding in branding the existing regimes and existing orders as illegitimate, and by winning mass support for this view even among persons who outwardly conform to the establishment culture, the Rastafari have made and are making an outstanding contribution to the Caribbean revolution.

Eusi Kwayana, Georgetown, Guyana – 1982

Introduction

"Rastafari has extended from a small and formerly undesirable cult into a dominant force which influences all levels of national life; and it has done so against formidable odds, political harassment and general condemnation. The Rastafari has dramatised the question that has always been uncomfortable in Caribbean history, and the question is where you stand in relation to blackness."

George Lamming, 1980

In his commentary on the Rastafari, George Lamming joined the ranks of those members of the Caribbean community who correctly noted that the Rastafari movement carried with it a certain continuity from the days of slavery, a continuity of resistance and confrontation with white racism.[1] The Rastafari movement, in all its contemporary manifestations, challenges not only the Caribbean but the entire Western World to come to terms with the history of slavery, the reality of white racism and the permanent thrust for dignity and self-respect by black people. The racial consciousness which was stamped yesterday in the Universal Negro Improvement Association, and which is today encrusted in the locks and beards of the Rastafari, stands as a potent force in the struggle for justice.

Race consciousness remains an integral part of the class consciousness of African peoples as long as Euro-American culture seeks to harmonise the economic and political domination of black peoples with attempts at destroying their cultural personality. Such a harmonising project of dehumanisation started in the era of the slave trade, when the day-to-day atrocities were unified by a cultural assault – whether French, Dutch, Spanish, Portuguese or British – to impose European ideas and values on the dominated Africans.

In the face of cultural resistance – manifest in religious practices, the preservation of African languages, African medicinal and healing crafts, and musical forms of communication – and open slave revolts, the slavers deepened their racist theories, building upon the original biblical justification for racial inferiority with the kind of pseudo-science which led to the theories of Arthur Jensen (that black people were genetically inferior to white people).

This study of the Rastafari spans the past fifty years, properly linking the emergence of Rasta to the roots of resistance to slavery. A recourse to the world of slavery, where the cultural and spiritual expressions of the slaves were preludes to armed revolts, begins in the analysis of resistance, centralising the role of religion among the slaves and their children, highlighting the importance of religious leaders such as Sam Sharpe and Paul Bogle.

Bogle's strident defence of the black poor, the Morant Bay Rebellion and the song 'Colour for Colour' laid the foundations for the development of Garveyism in the society. The incomplete crystallisation of the Jamaican working class, their dispersal by capital to Central and North America, the deformed racial hierarchy of whites, mulattoes and blacks, provided the background for the ideas of African redemption and deliverance which were to be so clearly articulated by Marcus Garvey. The convergence of the heritage of the Maroons, the religious movement – called Ethiopianism – and the emergent Pan-African movement which culminated in the U.N.I.A., were some of the forces which merged in the formation called *Rastafari*.

Rastafarians in Jamaica today see themselves as the conscious heirs of Garveyism. One Rastafari expressed this fact in the following manner:

> *"Many say Garvey is dead, yet it is clear that I and I sons of Marcus Garvey are still here making his philosophies a reality in 1980. Garvey was the undisputed champion of the black race, of the poor, of the working class and the downpressed. For this he was vigorously opposed in the land of his birth . . . I and I have been safeguarding Garvey's work for fifty years in an attempt to keep the predicted bloodshed within limits and to help the successors of Father Manley and Busta to solve the host of problems they take on their heads when they assume political power in Jamaica."*[2]

Here I. Jabulari Tafari was pointing to the role of the Rastas in the political life of the Jamaican society; and it is the continuity in the assertive racial identification of Garvey and the Rastafari which is the main thrust of this study.

The limitations of the all-class racial appeal of Garveyism were to emerge in the Rastafari movement, and nowhere clearer than when in 1980 a 'white' Rasta formation joined the white ruling class of Jamaica in quoting the anti-communist statements of Garvey during the 1980 electoral struggle. The problems of the racial divisions of the society are elaborated within the context of the capitalist depression of the thirties, which led to the massive revolt of 1938. The origins and growth of the Rastafari movement are explored against the background of the social conditions of colonial Jamaica, which led some of the rural poor to reject the British overlordship by identifying positively with the Ethiopian monarch, *Haile Selassie*.

This analysis of the Rastafari is developed to show the identification with Ethiopia as a profound response to the racial repression of capitalism. Rural Jamaicans were only one section of the black world which welcomed the crowning of this African King in an independent African Kingdom. This welcome had been preceded for a hundred years previously by an Ethiopian Movement which took the words of the Psalms – "Princes come out of Egypt, Ethiopia stretches forth her hands unto God" – to mean that Ethiopia would literally help in the emancipation of all blacks. Rastafari, who proclaimed that

Haile Selassie was the King of Kings and Lord of Lords, was taking the Ethiopian Movement one step further by centralising the person of Haile Selassie as the vehicle of liberation.

That the first Rastafarians were not madmen was clear to the society when both Rastas and non-Rastas raised their voices against the Italian invasion of Abyssinia in 1935. Leonard Howell, and those who sang that "The Lion of Judah shall break every chain and bring us victory again and again", found an international outlet for their ideas through the Ethiopian World Federation. The first doctrines of this young movement were linked, in this analysis of the Rastafari, to the writings of the *Voice of Ethiopia* (the widely circulated paper of the E.W.F.) to further underline the assertion that the ideas expressed by black Jamaicans that Haile Selassie was King of Kings (Ras over Rasses) was no mere millenarian escapism. The question which could be posed is: What made Jamaicans who positively identified with Haile Selassie millenarian, and those who identified with the images of the British King well-adjusted? The answer to this question is explored in the context of the idealism of the society.

The effects of this idealism could clearly be seen after the 1938 revolt, when the ideas of the Rastafari could not carry the sufferers forward. After the 1938 uprising, the working people of Jamaica were willing to downplay the strength of racial identification to accept the 'brown man leadership' of the fledgling two-party system. This compromise was a *holding action* which the working people accepted in order to oust the British overlords from the politico-constitutional sphere.

The continued wretchedness of the poor, the incipient political violence which was becoming a part of the political culture, and the leaderism and competition of the two-party system, had a debilitating effect on the unity and purpose of the working people. Membership of the Rasta groups increased in the fifties, accompanied by a strident call for repatriation, a call issued in protest against the massive population movement of the society. For between 1943 and 1970 the biggest movement of the population took place since the time of slavery, when over 560,000 rural Jamaicans were uprooted from their provision grounds by the bauxite tractors and earthmovers.

Herein lay the roots for the growth of the Rastafari movement inside Jamaica in the fifties. Because of the range of influences – Garveyism, anti-slavery resistance, Nyabingi, Ethiopianism – which came to bear on the growth of the movement, this study seeks to illuminate the elements which were paramount and does not seek to recount the history of Jamaica in this period. The richness of the pre-World War II struggles is captured by Ken Post in his book *Arise Ye Starvelings*; but the work has the limitations of representing the sufferers as Quashie and the Rasta as millenarian. Post's use of this formulation showed how pervasive the stamp of millenarianism had become. Both Marxists and non-Marxists took similar attitudes to this new force among the black poor of Jamaica, leaving behind a barrage of studies which have helped to create an image of the Rastafarians as 'escapists'.

Amilcar Cabral's notion of culture and resistance provides the theoretical foundation for this study in an attempt to bring a new approach to the analysis of the Rastafari. This African freedom fighter, who struggled for the highest form of cultural liberation, captured the essence of cultural resistance in the process of armed struggle against Portuguese colonialism, observing that:

> *"The value of culture as an element of* resistance *to foreign domination lies in the fact that culture is the vigorous manifestation of the ideological plane of the physical and historical reality of the society that is dominated or to be dominated. Culture is simultaneously the fruit of a people's history, by the positive or negative influence which it exerts on the evolution of the relationship between man and his environment, among men or groups of men within a society, as well as different societies. Ignorance of this fact may explain the failure of several attempts at foreign domination – as well as the failure of some liberation movements."*[3]

The resistance of the Rastafari to the neo-colonial society of Jamaica is examined against the background of positive and negative influences which this movement has exerted on Jamaican and Caribbean society. The rejection of the superstructural analysis of locks, beard and the chillum pipe is an effort to grasp the process and ideas which led to the development of the particular symbols of the Rastafari. Those studies which have been preoccupied with the external phenomenon of locks, beard and the divinity of Haile Selassie represent a particular world view, a view which supported the existing social order. This much was evident from the first major study of the Rastafari in 1960, which was seen as a "palliative to an explosive situation". The first *Report on the Rastafari*, published in 1960, set the agenda for future distortions of the Pinnacle settlement. Further research on the growth and the development of the Rastafari will help to correct some of the distortions, especially when the research is carried out from a perspective which is not anti-people.[4]

Efforts towards control of the Rastafari ranged from the ideological to the coercive, with the use of the Dangerous Drugs Law as the most prominent. At the ideological level, the incorporation of the Ethiopian Orthodox Church as a Church of State, subsequent to the visit of Haile Selassie to Jamaica in 1966, showed the failure of outright police harassment. It was not possible to keep on cutting the locks of the Rastamen and putting them behind bars; thus the sociology of 'political cultism' was taken off the library shelf to see if the movement could be isolated into the realm of an obscure 'sect'. But the movement kept on growing. The original spate of studies which stamped the movement with the 'escapist cult of outcasts' failed to explain the massive spread of the culture inside Jamaica, in the English-speaking Caribbean, and ultimately as the most dynamic force among the children of black immigrants in the United Kingdom.

There is no doubt that whatever the limitations of the cultural pluralist analysis, the emphasis on locks, ganja and Haile Selassie in this literature has had an impact on the development of the ideas of the movement. One only has to read the writings of the Rastafari in the fifties and the present organs of some Rastafari, such as the *Voice of Rasta,* to see the results of bourgeois sociology and anthropology.

Another of the original distortions of the movement which has gained currency is the stamp of criminality on the movement. From the original police harassment in the hills of Sligoville to the British police attitude towards the 'criminalised dreadlocks subculture', the ideas of those works which linked ganja to crime has given sustenance to State violence against the Rastafari. Rastafari confrontation with the State over the usage of ganja is examined to show the folly of the attempt to outlaw a popular custom, viz., the smoking of the chillum pipe.

However, as in all aspects of Rasta life, the dialectic of the positive and negative emerges in the form of the Coptics and the international trade in ganja. Similarities can be drawn between the takeover of the kola-nut trade in West Africa by the Afro-Portuguese in the era of the slave trade, and the intervention of the Ethiopian Zion Coptic Church in the new circuit of capitalist trade in ganja. The sophisticated methods of transport, procurement and harvesting of the Ethiopian Zion Coptic Church are a far cry from the original system of small farmers planting the weed as a crop to provide additional income. But, because the State has systematically used the Dangerous Drugs Law against the Rastafari, imperialism hoped to bind the brethren in a united bond with the Coptics, who wanted the weed legalised as a 'holy sacrament'.

The boast of the Ethiopian Zion Coptic Church in 1980 that "ganja saved Jamaica from Communism" raises further questions on the purpose of this 'white Rasta' formation which emanated from Star Island, Florida. The experiment in subversion by a pseudo-popular group had been duplicated in the other regions of the Caribbean, with the opposition elements in Grenada attempting to bind Rastafarians into supporting their international trading activities. From Handsworth, Birmingham, to St. Thomas, Jamaica; from the Turks and Caicos Islands to Soweto, imperialism has used the trade in this commodity to lure young blacks into the commodity fetishism of the capitalist order. Inside Jamaica the trade in ganja in the early sixties had provided the surpluses necessary for the growth of a lumpen stratum which was part of the ganja/gun/crime complex.

The Rastafari who had rejected the two-party competition were not aloof from the political struggles of the society. Instead of becoming pawns in the political game they used the medium of the Rasta song – reggae – to mobilise the people. Despite the promotion of religious forms, despite the distortions by the media and the infiltration of the ranks by lumpens (who wore locks), the Rastafari had begun to promote the cultural and musical forms in the search for a popular culture. Ras Daniel Hartman's depiction of the Rasta – as a lion-hearted man – complemented Count Ossie's use of the drum to fashion and deepen the music as a tool of communication, and become the Rastafari form of cultural resistance.

In analysing the culture of resistance, called reggae, it becomes clear that the conscious efforts to internationalise this music stemmed from the fact that the Rastafarians understood that in the neo-colonial society of Jamaica it was only the attainment of international recognition which would lead the music to become the music of Jamaica. Bob Marley, Jimmy Cliff and other reggae artists who took the music of the poor around the world were in the process of producing their music to contribute to a new anti-imperialist culture. Mastering the skills and technology of modern communication, the Rastafari song of defiance and inspiration took root in the world, spreading the anti-racist doctrines of the Jamaican movement to the Eastern Caribbean, and to the capitalist metropoles. Bob Marley's intervention on the side of the Zimbabwean guerillas, and his historic appearance at the Zimbabwean Independence Celebrations, signalled a shift in emphasis of the movement from the preoccupation with Haile Selassie and Ethiopia to the battles for liberation in Southern Africa. Peter Tosh, who as a youth had been arrested for demonstrating against Ian Smith in Jamaica, simply put the words to song in "We Must Fight Against Apartheid".

The Rastafari song – reggae – was the highest form of self-expression, an expression which was simultaneously an act of social commentary and a manifestation of deep racial memory. This memory had been kept alive by the attempt of the Rasta to build upon the foundations of the Jamaican language with their own contribution, called Rasta talk. The question of cultural resistance could not be examined simply within the context of music, since the food policy – called ital food – the language, and efforts at communal practices were as much a part of the rasta culture as the song of mobilisation which said "Get Up, Stand Up, Stand Up For Your Rights".

Walter Rodney's *Groundings* are analysed as part of the positive experience of a black intellectual who sought to "attach himself to the activity of the black masses". Rodney had perceived correctly that the Rastafari were "the leading force of the expression of black consciousness in the Caribbean", but he did not trail behind the movement; instead he brought his training as a historian to the movement, in an effort to lift the movement beyond the myths of Ethiopia and Haile Selassie. His exercise of *Groundings*, his clear identification with the most oppressed sections of the Caribbean people, were part of his awareness that the region should be liberated from foreign domination to be really independent. The Rastafari was one component of the people's right to their own history. He believed, as Cabral did, that the return to history could only be achieved when there was full development of the national productive forces. Cabral noted that:

> *"The foundation of national liberation rests on the inalienable right of every people to have their own history; whatever formulations must be adopted at the level of international law. The objective of national*

liberation is therefore to reclaim the right, usurped by imperialist domination, namely: the liberation of the process of development of national productive forces. Therefore, national liberation takes place when and only when national productive forces are completely free of all kinds of foreign domination. The liberation of productive forces and consequently the ability to determine the mode of production most appropriate to the evolution of the liberated people, necessarily opens up new prospects for the cultural development of the society in question, by returning to that society all its capacity to create progress."[5]

Walter Rodney, the Pan-African, Pan-Caribbean Marxist, saw within the racial expressions of the Rastafari a *possibility* of assisting the region to free itself from foreign domination. He was fully aware of the negative influences of the movement, but he was sure that if the positive attributes could be harnessed, without complexes and without underestimating the importance of the positive contributions of other cultures, the Rastafari movement could be part of the dynamic regeneration of the working people in their search for complete freedom from imperialist domination. Rodney used the tools of historical materialism to analyse the emergence of the Rasta, patiently pointing out to them that there was an Africa of the villages, and that only a small minority lived in Kingdoms.

The negative results of the question of race had put a brake on the unity of the working people of the Caribbean, with the Trinidadian and Guyanese working people burdened with racial insecurity. Rodney had grown up in a society where the politicisation of race and the manipulation of African and Indian workers had diverted the energies of the people. The spread of the Rastafari movement to the Eastern Caribbean was to be a major test of whether a movement which called for black dignity could manifest racial tolerance.

Conscious elements in the Eastern Caribbean identified the divisive racial alignments at the political level as a negative factor, and were working for a non-racial society, but those whose interest lay in exploiting the people would not want the Rastafari to prosper, hence they were seen to be subversive. The coercive legislation against the Dreads in Dominica, the discussion of the Rasta in Trinidad after Stalin's tribute to the *Caribbean Man*, and the subsequent role of the Rastafari in the Grenadian revolution in 1979 were clear signs that the Rastafari movement was destined to be part of a new Caribbean. Walter Rodney recognised this fact, and in his work with the Working People's Alliance of Guyana called for the recognition of the nature of the Caribbean working class which would necessitate the mobilisation of elements who were not at the point of production. Underdevelopment had rendered more than 40% of the population unemployed, and cosmetic measures such as 'Special Works' or 'Crash Programmes' could not deal with this fundamental problem of failure to fully mobilise the productive capacity of the working people.

The urgency of the task of harnessing the full potential of the working people, especially the Rastafari, became clear in the United Kingdom as the music of reggae took hold of the children of the immigrants. The explosion of this movement in the seventies confounded the social workers, leaving them to wring their hands while the police used all the power of the State against the youths who called themselves Rastafari. An elaborate system of social control over these youths, which began in the 'disruptive units' of the schools and ended for some in the Victorian prisons, was justified by State intellectuals who branded the Rasta with the stamp of criminality.

Building upon the foundations of the distortions which had been embedded in the first *Report of the Rastafari Movement in Kingston*, the Home Office and the media moulded a popular conception that the Rastafari formed a 'criminalised dreadlock culture'. British racism stared the Rastas in the face as a doctoral dissertation was woven to link Rastas to murder. The ensuing book, *Rastaman* by Ernest Cashmore, compared the Howell commune at Pinnacle to the murderous Charles Manson cult of California. Such distortions of the purpose of the Rasta call for more research and writing on the Rasta from a perspective which examines the social conditions of society which produces Rasta. More and more it is important that there is a need to study the institutions which oppress the Rasta and other black working people, instead of retracing the old ground broken by the first report in 1960.

It is inevitable that the Rastafari movement in Britain would be affected by the level of ideological development in the capitalist metropoles. The virulent white racism of the society and the befuddling of the working people with national chauvinism led to the impoverishment of ideas in this crisis-ridden capitalist centre. Caught in the society of militarists and racists, some of the negative ideas of the Rastafari came to the fore, and these were to manifest themselves in inter-personal relationships, with the Rasta women being burdened with the view that "women could only see fari through their men". Some elements sought biblical justification for their actions, as they manifested practices which were not particularly progressive.

Twice removed from their homeland in Africa and from their adopted home in the Caribbean, the Rastafari, as a part of the black population of Europe, yearned for a land which they could call their home. The sentiments towards repatriation, which were issued in the cry of the fifties – Ethiopia Yes, England No – re-emerged as the black immigrants sought to escape the growing racist attacks on the streets of Britain. Some young Rasta translated this yearning into a passionate appeal for repatriation.

Herein lay another contradiction, for the Rasta youths were calling for repatriation at precisely the time when the racists in the State apparatus were articulating the Nationality Bill and speaking about repatriating black people. Those who did not know African history were not to know that in another epoch there had been a convergence of a racist/humanist project in the Sierra Leone settlement. The chapter on Repatriation and the Ethiopian Revolution attempts to show the results of three former schemes of repatriation: the Sierra Leone forced deportations of 1786, the colonisation scheme of Liberia, and the

Shashamane settlement.

The Liberian Scheme has shown concretely that those who sought black dignity had to return to Africa with more than the search for respect, or they would carry with them the capitalist values of exploitation, as shown in the experience of the relationship between those who returned and the indigenous population. The settlement in Shashamane, Ethiopia, remained small, but similar problems of individualism and competition had dogged the settlement, especially when it was tied to the royal household.

It remains the right of any black person, whether or not they are Rasta, to repatriate to Africa, but such a move cannot be carried out under any illusions as to the nature of contemporary African society. That the continent of Africa is in ferment and that not even Rastas can remain aloof from this ferment was demonstrated in Shashamane when the Ethiopian people expropriated the land of the settlers in 1975. This act of expropriation was the way in which the peasants of Ethiopia, in the process of the Ethiopian revolution, were saying to the Rastafari that the Haile Selassie that they deified was not the same Haile Selassie who helped to mobilise the people against Italian fascism.

Would the Rastas listen to the people of Ethiopia and have the humility to understand that their embrace of Haile Selassie was an affront to the struggles of the African people? This question remains a burning issue, especially for those who have consciously built up rituals and hierarchy to create the Rastafari religion. Those who have not been carried away with the rituals are responding to the struggles of the people of Southern Africa, with the Grenadian Rastas showing that wherever there is clarity of purpose, the Rastas can be mobilised to struggle where they live.

The struggle in Southern Africa calls for Rastas to transcend the forms of cultural resistance to embark on a programme of cultural liberation which would release the creativity of black peoples everywhere.

Horace Campbell, September 1981, London

FOOTNOTES

1. Statement by George Lamming on the Rastafari, *Daily News*, Jamaica, Sept. 28, 1980.
2. I. Jabulari Tafari, "Rastafari and the Coming of Black Power", *Daily News*, Jamaica, Sept. 14, 1980.
3. Amilcar Cabral, *Return To The Source*, Monthly Review Press, 1972.
4. See the work of Robert Hill on Leonard Howell. Howell, one of the founders of the Rastafari movement, died in 1981.
5. Cabral, *op. cit.*

Chapter One

DO YOU REMEMBER THE DAYS OF SLAVERY?

Part I

Slavery and the Roots of Resistance

The atrocities of the Atlantic trade in human cargoes formed an indelible part of the consciousness of the African people of the New World as they daily toiled to produce wealth for Europe. The horrific Atlantic slave trade lasted for more than four hundred years and involved three continents – Africa, Europe and America.

Every Western European State, from Sweden in the North to Portugal in the South, participated in the commerce which was to change world history. The aboriginal peoples of the Caribbean and Central America were virtually exterminated in the wake of the search for gold and silver. In Jamaica and Barbados, the indigenous Arawak population and the Caribs were murdered by the buccaneers and pirates who roamed between the islands.

The Spanish were the most active in the Caribbean, a region of perhaps 50 insular settlements and over 2000 miles of sea. The sea dominates the region, with societies ranging from a few square miles and population of a few hundred, to the large island of Cuba with a territory of over 44,000 square miles.

It was in the waters of the Caribbean Sea that the European pirates fought each other for supremacy. The island of Jamaica was central to the struggle of the pirates, situated as it is in the middle of the Caribbean Sea, on the direct sea routes between North and South America, and between Europe and Panama. As a central station of the pirates, the notoriety of this island reached its zenith with the concentration of plunderers and explorers at Port Royal. The wealth accumulated from the piracy on the high seas and the plunder of the Central American civilisations went towards the setting up of plantations to provide sugar, tobacco and cotton for Europe.

Piracy on the high seas was transformed into piracy on land to exploit the labour of first the Indians, and later the African slaves. Christopher Columbus, the adventurer who laid the foundations for the Spanish military occupation of the region, had previously traded in slaves on the Upper Guinea Coast of Africa. Portuguese explorers had arrived in West Africa shortly before the middle of the 15th century and immediately started seizing Africans and taking them to work as slaves in Europe. This elementary trade was soon superseded by large-scale trade, when the European traders and bankers realised that they could earn enormous profits by using the labour of Africans to exploit the enormous wealth of the Americas.

This long-distance trade effected a form of organisation and support which strengthened Europe in the same way in which Africa was weakened. By the end of the Civil War in Britain, the English merchants, with the support of the Crown, threw all their resources into the slave trade. By the beginning of the 18th century Britain was the dominant slave trade State, ruling the high seas and binding the Spaniards with the right to supply slaves to Spanish colonies in British ships.

There was hardly a trading or manufacturing town in Britain which was not in some way connected with the triangular trade. In this trade, ships fitted out by European nations sailed to Africa, where slaves were bought for trinkets, cloth, guns, or alcohol diluted with sea water. These African slaves were then taken to the Americas where they were sold in return for goods produced by the very same slave labour. The precise numbers of Africans taken in this trade will never be known, because many perished in the Middle Passage (between West Africa and the Caribbean). It has been estimated that over 15 million Africans landed alive in this hemisphere, but for every African who reached the West, there was one who was killed in the process of the slave hunt, and between 25-35 per cent died during the crossing of the Atlantic.[1]

This savage trade laid the foundations for the primitive accumulation of capital to be re-invested in Europe, which ultimately made Europe the most powerful continent, such that by the 19th century they could militarily subjugate the richest continent on earth – Africa.

Eric Williams was very precise and detailed in illustrating the connections between British capitalism and the enslavement of Africans.[2] The wealth accrued to Europe was the other side of the barbarism and destruction unleashed on Africa. The African countryside, especially along the West Coast, was depopulated as the European nation states set about organising one of the biggest transportations of slaves in the annals of world history. The forts dotted along the coastline of West Africa today are the bloodstained records of a process which initiated the present underdevelopment and poverty in Africa.

Though the subjugation of the African societies was slow, it was a cumulative process which in the end engulfed even those functionaries who participated as intermediaries for Europe. Once the trade in slaves had begun, it was beyond the capacity of any single African State in any part of Africa to change the situation. The combined naval and economic power of the European nations, which were moving from feudalism to capitalism, ensured a level of technological superiority in important spheres of production, especially in the production of weapons. What the Europeans did was to take advantage of the divisions within Africa in choosing their allies. In the process, incipient differences between clans and embryonic nation states (called tribes by Europeans) were exploited; so that if the Europeans saw two sets of Africans at war with each other, they supported one side and helped them to achieve victory so as to be able to obtain captives.[3]

The Europeans managed to get prisoners of war from both sides. One group would be supported with guns made in France, while another group would be supported by the Danes, and yet another group by the Portuguese, but the end result was that Africans were sold and carried across the seas.

War and violence prevented the consolidation and unification of the nation state, such that even those societies which had developed beyond communalism to form powerful kingdoms[4] were weakened. As the most productive units of the society, the young and able-bodied, were sold into bondage, the challenge of eking out an existence was so much more arduous that those who remained were prone to epidemics and diseases. The ecological balance was changed in such a way that the depopulation was followed in later years by periodic catastrophes of rinderpest and tsetse fly infestation.

During the whole period there were African chiefs and headmen who were prepared to sell their fellow men in exchange for the trinkets of Europe. And yet these Africans, who allowed whites to build forts and send out raiding parties (graphically documented in Alex Haley's *Roots* in the capture of Kunta Kinte), did not have any control over the trade. Though it was only in the last resort that the invaders needed to use armed force, they were not hesitant to use this force, even against their 'allies' who had previously hunted slaves in the interior. Walter Rodney, in his reconstruction of the history of the Upper Guinea Coast, remarked that the only order or production which was possible was that imposed by the Europeans.

> *"Order, for instance, was introduced only in the sense that Europeans ceased direct raiding and turned to trade. But rapine and plunder, organised merchants, kidnapping that bred more kidnapping, deterioration in the customary law – all these lay behind the façade of relatively orderly and peaceful agreements between European slavers and coastal chiefs."*

Commenting on the actions of Africans towards Africans in fostering the underdevelopment and weakness of their land, he observed:

> *"In modern capitalist society, rules are drawn up to protect members of the possessing class from devouring each other raw; but on the Upper Guinea Coast and the West African littoral as a whole, capitalism paraded without even a loin cloth to hide its nakedness. With no restraints on either side, the confrontation of the two cultures was neither peaceful nor orderly, contrary to exploratory revision, and it proved entirely detrimental to African society which was the weaker party."*[5]

This destruction of Africa had to find expression in the realm of ideas; and the church in Europe, which was the principal ideological organ of the State, found biblical justification for the enslavement of blacks, turning the poetic "Songs of

Solomon" into the rationale for the bloody trade. Quoting "Songs of Solomon" Chapter One, verse five and six, priests blessed the Africans boarding the slave ships, while at the Vatican they debated whether Africans were humans or beasts. While the pontification as to whether slavery was divinely sanctioned was going on, the slave traders, merchants and bankers exposed the fact that the need for profits dictated the ideas with respect to the relationship between Europe and Africa. The bankers, shippers, and iron masters, who made the chains and anchors, pressed ahead with making their fortune, quietening even those who were appalled at the murders on the ships.

'Do You Remember On The Slave Ship, How They Brutalised My Very Soul?'

For those who were captured and chained, the ordeal on board the ship reinforced the conditions of kidnap and the forced march to the coast. Africans were packed like sardines in the hold of the specially made ships, and large numbers died of suffocation. The space allotted to each slave measured five and a half feet in length and six inches in width. Slaves were chained two by two, right leg to left leg and right hand to left hand, and each slave had less room than a man in a coffin. The well publicised hold of the typical slave ship showed how closely packed were the chained Africans on shelves and rows. The slave Equiano, who has left a written record of his capture, gagging and terror, had this to say of the hold of the ship on which he travelled across the Atlantic:

> *"The closeness of the place, and the heat of the climate added to the number in the ship, which was so crowded that each had scarcely room to turn himself, almost suffocated us. This produced copious perspiration, a variety of loathsome smells and brought a sickness amongst the slaves, of which many died, thus falling victims to the improvident avarice, as I may call it, of their purchase. This wretched situation was again aggravated by the gulling of the chains, now become insupportable, and the filth of the tubs into which the children often fell and were almost suffocated. The shrieks of the women and the groans of the dying reduced the whole to a scene of horror almost inconceivable."*[6]

Equiano's narration of the atmosphere of the ship revealed the greed of those insurers and bankers who profited from this cargo. And yet, despite these chains, when the slaves were taken on deck for exercise they struck, undid the chains, hurled themselves against the crew in attempts at insurrection, and oftimes threw themselves overboard. It was on the ship that they cemented bonds of unity and solidarity, and they were strongly attached to those companions who had come with them on the same ship from Africa. The term 'shipmate' symbolised the first Pan-African sign of solidarity and unity which went towards resisting the oppressive conditions of the plantations.

'When I Hear The Crack Of The Whip, My Blood Runs Cold!!!'

This refrain by Rastafari in the 1970s reinforced the brutalities of the passages to those who were unaware of the primary relationships formed on the ships. For the capture and middle passage crossing, where at least 30% of the cargo was fed to sharks, was reinforced by the seasoning process, or the struggle to break the spirit of resistance among the Africans.

On the auction block the white buyers examined the Africans as if they were examining cattle, and upon purchase they would be branded and given a European name. A red hot iron thrust into the flesh was the mark of being chattel slaves. The new name and the red hot iron rod were the first actions in the creation of a new docile chattel, but it took three years of seasoning, with the whip, to fully break the will of the stronger Africans. During this period of 'adjustment', which lasted between one and three years, between one-quarter and one-third of the Africans died.[7] This high mortality rate, even before the slaves began working, was such that slaves seldom lived for 9 years after their capture in Africa. One reason was that the owners found it cheaper to work them to death and then buy new slaves. While sugar was 'king', the slave masters found it cheaper to buy slaves than to rear children, and the slave population could not reproduce itself.[8]

This treatment gave an added impetus to the slave trade and Jamaica was not only a plantation colony, but it was also a centre for re-export to other British and Spanish colonies. Over a million slaves were brought to Jamaica during the period of slavery, of which 200,000 were re-exported. The very fierce slaves remained in Jamaica, and by the end of the slave period, there were only 323,000 slaves who survived.

As a centre for re-export, Jamaica was the prize of the British possessions, and the planters in Jamaica were the darlings of the British aristocracy in the 18th century, when the wealth of the slaves supported Earldoms and safe parliamentary seats. The organisation of the plantations, which supported the planter class, encompassed the highest form of capitalist organisation at that time - a form of organisation where the instrument of labour, the slave, was at the same time a commodity which could be replaced after being worked to death.

The sugar plantations required levels of capital which placed ownership outside the reach of the small white farmers. These whites employed jobbing gang slaves who would be hired out to the bigger planters. The production of sugar required costly machinery and equipment, and plantations were linked directly to the merchant houses of London, Liverpool, Bristol and Glasgow. The average estate in Jamaica ranged from 800 to 3000 acres, with the plains for growing cane, the rocky hills for the provision grounds of the slaves and the grazing ground for the cattle – the principal means of transport.

Because of the intensive use of cattle for transport, for turning the sugar mills, and for manure, the breeding pen was an important sector of this economy, and a class of pen keepers emerged in the society. Up to the present many place names in Jamaica bear the names of these pens, e.g., Slipe Pen, Rollington Pen, Admiral's Pen, May Pen, etc.

In essence the cows in these pens were treated better than the slaves, for the field slaves were driven as if they were the lowest form of animal. Because sugar production accounted for the bulk of the labour used in the slave society, it has been the focus of research and documentation. It was a system of production, like the production of tobacco and cotton in the Southern States of the U.S.A., which required hordes of cheap labour. The production process centred around the sugar factory, involving a complex system of production, with five main stages:

1. from the planting to the cutting of the ripe cane;
2. the transporting of the cane to the mill where the juice was crushed from the cane;
3. the boiling house where the juice was evaporated to a syrup and sugar was crystallised;
4. the curing house where the molasses drained from the sugar; and
5. the distillery where the molasses were made into rum.

This process called into being a wide range of workers, from the skilled slaves, such as carpenters, coopers, masons, sugar boilers, distillers, to the slaves who did the most arduous tasks –the field slaves. These slaves were distinct from that layer of 'house slaves' – the maids, butlers, cooks, gardeners and coachmen who acted as spies for the masters; and often the overseers would keep a string of mulatto women so that they could be kept informed of the rumblings of the field slaves.

Field slaves were expected to open up at least one hundred holes a day for planting the cane, and failure to do so was punished by whipping.* The slave started working at 4 a.m. and several jobs had to be completed before going to the fields; these included carrying mould to the cattle pens, cutting up the dung, making mortar, carrying white lime to the works, and doing various odd jobs. It was during crop time, when the cane was reaped, that the slaves were driven to exhaustion, because it was on the plantations that the factory system was perfected in preparation for the industrial revolution in Europe. Those estates which could not afford jobbing gangs worked two shifts, one beginning at twelve noon and the other at midnight.

*Some of the forms of punishment for the slave included "Burning them by nailing them down on the ground with crooked sticks on every limb, then applying fire by degrees from the feet and hands, burning them gradually up to the head, whereby their pains are extravagant.... For crimes of lesser nature Gelding chopped off half of the foot with an ax ... For running away they put iron rings of great weight on their ankles, or Pottocks about their necks, which are Iron Rings with two long Necks rivetted to them, or a spur in the mouth... For negligence they are usually whipped by the overseer with Lance-Wood Switches, till they be bloody, and several of the Switches broken, being first tied up by the hands in the Mill Houses. After they are whipped till they are Raw, some put on their skins pepper and salt to make them smart; at other times their masters will drop melted wax on their skins and use several exquisite tortures...." Patterson, *The Sociology of Slavery*, pp 82-87.

> *"The boilers and other Negroes who formed the spell about the works went to the field to cut the canes about 1.30 p.m. and continued to do so until it became too dark, about 7 p.m. They finished off by carrying cane tops or grass to the cattle pens and then rested for about four hours. At 12 midnight they received the spell in the boiling house and the rest of the works which had relieved them the previous noon. The relieved spell then rested until about 4.30–5 a.m. when they worked until 12 noon at which time they went to lunch and then returned to the works at 1.30 p.m., and so the cycle continued."*[9]

The field slave worked an eighteen-hour day and during his lunch break was expected to work in his provision ground, for the slavery form of capitalism did not take care of the subsistence cost of labour. Legal statutes compelled the planters to keep a small plot of land where each slave cultivated yams, plantains, and those agricultural products which they had planted in Africa.

In order to maintain the pace of the 16- or 18-hour day, the overseers employed *slave drivers* who were armed with special whips which, when cracked, sent a loud sound all across the fields, and left deep wounds in the flesh of the slaves. Some of the more renowned whips were the supple jack, cat-o'-nine tails and bamboo switch. These drivers, themselves slaves, often abused their authority and could themselves be whipped by the overseer for not forcing enough work out of the tired slaves.

Because slavery was not calculated to bring out the best in those who fell under its sway, whether owner or slave, the system had a debasing effect on the character of those involved. This was explicitly so for those tyrants who were head gang-men or drivers. These representatives of capital in the field, along with the house slaves, were permeated with the vices of their white masters and scheming bored mistresses, and they despised the slaves in the field. They internalised the ideas of their masters and were imbued with self-hatred.

Apart from the physical violence, the field slave was exposed to every form of outrage and mortification to break his spirit. There was no law to protect the slave and the institution of slavery was stamped in the colour of his skin. Race prejudice was emphasised to demoralise the blacks. Despite the efforts of the apologists who try to compare black slavery with the slavery of the Roman era, they forget that the children of Roman slaves were usually born free, and slavery was never reserved for one race. From the earliest days of Spanish occupation, indentured whites could be seen in the fields with blacks. This was soon deemed dangerous; colour was the most obvious sign of differentiation; and it became the legal and rational basis for keeping blacks in servitude. Slavery or bondage was deemed the natural role for blacks, and overlordship the right of the whites.

This distinction between whites and blacks was most fundamental to those whites who saw their white skin as the sole basis for their superiority to blacks. This was especially so where there were many poor whites, as in 18th century Haiti and in the Southern States of the USA in the 19th century. Spokespersons and the ideologues of that period refined the theory of racism to the point where some whites assiduously maintained that Africans were not human beings, but a lower form of animal, ordained by God to be the white man's beasts of burden.

The rise of white racism as a deeply rooted element in European thought took a leap in that period and can now be distinguished from all other forms of prejudice in the annals of human history. This was because no other system had claimed universal dominance as the world capitalist system did. The whip on the plantation in the 'New World' was only a lever in the long process of exploitation which centralised the wealth of the world in Europe, and later in North America. The well preserved records of the Jamaican plantation, where 300 years of continuous oppression of blacks were commemorated in 1970 in a document entitled *A Jamaican Plantation, The History of Worthy Park 1670-1970*, have given some idea of how much wealth was gleaned from Jamaica over the period. In addition, Eric Williams' *Capitalism and Slavery* states:

> *"In 1773 British imports from Jamaica were five times the combined imports from the bread colonies; British exports to Jamaica were nearly one-third larger than those to New England and only slightly less than those to New York and Pennsylvania combined."*

When in 1783 the abolitionists began their campaign, Lord North, the Prime Minister, reminded them that "the slave trade had become a necessity to every European nation". Planters from Jamaica also told these humanitarians that between 1790 and 1791 Jamaica sugar alone added "at least £1,600,000 sterling to the balance of trade in favour of the parent state".[10]

The Westindian islands were central to the accumulation process in Europe, and while many economic historians today examine the Jamaican economy or the British economy as if they were entirely autonomous, European economists in the 18th and 19th centuries had no illusion about the interconnections between their 'national' economies and the world at large. England, the seat of the industrial revolution, was the chief beneficiary of this plunder, for the county of Lancashire was for a very long period the entry port for the slaves at the port of Liverpool. The economic advance from ship building and banking at the Port of Liverpool led to investments in the textile mills which used cotton planted by the slaves in Montserrat and Georgia.

Eric Williams showed some outstanding examples of traders, insurance brokers and iron foundries which boomed out of sugar and slaves. The Barclay family owned slave plantations in Jamaica and it was from this accumulation that they were able to set up Barclays Bank, one of the foremost trans-national banks in the 20th century. A similar economic foundation led to the development of Birmingham as an industrial centre. Probably the most outstanding contribution the slaves made to the world of science was to provide the capital to finance James Watt and the steam engine.

A similar path of development took place in the United States of America, where the Northern colonies had direct access to benefits from slavery in the

American South, and in the British and French Westindies. As in Europe, the profits made from slavery went firstly to commercial ports and industrial areas, mainly the Northeastern areas of New England and New York. While the centre of capitalism boomed, the periphery of capitalism exuded forms of economic and intellectual backwardness which deformed the societies. The plantation society was fraught with debauchery, drunkenness and the kind of mental enslavement of those who kept blacks in bondage. Hence, the only source of creativity in the slave society were those who were supposed to be beasts of burden for Europe, the hewers of wood and drawers of water.

The slaves were fashioning a lifestyle of *survival* in the face of the bizarre mutilation which was meted out to them. A culture of resistance, which developed in a slow undramatic manner, exploded in massive slave revolts, and the planters were enslaved to the dread and terror that one night the slaves would organise to rid the world of racial slavery. Thus, two cultures were boiling in the Caribbean, one of domination and oppression which involved economic, political and racist subjugation, and a culture of resistance where the slave even transformed his personality to preserve his humanity, hiding the plans for open revolt. These two cultures struggled for dominance and it is only in the era of Rasta that the white culture is being beaten back. It is this resistance which links the revolt of the slaves to the present Rastafarian movement.

Resistance to Slavery in Jamaica

> *"I would rather die upon yonder gallows than live in slavery"*
>
> *Sam Sharpe, 1832.*

The existence of a repressive culture which harmonised the economic exploitation of black people with the idea of white supremacy prevented the constitution of a Jamaican national consciousness, hence the black man's consciousness as an African constituted the centrepoint of his identity. It is this identification with Africa which laid the foundations for the doctrine of Rastafari – an ideology which combined the resistance against oppression with an underlying love for the freedom and emancipation of Africa and African peoples.

African resistance to slavery began on the slave ship and continued up to the present. It was the struggles on the slave ship which led to the chaining of the slaves. The restlessness of the slaves caused revolts to be endemic and the slaves broke tools, committed suicide, ran away*, and mothers preferred their children to die at birth rather than to grow up as slaves. As early as 1522 slave revolts were taking place in the Americas, long before the slave trade had become central to the triangular trade. The rebellious nature of the slaves differed according to the areas which they came from in Africa. The Gold Coast slaves – usually called Coromantees – were supposed to be the most fierce. These slaves, from the Ashanti-Fanti speaking peoples, were the most feared by the slave dealers, and they featured prominently in the revolts. It is from the ranks of these Gold Coast Africans that the Maroons emerged.

The core of the Maroon community was the small band of slaves left behind by the Spaniards when the English captured Jamaica in 1655. These slaves formed the free communities which gave refuge to the runaway slaves. Major uprisings in 1673 and 1685, when the slaves rebelled in plantations in St. Ann and St. Catherine, increased the number of slaves living in the free communities in the hills. These slaves, called Maroons, carried out detailed studies of the soil, topography and climate which aided their strategy of guerilla warfare. This system of guerilla warfare, where the Maroons attacked the plantations at night, undermined the whole system of slavery.

The survival of the Maroon communities depended on the mode of social organisation of the villages. In order for the Maroons to survive they had to organise a system of production and exchange, superior to the plantation levels of co-operation, reminiscent of African communalism where they divided the tasks as they hunted, fished and gathered wild fruits.[12] Their scouts carried out intelligence activities on the white plantations to learn the military movements of the white people's army; they never confronted the whites on the plains and blew the *Abeng* horn to forewarn their villages of the impending attacks. This Abeng horn was made from the horn of a cow; the top was cut off, leaving a small opening about 1½ inches from the top end. There was also another opening over which the blower placed his mouth. The sounds were controlled with the thumb, opening and closing the small hole at the top end of the horn.

This *Abeng* horn became the sound of warning, war, and battle among the first band of Africans whose struggles were recounted throughout the world of slavery. For fifty years the British tried to suppress these offspring of Africa who, like the Saramaka Maroons of Surinam and the Cimaroons of Santa Domingo, challenged the system of bondage. The major Maroon War in Jamaica, 1729-1739, was fought under the leadership of Cudjoe, the son of Nangua, a proud Ashanti. Cudjoe had sworn that he would never become a slave and waged war for ten years, co-ordinating his battles with the Maroon

*This was the most widespread form of resistance, desertion from work. In Cuba the slave Esteban Montejo lived to tell his story of how he ran away from slavery. See Esteban Montejo, *The Autobiography of a Runaway Slave*, Penguin Books; London, 1970. Meanwhile, in the USA the runaway slave perfected desertion in the setting up of the 'underground railroad.' Harriet Tubman, herself a runaway slave, became the most renowned conductor in this struggle. For an analysis of the role of black women like Harriet Tubman, see Angela Davis, "Reflections on the Black Woman's role in the Community of Slaves", *Black Scholar*, No.4, 1971.

communities spread out over the island. They neutralised the superior weapons of the redcoats and lured them to mock villages where they would be surrounded and attacked from all sides. So successful were these blacks that the British army begged them to sign a peace treaty. Richard Hart quoted the desperate call by these whites, who called for more help from Britain in these words:

> *"We do ... apply to your majesty to implore your most gracious assistance in our present dangerous and distressed condition – the danger we are in proceeds from our slaves in rebellion against us ... our attempts against them having been in vain, only convinced us of our weakness; so great, that instead of having been able to reduce them, we are not in a condition to defend ourselves. The terror of them spreads itself everywhere ... The evil is daily increasing, and their success has had such influence on our slaves, that they are continually deserting to them in great numbers; and the insolent behaviour of others gives us but too much cause to fear a general defection; which without your majesty's aid and assistance must render us prey to them."*[13]

It was against this fear of losing their lives and after spending £100,000 that Britain signed a peace treaty with Cudjoe in 1739. By the terms of this treaty, sealed with blood, the Maroon communities were guaranteed a level of autonomy and independence which was unthinkable for blacks ir the 18th century. The four main terms of the treaty were:

(1) that the Maroons should govern themselves in their own communities in five main settlements – Moore Town, Nanny Town, Charles Town, Scotts Hall and Acompong Town;
(2) that the British should discontinue efforts to enslave the Maroons;
(3) the right of the Maroons to hunt and fish unmolested; and
(4) the continued ownership and occupation of Maroon lands.

It was over this final point that the British extracted a compromise from the Maroons not to give solace to runaway slaves. Britain hoped to use the ruse of taxation to force them to pay for the land, but they rightly asked why they should pay taxes or pay for the land when they were settled there before the British. So, while the British accepted that the Maroons could own the land, the Maroons promised never to give refuge to runaway slaves. This agreement paid dividends in 1865 when the Maroons saved the whites from being driven into the sea.

Going Back To Africa, Cause I'm Black

However, this treaty proved tenuous because the whites did not feel bound to honour the agreement, and in 1795 a second Maroon War broke out over the question of the flogging of two Trelawney Maroons in Falmouth. The British governor tried to enslave the Maroons, who insisted that by the 1739 treaty they should be tried in their own courts and any offence should be dealt with in their communities – they should not be whipped under the white man's law. With this provocation the Maroons resorted to guerilla warfare and inflicted serious losses on the local militia.

In desperation, the Governor imported large hunting dogs from Cuba. The impending use of these dogs led the Maroons to propose a second treaty which was quickly accepted by the Governor; but in a proper British manner the Governor organised the illegal deportation of 556 of these Maroons – they were taken to Nova Scotia in Canada. Mindful of their military skills, they were called upon to fight in the Napoleonic Wars against the French. There they acquitted themselves well in battle and after the war agitated to be settled in Africa. Fearing another outbreak of violence, and at the urging of the abolitionists, these Maroons were returned to Sierra Leone in Africa. They were the first group of blacks in the New World to be resettled in Africa.[14].

Me No No Quashie

The majority of slaves never accepted the system of slavery, contrary to the historical accounts which referred to the slaves as docile, lazy and child-like in character. This slur on the character of the black and African person has become entrenched in European thought, and in the Caribbean it is taught in schools, in the history books written by Carlyle, Trollope and Froude. But what the chroniclers of slavery did not understand was that the peculiar personality trait of the slave was in itself a response to and a form of resistance to slavery.

The black man, knowing that the planter expected him to be a dumb beast, acted his part well. It is from this personality trait that the "smart-man" Anancy character emerged, where it was said that Anancy "play fool fe catch wise". The majority of slaves adopted an attitude of wooden stupidity before the planters, and if asked an indifferent question, he would seldom give a prompt reply – pretending not to understand what was said, forcing a repetition of the question so that he or she could have time to consider, not what the true answer was, but what was the most expedient one to give.

Unfortunately, even recent writers on slave society have misunderstood this form of resistance and sought to give some intellectual support to the concept of lazy Quashie*. Being owners of the means of production and controllers of the State, the planter class were in a position to pursue policies which shaped the society, seemingly to justify the stereotype Quashie. It was a pity, therefore, to see Orlando Patterson quoting from pro-slavery journals of the time and seeking

*Quashie is the Akan name for a male child born on Sunday. It is used in Jamaica to refer to someone who is foolish or stupid.

*This line of reasoning, which gives a seemingly critical account of Quashie, is pursued by Ken Post in *Arise Ye Starvelings*.

to give an ambiguous account of Quashie without understanding how the African could change his very character to fight the unjust system*. Those who took the trouble to observe the slave outside the shadow of the whip were astounded at their dual personality. One white commentator, who gained the confidence of the slaves, remarked that:

> *"One has to hear with what warmth and volubility and at the same time with what precision of ideas and accuracy of judgement this creature, heavy and taciturn all day, how squatting before his friends tells stories, gesticulates, argues, passes opinions, approves and condemns both his master and those who surround him."*[15]

The slaves were fond of mocking their masters. They could laugh and talk about anything reprehensible that their masters did; they could invent nicknames which were most appropriate and would stick. This so-called Quashie could laugh at himself, his master and others around him, and this stood high to his credit.

It was at these nocturnal sessions that African stories were told; there was the telling of folk tales and the use of oral history to solidify the consciousness of being an African. In these sessions the hero was none other than Anancy, and stories of his genius were told with such precision that it played a part in moulding the cunning and guile necessary to turn the tables on the oppressor. Anancy symbolised the possibility of the underdog emerging triumphantly against the strong. The tales of Brier Anancy and his son Brier Tacooma reinforced the influence of the Ashanti among the slaves, and provided the psychological release necessary to face the day-to-day task of providing surpluses for Europe.[16]

The retention of African culture and religious expressions in Jamaica was enhanced by the continuous flow of new slaves to Jamaica. As a result, there was always a large proportion of slaves who remembered Africa, and these Africans commanded great respect, especially those with a knowledge of African medicinal practices and religious rites. They were in the forefront of transmitting the tradition of oral history and restoring those African beliefs to slaves who were being creolised.* It was these slaves who generated and stimulated the practices which resisted the cultural and ideological domination of Europe, and their religious rites symbolised the struggle for self-expression and dignity.

In every sphere of life, in language, in the planting of his provision ground, and in the burial of the dead, the slave sought to preserve his dignity as an African person. This was so marked that in death the slave believed that they would once again return to Africa; consequently, their relatives and friends would leave rum and food at the graveside so that the departed one would not go hungry on his journey to Africa. Funeral rites were accompanied by music,

*This word, creole, has been handed down in Caribbean literature to depict the mulatto culture of ambivalence.

dance, drumming and song. The jubilation at the return of the spirit to Africa was not tempered with grief; many slaves committed suicide rather than live in slavery. The songs and lamentations sung at the graveside were of hope. One popular song, sung by Africans throughout the New World and later featuring prominently as a Negro spiritual, said:

> *"Oh Freedom, Oh Freedom, Oh Freedom I love thee*
> *And before I'll be a slave, I'll be buried in my grave*
> *And go home to my Lord and be Free."*

This song depicted freedom in a promised land, in this case consistent with the promise of freedom in the life hereafter of the Christian religion. In Jamaica, the religion of the slaves was distinct from the religion of the masters until the end of the 18th century when Baptist missionaries began to be active among the slaves.

Formerly the planters were opposed to any religious instruction being given to the slave, and when the Moravians and Baptists insisted that by Christianising the slaves they could make them better slaves, the masters refused to countenance the possibility of any religious teaching which could make the slaves literate. Even so, the blacks resisted the Christian religion and only a section of those exposed to free black ministers, like the ex-slaves George Lisle and Moses Baker, were responsive to the European version of Christianity. In the main African religious expression held sway in the hills.

Of the Spiritual World and the Material World

The era of the renaissance and enlightenment in Europe led to a sharp division between the spiritual and the material worlds. The philosophy of mechanistic materialism, which was consistent with the rise of capitalism, separated matters of the soul from matters of science and technology. The ideology of enlightenment postulated that science and technology, by their 'progress', determined every sphere of life, transforming social relations in the process. Feudal ideas which said that progress was guided by God were superseded by the notion that this function was fulfilled by the 'laws of nature'.

In this way, religion was retailored to conform to the reproduction of alienation and to justify capital exploitation of labour. The Christian religion, like all other religions, then settled the problems of relations between people and nature and the relations among people (social classes). In the process, myths concerning the European variant of Christianity were developed to justify the plunder of the globe. The European mode of social organisation and concomitant ideological (religious) formulations, claimed universal validity in that the capitalist system was the first global system. Thus as a universally valid religion, the ideological organs in the form of the established churches, whether the Dutch Reformed, the Anglican or the Catholic Church, rationalised and blessed the plunderers of the globe.

It was therefore not surprising that for three centuries the slaves resisted this ideology, and the European religion was practised only by those slaves who were creolised. For those Africans who held on to the vision of Africa and the religion of their ancestors, their ceremonies were carried out in the hills and slave huts, out of the reach of the masters and their mulatto underlings. In the eyes of the established church, where the debauchery, rape and kidnapping was sanctioned, the religious rites of the slaves could only be pagan and cultist.

This ideation has been handed down and reshaped by modern anthropologists and sociologists, who term African religious practices which they cannot control 'cultist' or 'millenarian'. Laws were passed against African religious expressions such as Cumina and Shango, and the use of the drum, the main instrument in the outpouring of emotions which went with these ceremonies, was banned. This attempt at legal extermination forced the most overt African expressions underground, and it is not surprising that they only emerged in the revival of 1860-61, and the more African form, called Bongo cult, was not observed until the 1950s.[17] The Bongo men were slaves who defied authority and recognised no authority higher than themselves.

Europeans denigrated African religion both in the New World and in Africa. A barrage of derogatory treatises were written in Europe which called African religion ancestor worship, superstition, magic, fetishism and paganism. But the Bongo men who resurfaced were the product of African religion, the product of centuries of development and the accumulated experiences and ideas of generations. These religious and cultural experiences (developing independently according to region) were interwoven with religious ceremonies, rituals and beliefs, and guided the evolution of customs.

Because the crude materialism of capitalism did not exist in Africa, the spiritual world was not separated from other spheres of human endeavour. All things, material and immaterial, were linked to the spiritual needs of the society. Hence, various foodstuffs, tools, utensils, clothing, shelter, art objects, the drum, and collective monuments were all linked to the spiritual needs of the society so that these objects served as use-values, while at the same time being the means of expressing scientific ideas and beliefs, and satisfying emotional needs. An African utensil was not just a utensil, it was a work of art and an expression of religious emotion as well.

This is why all over Africa scientific achievements, such as the building of pyramids in Egypt, the acropolis in Zimbabwe, or the Axum temples in Ethiopia, were linked to religious expression. There was no need to separate science from religion, and religious leaders had high standing in the communities. This is not to say that there was no social differentiation, for myths concerning natural phenomena and the means of placing them at the service of the community were integrated in a broad philosophy to justify the social order.

This was most pronounced in those areas where the State had emerged (particularly in the great Kingdoms of Axum, Egypt, Nubia, Mali, Songay and Zimbabwe). In these States religious ideology functioned to justify the paying of tribute by the toiling masses. Like the great religions of the East – Islam, Buddhism, Hinduism – African religions served the reproduction of social hierarchy, and the more developed the society, the more important religion was in stabilising the system.

Religion and Resistance

For three hundred years the religion of the slaves' ancestors survived in the New World, and in Jamaica it was not until there were native literate preachers that the Christian religion began to gain some currency. The history of the Baptists in Jamaica is replete with the struggle to convert the slaves while maintaining some sense of dignity in being African. Black preachers who were literate began to gain influence at the end of the 18th century, because they could read and write, and in this way they could interpret the great debates which were raging in England between those who wanted the slave trade abolished and those who spoke for the local assembly and called for even more brutalities.

It was this quest for literacy which began to influence the slaves towards Christianity, for the literate Mandingos could not read the English language. Black preachers of the Baptist denomination used the bible as an ideological tool, preaching deliverance, and the stories of the bible which depicted resistance were the most popular among the slaves. Outside the organised churches, the fusion of African religious ceremonies and the words of the bible were best expressed in a religious formation called *Pocomania*.*

The modern Pocomania was a spin-off of an African religion called Cumina, and the intense drumming of the ceremonies was considered subversive by the planters. The planters had good reason for fearing these religious practices, because those Africans who possessed training as spiritual leaders commanded great respect, and they were usually the ones in the forefront of revolts.

Jamaica acquired special significance during the period of slavery, not only because it was the most prosperous of the British colonies, but also because it was the area of the most slave revolts in the New World. There were more than 400 revolts with major confrontations in 1729-39, 1760, and 1831-32, each involving over a thousand slaves. The Akan slaves were militant, and the ones called Coromantees shook the hearts of the planters.

The Armed Slave Revolts – From Tacky to Sam Sharpe

The 1739 peace treaty between the British and the Maroons had made the problem of revolt more difficult, but this did not stop the regular uprisings. Numerous organised plots emerged, only to be given away by weak-hearted slaves or those mulattoes who were the eyes and ears of the masters. One of the

*This Pocomania is still a very powerful force among the working people of Jamaica. It is derived from the *Cumina* religion, a form of religious expression which was accompanied by elaborate ceremonies, drumming, singing and spirit possession. See Leonard Barrett, *The Sun and the Drum*.

most organised revolts, after the Maroon War, was the rebellion of Tacky, another Gold Coast African. The rebellion was planned in secrecy among the Coromantees throughout the island, who aimed at "a total massacre of the whites and to make the island a Negro colony".[18]

More than a thousand slaves were involved and for six months in 1760 they fought the planters. It was only after Tacky, the strategist, was killed that many of them committed suicide rather than allow themselves to be enslaved. The usual vengeance of the white population was meted out. During the course of the rebellion 60 whites were killed, and in the aftermath 600 slaves were executed. Patterson details 18 plots between 1765 and 1784. In one case, in 1776, when a plot was discovered in St. James, the whites reacted with their developed and cumulative brutality; those involved in the plot were gibbeted, burnt alive, hanged or transported out of the island.

The struggle for freedom and independence epitomised by the Maroons and articulated by Tacky was carried to its historical conclusion by slaves in Santa Domingo – now called Haiti. The rebellion of the Africans in Haiti shook the foundations of slavery and capitalism in the Caribbean, North America and Europe. This revolt exposed the military genius of the black general, Toussaint L'Ouverture, and led to the creation of the first black independent State in the New World. This revolt – the Haitian Revolution of 1804 – was the only case of a successful rebellion in Caribbean history, not only on the cultural plane but also on the political and economic planes.[19] René Depestre, the Haitian revolutionary who has himself seen the limitations of this cultural and nationalist victory, conceded that:

> *"This successful slave revolution – the only one known in human history – was in itself a glorious act of identification for the black man. It showed the entire world that liberty and human dignity also have a black face in the history of civilisations. It further highlighted, in universal life, the personality of the black man by giving full exposure to great men like Toussaint L'Ouverture and the heroes of the early independence era in Haiti.*
>
> *"The Haitian revolution also allowed the Negro, wherever he is in America, to acquire a new vision of himself and to begin to destroy all the stereotypes of the Negro which had been created by colonialisation."*[20]

This act of liberation in Haiti was an inspiration for slaves in the New World in the same way in which it deepened the fear of the whites. Jamaican slave-holders trembled for their safety as they followed the victories of the black freedom army and their already precarious sense of unease was further jeopardised by the appearance and tales of those refugees arriving in Jamaica. Slaves and mulattoes who had been pressed into the Westindian regiment to fight their brothers in Haiti were refused permission to re-enter the island. They happily returned to join the Haitian Revolution. Even the much celebrated philanthropists in the United Kingdom were shaken by the fact of black people making their own history. In Haiti slaves had given wider meaning to the concepts of liberty and equality evolved by the bourgeois philosophers of the French Revolution; and the British abolitionists were blind to the possibilities of slaves involving themselves in their own liberation. In essence, the anti-slavery movement was distressed by every sign that slaves intended to take matters into their own hands.

Pressures in England at that time consisted of parliamentary initiatives towards amelioration of the whippings and wanton brutalities. But in Jamaica, the planters panicked and vowed never to give up their 'right' to enslave black men. This was the political expression of a dying stratum; by the beginning of the 19th century the changes from mercantile capitalism to industrial capitalism was such that the leading capitalists (the industrialists) found that the trade in slaves and the use of slave labour were no longer in the interest of further development. The spokespersons for the industrialists were the abolitionists, such as William Wilberforce, who understood that the transformation of slaves into wage labourers would mean an increased market for the rising industrial bourgeoisie, increased production, and increased profits. These abolitionists saw the process of emancipation emerging gradually over 40 or 50 years, and though the trade was illegal after 1807, they deliberately decided to go easy on the question of full freedom.

While they equivocated, the slaves decided to take matters into their own hands. Those slaves who could read and write eagerly read the reports of the anti-slavery movement, and the insurrectionary movement swept the islands. There were rebellions in Barbados in 1816 (involving over 13,000 slaves), in Trinidad in 1819, 1825 and 1829, and in Antigua in 1831.[21]

The year 1831 also witnessed a major revolt in the United States when a literate preacher, Nat Turner, started with a force of six men and swept the State of Virginia, moving from plantation to plantation, freeing the slaves. All these rebellions were discussed with trepidation by the planters, who openly expressed their determination to defy any Act of Parliament to abolish slavery.

To demonstrate their will to be free, the slaves in Jamaica organised the biggest slave revolt in the Western part of the island when over 20,000 slaves rose up and for two weeks set free the slaves in the parishes of Trelawney, St. James, Westmoreland, Hanover and St. Elizabeth.

The widespread nature of the revolt and the organisational skills which went into the planning was the result of a new kind of leadership; this was the leadership of the religious preacher, literate in the English language and in the African religious practices, who combined the ideas of deliverance and resistance. It was a leadership which could read the newspapers and interpret debates to fellow slaves.

Such a leader was Sam Sharpe, who was a 'native' Baptist lay preacher. He worked in close co-operation with other leaders such as 'Daddy Thorpe', an African religious teacher whom the whites called a myal man.

Sharpe used the freedom of movement which he earned as a lay preacher to mobilise the slaves on the plantations in four parishes. He carefully laid his plans from August 1831 and ensured that there were no weak-hearted men among his cadres. When the whites thought they were holding prayer meetings, Sharpe was holding forth on the evils and injustices of slavery, and then binding his followers with an oath telling them that "if black men did not stand up for themselves and take their freedom, the whites would put them out at the muzzle of their guns and shot them like pigeons".

The plot was simple. The slaves planned to use the period of the Christmas break, 1831, to lull the whites into believing that the merrymaking and dancing of 'John Canoe' was a sign of contentment. Three days after Christmas, when the slaves were supposed to return to work, the signal to begin the battle was given when slaves at Kensington Estate (on the hills overlooking Montego Bay valley) burnt the trash houses. That very night the fire and drum signalled the beginning of an all-out attempt by the slaves to free themselves.

Local commanders, who had previously taken on the guise of deacons, proceeded to march from plantation to plantation freeing the slaves and burning to the ground the homes of the most vicious planters. The drum, conch shells and the blowing of horns called other slaves to the ranks, so that before the night was out 20,000 supposedly docile slaves were precipitating the death-blow to slavery in the British domains.

As usual, capital was called upon to defend its own interests and one of the most feared overseers, Grignon, assumed the rank of Colonel to command the Western Interior Regiment to defend the estates. But the determination of those who stood up for their rights was such that Grignon soon had to retreat to the sea, along with those whites who had already been put out to sea in the Montego Bay Harbour. This retreat left the countryside to the slaves, who pushed from Montego Bay to Savanna la Mar, freeing slaves and blowing the horns of freedom.

From the safety of the harbour Grignon sent a column of 'coloured' troops to engage Sharpe's liberation army, but the slaves retreated only to attack when the militia were on the defensive. In one battle, when the whites were retreating from Montpelier, the slaves attacked and forced the whites down towards the sea. All the plantations were under the control of the slaves and the Governor declared martial law when over £1 million of plantation property had been razed to the ground.

Knowing that the slaves believed that Parliament had abolished slavery, the Governor declared an Amnesty for those slaves who would surrender. This call for Amnesty was couched in language which suggested that slavery had indeed been abolished and that the British Army would do them no harm.

The promise of Amnesty led the slaves to lay down their arms, but the whites who had been held prisoner now carried out their blood-thirsty passions. The blacks had allowed some whites to flee, and during the two weeks that the slaves held control of the plantations, only fourteen whites and three mulattoes were killed. Yet after surrendering thousands of Africans were put to death by bullets, firing squads and by a gallows which was erected in the central square at Montego Bay. Those who escaped death faced the lash: 500 lashes, 300 lashes were the order of the day.

Henry Bleby, a missionary who recorded for posterity the atrocities of the whites, tried to induce confessions from the slaves who were on the way to the gallows; but Sam Sharpe, who was executed in Montego Bay on May 23, 1832, refused to utter a word of remorse, telling Bleby that:

> *"I would rather die a slave upon yonder gallows than live in slavery."*[22]

Bleby and other commentators were astounded at the richness in spirit of the leaders of the revolt. They were amazed at the capacity for reasoned discussion and clear exposition of ideas exhibited by Sharpe and his deacons. For in the consciousness of those who had internalised the idea of the black man as a beast, the intelligence of Sharpe and his organisational skills were a rude awakening. Bleby accurately understood the implications of this revolt and he remarked:

> *"The revolt failed of accomplishing the immediate purpose of its author, yet by it a further wound was dealt to slavery, which accelerated its destruction, for it demonstrated to the imperial legislature that among the Negroes themselves the spirit of freedom had been so widely diffused, as to render it most perilous to postpone the settlement of the most important question of emancipation to a later period.*
>
> *"The evidence taken before the committee of the two Houses of Parliament made it manifest that if the abolition of slavery were not speedily effected by the peaceable method of legislative enactment, the slaves would assuredly take the matter into their own hands, and bring their bondage to a violent and bloody termination."*

The Sam Sharpe rebellion forced the question of abolition in England, and the British Parliament legislated for the abolition of slavery in all British dominions on August 1, 1834.

Part II

From Emancipation to The Morant Bay Rebellion of 1865

"Blood, blood, we must humble the white man before us."

When the emancipation proclamation was read on the steps of the government buildings in Spanish Town on August 1, 1834, there was jubilation, singing, drumming and shell blowing. But the dancing did not end before it sunk in to the former slaves that £20 million compensation had been paid to their masters and they had to serve a four-year mandatory period of apprenticeship.

Apprenticeship was a transitional expedient to convert slave labour into wage labour. The planters tried to get the maximum amount of labour out of the workers, while the blacks preferred to do their compulsory 40½ hours in the first four days and then have the other three days to work on their provision grounds. Those planters who had used the shift system during crop time now found that blacks refused to work at night, and in the confrontation between estate capital and labour the whites used coercion and legal fiat in their hope to survive on the estates.

However, changing conditions in Europe made the demands of the Westindian sugar interests subsidiary to those of the rising industrial bourgeoisie; and in any case, the sugar importers could buy sugar cheaper from Brazil and Cuba, where slave labour was still being used. Planters tried to control workers by levying rents on their houses and provision grounds. When they realised that the Africans placed great importance on the burial places of their ancestors, the planters taxed the grounds as a way of ensuring that the blacks supplied a continuous flow of labour. Use of taxation as a means of alienating labour was enacted in Jamaica prior to its widespread use in colonial Africa.

The response of the blacks was to leave the sugar and coffee estates and go to the hills. When the planters clamoured for more cheap labour the colonialists imported Asian indentured labour in order to cheapen the cost of labour, and between 1834 and 1865 6,000 Indians were imported into Jamaica.[23] However, the number of Indians imported was insufficient to affect the demands of the blacks, and this did not have the divisive effect on the class struggle that it had in Trinidad and Guyana.[24]

Black workers employed varying tactics in their struggle with the planters, who had become so accustomed to slave labour that they made no effort to improve the conditions of work by introducing new machinery or an economic infrastructure capable of properly utilising the resources of the society. Those who survived exported their profits to England, wallowed in conspicuous consumption and cursed the hard-working blacks as being lazy; thus laying the cornerstones of the economic dependence which still plagues Jamaica.

It was a parasitic stratum which aspired to give social and cultural leadership to the society and found that they had to build upon the foundations of racism to maintain their social position. The decline of the plantation system led to bankruptcies, and by 1860 half of the plantations had folded up. Jamaican planters did not have the resources to entrench the system of peonage, like that of the sharecropper system of the USA after slavery, where blacks were permanently indebted to big landowners.

In Jamaica the merchants and the Jews took advantage of the plight of the bankrupt planters to buy up many of the deserted properties, so that by 1860 the Jews, who had hitherto been discriminated against, began to call for a share of political power in the society.*

The strict and deformed racial hierarchy of the post-slavery society vested political power in the hands of the white planters. Below these planters were the Jews and an energetic stratum of mulattoes, the product of white and black miscegeny. By 1860 the Jews had begun to dominate local parish politics, while the mulattoes spurned agricultural work and sought to dominate the professions which serviced the plantation system. The mulattoes wanted to avoid agricultural work, for it reminded them of the rapacious activities of their fathers and their link with the black man.

Indeed, the sexual exploitation of the black women by the white men was one of the most disgraceful and iniquitous aspects of slave society.

> *"Rape and seduction of infant slaves, the ravishing of common-law wives of male slaves, under threat of punishment, and outright sadism involving the most heinous forms of social torture were the order of the day. It was common practice for a white man visiting a plantation to be offered a slave girl for the night ... Many of the white employees on the estate had a rotation system whereby they seduced every desirable female on the plantation over and over again."*[25]

It was this rapacious and dehumanising activity which gave rise to the 'coloured' or mulatto stratum who resided in the towns. Numerically, the mulattoes came to outstrip their fathers not only by natural increase, but because efforts towards settling white immigrants after slavery failed in the stagnant economy. Most mulattoes clung to forms of behaviour which were even more pro-British than those of the planters in terms of language, dress and religion, in order to identify themselves outwardly as a community with a different heritage from the mass of blacks.

*Because Jamaica had been a centre for slave buying and selling in the boom days, the Jewish merchants, who were the descendants of Portuguese and Spanish Jews, made money as slave dealers. However, they were discriminated against by the English and when the blacks began to stir, the whites found them willing allies. For a discussion of their political struggles in the 19th century see Jacob Andrade, *A Record of the Jews in Jamaica from the English Conquest to the Present Time* (1940), Kingston, The Jamaican Times Ltd. 1941. See also Benjamin Schlesinger, "The Jews of Jamaica", *Caribbean Quarterly*, Vol 13, No. 1, 1967.

They concentrated in the urban areas where there were opportunities for educational and political advancement; so much so that in the 19th century economic differences between town and country took on racial overtones. The mulattoes accepted the superiority of the whites and the inferiority of the blacks. Special schools, such as Wolmers Boys School, were organised for them, and many became clerks, journalists, lawyers, teachers, actors and preachers.

At the bottom of the society were the ex-slaves; but the black population was not entirely homogeneous. There were distinctions between children of the freeborn and the children of the slave drivers: they were alike in that they were invariably the blacks who were able to set up plots with land titles. Differentiation of land holdings took place within African ranks, and a few successful farmers of provisions and sugar cane could employ mules to make their own sugar.

Douglas Hall estimated that of the 317,000 Africans in Jamaica 218,530 were freed in 1838 and by 1840 there were approximately 3,000 who owned land of over 10 acres. About 20,000 owned plots of 2-10 acres, while the vast majority were strugglers who operated as workers and small farmers. It was this mass of struggling blacks who formed the embryo of the Jamaican working class.

These blacks, who removed themselves from the estates to set up free villages, have been described as 'peasants' in spite of the fact that some of them continued to work full-time on the estates, while an even greater number were part-time workers. In some sense their relationship was partly determined by geography: the blacks of Vere, St. Catherine, Westmoreland and Trelawney had little scope for bargaining as there were fewer opportunities for growing provisions in the hills.

The crude interpretation of the 'rise of the peasantry', with all its political implications, has been repeated in recent books on the struggles of the Jamaican people; but it overlooks the behaviour of the African wage earners in the period after slavery. The movement of the ex-slaves away from residence on the plantations has been wrongly identified with the movement away from estate employment; but the owners of the estates in their negotiations over rents and provision grounds understood that they had to bargain with the former slaves.

These ex-slaves were acting as a wage earning proletariat in their struggle for independent action within the limits of the plantation system.[26] Village residence farming and petty trade (hawking) were both discouraged by the planters, not only because these activities removed labour from the estates, but also because it increased the scope for independent action on the part of those who remained. The planters were vehement in their opposition to free villages such as Sligoville which had been set up by the Baptists, for these villages reduced the number of workers available and enhanced the industrial strength of those who remained.

The movement of the slaves to the hills to form free villages was a clear example of the quest of the black man to have some control over his labour. A frequent pattern was for the ex-slave to divide his time between working on the estates, farming his own plot and selling provisions in the market.

Despite this form of struggle, as the sugar industry declined the starvation and privation grew worse without any sign of relief. The only measures taken by the local planter government were the increases in the rate of taxes. Heavy taxes were placed on the imported staple food of the black man. Exorbitant road taxes and toll charges led blacks to transport their provisions by sea. Even then the State levied taxes on canoes, on top of the tax on donkeys. So opposed were the blacks to these taxes that there were toll gate riots in 1859 in Trelawney and Westmoreland.

Whites would shoot the pigs and goats of the poor, and vicious coercive laws proscribed the movements of the blacks. The vagrancy law, the Trespass Act and the Ejectment Act were class laws which were added to the Police Act of 1833 and 1839 providing for the arrest of any person carrying agricultural produce without a note of permission from the owner of the land on which it was grown.

As the injustices mounted, strikes broke out on many sugar estates in 1863 and 1864, but the black workers lacked strong cohesive organisations to defend themselves, and the free village communities became the centres of protest. In these villages the black man had to depend on those skills which had been preserved from Africa, in agricultural production, in oral history, in housing. The wattle and daub structures which were supposed to be houses were blown away with the periodic hurricanes. There was no system of public health, and between 1850 and 1851 20-30,000 died from a cholera epidemic.

Because there were no schools in the villages, no hospitals and no system of public health, the medicine man and those whose parents had retained the knowledge of the herbs and other forms of healing achieved important standing in these free villages. Old slave laws which outlawed obeah were invoked against the herbalists, for invariably the practitioners of African medicine were the ones who claimed to have mystical powers and the power to cast out evil spirits. And the importance of the spirit would call into being many charlatans who claimed to have powers over the devil.

It was the complex of religious revivalism and African religious survivals which intensified in the period of crisis. Religious expressions of resistance called Myalism and Pocomania surged throughout the island with major religious processions proceeding throughout the rural areas. The whites who had passed laws against drumming and shell blowing alleged that this revival of 1860-61 was another manifestation of the laziness of the blacks. A spasm of fear went down the spine of the whites when they heard the reverberating sound of the revival drums. Phillip Curtin summed up their fear in this way:

"Until the 1860s the planters' racial fear was only a latent consciousness, it grew into something close to a real feeling of terror whenever the Negroes had a noisy prayer meeting or the revival drums sounded from a Negro village, the word passed around, 'The Blacks are drilling'."[27]

And drilling they were, for the revival meetings in St. Thomas were smokescreens for one of the biggest revolts in Jamaican history.

"Cleave To The Black"

1865 has become a focal point in the class and racial struggles in Jamaica and forms part of the foundation of modern Rastafari and the Jamaican working class movement. It was not insignificant that the issues involved trespassing, the control over labour, the right of the poor farmers to till the soil, and all those issues which exercised the poor blacks.*

The parish of St. Thomas was the centre of cultural resistance to the sterile aping of everything European. The rebellion broke out as the cumulation of the grievances of the poor, which all had noticed such that some of the more humanitarian missionaries were moved to write to Britain complaining of the wretchedness of the condition of the proletarian masses: of the starvation, the unjust taxation and denial of political rights. Black people noted the petitions and letters to the crown but decided on their own form of struggle for self-determination. Their leader was a black lay preacher by the name of Paul Bogle.

Bogle was the spiritual leader of a free village community called Stony Gut, a former estate where the land had been leased out to the blacks after apprenticeship. The occupants of the land refused to pay rent to the magistrates in Morant Bay, for they maintained that by virtue of their settlement there the land was theirs.

Efforts by the local planters to evict these small farmers were resisted, and after a period of continuous harassment and arrests the planters decided to use legal processes to humble the poor. Bogle saw the implications of the struggle and in order to cover his rear, he went to meet the Maroons to explain the need for a revolution. He outlined the problems of undue imposition of taxes, the non-payment of sufficient wages, and the need to beat the browns and the whites out of the country.

Despite a cool reception, Bogle pressed on with his plans and on October 7th 1865, when one of the villagers of Stony Gut appeared in the magistrates† court in Morant Bay, Bogle and his men were ready. Let the record of the colonial

*Wages actually fell in the period between 1840 and 1865. These figures can be found in *Free Jamaica*, by Douglas Hill, pp 44-45.

†The magistrates wielded tremendous control over labour. For example, in St. Ann the manager of the leading mercantile firm, Messrs Bravo, was at the same time clerk of the magistrates court and sat in the local vestry. A large proportion of the cases for adjudication involved Messrs Bravo.

State bear witness:

> *"Whilst a black man was being brought up for trial before justice, a large number of the peasantry armed with bludgeons and preceded by music came into the town, and leaving their music at a little distance surrounding the court house – openly expressing the determination to rescue the man about to be tried. One of their party having created a considerable disturbance in the court was ordered into custody, whereupon the mob rushed in and rescued the prisoner and maltreated the policeman in attendance."*[28]

The so-called disturbance in the court was a shout for the defendant to pay the fine and not the costs. Such an act of defiance shocked the planters and the Custos, Baron Von Ketelhodt, an immigrant who owned five plantations, despatched a group of policemen to arrest Bogle and his villagers. The same record reveals:

> *"On Monday 9th October the Justices issued a warrant for the apprehension of the 22 principal persons concerned with the disturbance. Upon arrival at the settlement – Stony Gut – about 3 miles from Morant Bay – a shell was blown and negroes collected around with guns, cutlasses, picks and bayonets – put the police in handcuffs and administering to them an oath upon the bible which they had ready, binding them to desert the whites and join the (that is the black) party."*

It was clear that the villagers wanted to unite all black men, for those who took the oath were set free. The next day, Bogle and his men marched into Morant Bay and on the way they administered the oath and shouted *"Cleave to the black, Colour for colour"*, and that they would kill all white men. Blowing the conch shell as a sign of war and beating the drums, the soldiers of Bogle's army reached the court house, where the planter Baron was trembling as he read the riot act. Before he could finish ordering the police to shoot, Bogle and his men surrounded the vestry (Parish Council). The Baron was killed and his assistants were roasted in the fire which razed the court house. The prisoners, mostly tax defaulters, were set free.

Bogle then left a contingent in charge of the town, proceeded to his village to regroup and then went to the other estates to liberate the oppressed workers. Chanting slogans, waving flags and beating drums, they sang songs of deliverance and echoed "Cleave to the black". Estates at Bath, Amity Hall and Golden Grove were captured, and Bogle told his men not to set fire to these estates for they wanted to take them intact. Bogle showed that he was aware of the social and economic realities of his society, dealing with those whites who were vicious while sparing any who were sympathetic to the cause of the blacks.

One of the sympathisers of the blacks who had spoken out against their deprivation was a mulatto by the name of George William Gordon. He had been

Paul Bogle raised the cry 'Cleave to the Black'.

pressing for changes in the constitution in order to break the political power of the whites. In his push for the mulattoes he was conscious of the misery of the blacks, for as a Baptist preacher he came into contact with blacks on a regular basis. Because he had been in the forefront of the call for better conditions, he was hanged by the whites for planning for revolt, even though when the armed struggle began he was not in St. Thomas.

Bogle had been in contact with Gordon but did not depend on him or the mulattoes for leadership. Bogle and his army spared those whites who were friends of Gordon. At Amity Hall Estate when a white man, Mr. Jackson, was attacked the rebels rubbed him up and revived him when they learnt that he was a friend of Gordon. While they shouted *"Blood, Blood, we must humble the white man before us"*, they dealt with the house servants. When the rebels attacked a house negro, a Mr. Price, some within the ranks begged that his life be spared because he was a black man; but the others retorted "he has a black skin but a white heart".

For three days the rebels took control of the parish of St. Thomas in a 30-mile radius around Morant Bay and tried to extend the armed struggle beyond the east, but the prospect of the whole island engulfed in rebellion led to the declaration of Martial Law and the whites, Jews and mulattoes were issued with arms to patrol the island. Meanwhile a British gunboat, HMS Wolverine, which was stationed in the island, rushed troops from Kingston to Morant Bay.

The Maroons were induced to protect the town of Port Antonio and others were promised a bounty to capture Paul Bogle. These Maroons were instrumental in capturing Bogle, while the British went for a scorched earth policy. Thousands of dwellings were burnt to the ground and more than one thousand blacks were rounded up and hanged. 400 were flogged. Paul Bogle was hanged on the British ship HMS Wolverine on the 24th October, 1865.

The colonial authorities and the local Governor feared the call for self-determination, for they could not bear the possibility of another independent black republic at a time when Britain and European capitalist states were contending to divide and exploit Africa. Black Haitians who lived in Jamaica were deported, and the State sought to block all but biblical ideas from circulating in the society. To frustrate the call of the vigorous mulattoes for political representation (which they were sure the blacks would later demand) the old representative assembly lost its autonomy and Jamaica became a Crown Colony.

Nevertheless, British capital was not destined to dominate the economy: for Canada and the USA had given notice, towards the end of the century, that they were ready to join the exploitation of black labour in the Caribbean. Banana companies from Boston bought out some of the sugar lands and Canadian banks joined in the rush to exploit the resources of Jamaica. The response of the coloured population was to call for assimilation with the whites. As early as 1862 one of their newspapers editorialised:

> *"Let the coloured men of Jamaica be true to themselves and their progress will be certain; their best policy is to form a bond of union with their white brethren, and if this is done, no Governor will presume to keep from them the rights to which they are entitled as loyal subjects of the sovereign of Great Britain."*[29]

Those blacks who were better off translated their earnings from provisions into educational opportunities for their children, who formed the embryo of a literate and active stratum: primary school teachers, junior clerks, ministers and even lawyers. The black masses continued to organise strikes on the estates and to retreat into the village communities, and began to migrate to the USA, Canada, Costa Rica, Panama and Cuba in search of better conditions of employment.

This out-migration served as a means of opening up the horizons of the poor, and those who returned enriched the life of the villages with stories of resistance in the African world. The legacy of Tacky, Cudjoe, Nanny, Paul Bogle and Sam Sharpe was linked to the struggles of Harriet Tubman, Sojourner Truth, King Ja Ja, Chaka Zulu and King Menelik of Ethiopia.

These tales reinforced part of the consciousness of the rural poor of their African heritage and formed part of the cultural and ideological struggle in the society between those who wanted to maintain the oppression of the ex-slaves, and those who wanted to overthrow the relations of exploitation. The ideas of deliverance in the bible became important since formal knowledge and a systematic set of ideas were barred from the rural communities.

Hence, by the end of the 19th century the class struggle took on racial and religious overtones. It was in this society that Marcus Garvey grew up.

Every society interprets its history to reinforce national pride, but in post-emancipation Jamaica those blacks who were fortunate enough to go to school were taught that the heroes of the society were Columbus, Drake, Hawkins and the pirate Captain Morgan. Blacks could not therefore identify with the heroes of the British and were forced to fall back on the resilience of African cultural traditions in the village. This was in the face of an explicit policy to keep blacks ignorant of African achievements. The purpose was to build up a picture of barbarous Africans so that the ex-slaves would be ashamed to admit that they were from Africa.

Blacks were forced to deny a decisive part of their social being: to detest their faces, their colour, the peculiarities of their culture, and their specific reactions in the face of life, love, death and art. All this was done so that they would idealise the colour, history and culture of Europeans.

But the rural poor turned this cultural attack on its head and searched out those ideas of resistance in Africa. Through the medium of oral history, folk tales, Anancy stories, the elders retold the stories of capture in Africa, of Cudjoe and Sam Sharpe, in order to inspire the youth. And the youth responded by playing the drums of freedom, telling all that they survived slavery and that they would survive colonialism. "Time longer than rope," they said.

These were the forebears of the modern Rasta. The tales of Ethiopia, Nyabingi and Marcus Garvey shaped a consciousness which emerged as *Rasta*.

FOOTNOTES

1. See Richard Hart, *Slaves Who Abolished Slavery*, Volume I, *Blacks in Bondage*, Institute of Social and Economic Research, U.W.I., Jamaica, 1980, for some figures of the numbers of slaves, chapter four "The Advantage of It". See also Phillip D. Curtin, *The Atlantic Slave Trade, A Census*, Madison, Wisconsin, 1969.
2. Eric Williams, *Capitalism and Slavery*, Chapel Hill, 1944.
3. The method employed by the Europeans is elaborated in *West Africa and the Atlantic Slave Trade* by Walter Rodney, East African Publishing House, 1967.
4. For an analysis of the tributary mode in Africa see Samir Amin, *Unequal Development*, Harvester Press, 1976.
5. Walter Rodney, *A History of the Upper Guinea Coast 1545-1800*, Oxford, Clarendon Press, 1970, pp 254.
6. The interesting narrative of the life of Olaudah Equiano or Gustavus Vassa, the African, written by himself, London 1809. In this work Equiano told how at the sight of the ship and the whites he was convinced that the whites were cannibals and intended to eat the slaves.
7. For a description of the seasoning process see Orlando Patterson, *The Sociology of Slavery*, McGibbon and Kee, London, 1967, pp 98-101. This work is useful, though it cast the history of slavery in the ideological mould of pluralism despite the evidence pointing to the violent conflict of European and African culture in Jamaica.
8. The appendix to Patterson's work contains a useful table of the numbers of slaves imported into Jamaica between 1702 and 1775 and from 1776-1787. See ibid.
9. O. Patterson, *op. cit.*, p. 67.
10. Richard Hart, *Slaves Who Abolished Slavery*, p. 161.
11. See "The Negro Slave" by Walter Rodney and Earl Agustus, *Caribbean Quarterly*, Vol. 10, No 2, 1964.
12. C. McFarlane, *Cudjoe of Jamaica*, Ridley Enslow, Short Hills, New Jersey.
13. Richard Hart, *Black Jamaicans Struggle Against Slavery*, published by Community Education Trust, London, 1979, p. 8.
14. Robin Winks, *The Blacks in Canada*, Yale, 1971. See the Chapter "Back To Africa", pp 61-95.
15. Quoted in "The Negro Slave" by Walter Rodney and Earl Agustus, *Caribbean Quarterly*, Vol 10, No 2, 1964, p. 44.
16. The retention of African culture in the Jamaican countryside has intrigued anthropologists for a century. For the analysis of an American anthropologist in this century see Martin Beckwith, *Black Roadways: A Study of Jamaica Folklife*, Chapel Hill, North Carolina, 1929.
    For the account of a Jamaican who actually went to West Africa to seek out his 'roots' see Leonard Barret, *The Sun and the Drum*, Heineman, 1976. See also *Soul Force: African Heritage in Afro-American Religion*, New York, Doubleday, 1974.
17. It is significant that the first Rasta men were called Bongo men. It was not until 1955 that an American anthropologist first noticed this 'peculiar' religious group in Jamaica which he called the Convince or Bongo Cult. He said that this religion, practised exclusively among the lower classes of St. Thomas, rests on the assumption that men and spirits exist within one another and influence each other's behaviour. See Donald Hogg, "The Convince Cult in Jamaica", *Yale University Publications in Anthropology*, No 58.
18. O. Patterson, *op. cit.*, p. 271.
19. C.L.R. James, *The Black Jacobins*, Allison & Busby, London, 1980.
20. René Depestre, "Problems of Identity for the Black Man in Caribbean Literature" in *Caribbean Quarterly*, Vol 19, No 3, 1973.
21. Richard Hart, *op. cit.*
22. Richard Hart, *op. cit.*, p. 31.
23. Douglas Hall, *Free Jamaica*, Yale University Press, 1959, pp 271-272.
24. Walter Rodney, (i) "Subject Races and Class Contradictions in Guyanese History" and (ii) "Immigrants and Racial Attitudes in Guyanese History". Seminar papers at the Institute of Commonwealth Studies, 17th May and 31st May, 1977, London.
25. O. Patterson, *The Sociology of Slavery*, p. 42. And yet Patterson could not understand Sabina Park who killed her three-month-old child because she "had worked enough for buckra (master) already and would not be

plagued to raise the child ... to work for white people". Patterson decided that this woman was mad (pp 106-107).

26. The record of Worthy Park showed the desperation of the planters in the period after slavery and the efforts made to conciliate the blacks. See *A Jamaican Plantation: The History of Worthy Park 1670-1970*, by Michael Craton and James Walvin, W.H. Allen, London, 1970. See chapter 9 on the period 1834-1863.
27. Phillip D. Curtin, *Two Jamaicas*, Harvard Press, 1955, p. 174.
28. CO 137/411 discusses the rebellion and includes the Commission of Inquiry set up by the colonialists. This colonial report provides a clear exposition of the widespread nature of the rebellion.
29. P.D. Curtin, *op. cit.*, p. 175.

Chapter Two

ETHIOPIANISM, PAN-AFRICANISM AND GARVEYISM

"Africa for Africans at home and abroad."

Marcus Garvey

"Marcus Garvey words come to pass, can't get no food to eat, can't get no money to spend."

Burning Spear, 1975

The social movements and political actions of all peoples are guided by their history, their culture and the reproduction of the material and non-material values necessary for the functioning of society. Men and women produce and reproduce themselves as human beings in the process of producing the social needs of society. The reproduction of society requires the organisation of its values through cultural forms, through social institutions, through the family and through the forms of producing food, shelter and clothing.

In the colonial society that Jamaica had become by 1900 culture was an instrument of class domination to the point where the colonisers would sing that Africans had no culture. Through the principal institutions of the colonial State, the ideas of white supremacy were circulated to justify the exploitation of black labour.

For the poor, the workers, the small farmers and the unemployed, their social consciousness was formed by the reality of the duality of racial discrimination and economic exploitation and thus nurtured searches for identification with the glory of the African past. This search was the beginning but was linked to the search for levers of power outside the rigid industrial framework of the plantation economy. The children of the slaves who had rebelled at Morant Bay and in different parts of the Caribbean found that Britain was violently opposed to any form of political rights for the mass of black people.

Britain had accepted the granting of dominion status to its old colonies of white settlers in Canada, Australia and New Zealand, but withdrew self-government from Jamaica when the white planters feared the political challenge of the mulattoes, because they perceived this as the first step in giving in to black self-rule. Stripped of all political rights and locked into producing sugar, coffee and bananas for the consumption of other societies, the idea of resistance flourished in the hills and in the villages; while in the urban areas the cultural values of Europe were imitated, the children of the slavedrivers internalising the

European version of the world, with a deepening sense of self-hatred.

Jamaican society produced a deformed system of racial degradation, with the colonialists strengthening the system of racial hierarchy by giving out favours according to gradations of skin colour and texture of hair. Degrees of colour became determinants of class, with the mulattoes reflecting the most pathological aspect of the racial prejudice of the society. These offspring of Europe and Africa were promoted to the middle levels of the colonial economy through a limited educational system which ensured that only the chosen few had access to a systematic set of ideas.

Poor Jamaicans who sought to escape the crude subjection of Britain in the rural areas found out that there was a universality to the conditions of black people, as they crossed the Caribbean Sea to search for employment and further educational opportunities. They brought back tales of the social conditions of Central America, along with the horrifying tales of the struggles in Europe for Africa.

From the era of 1865 to the present the system of out-migration to find employment became a safety valve for those who wielded political power. In moving from the rural areas to build the Panama Canal, and to establish plantations in Costa Rica and Nicaragua, the poor Jamaicans were responding to the extension of capitalism which was giving rise to territorial expansion and economic growth for European and American capitalists. The devastation of this expansion, especially in Africa, had a profound impact on the consciousness of the black people in the Caribbean and the United States of America.

The Scramble for Africa

When Jamaican workers went to Central America to lay railway tracks, they were involved in the expansion of capitalism, which was at that time in transition from industrial capitalism to monopoly capitalism. Internationally the consolidation of monopoly corresponded with the search for new areas of the globe to plunder for both labour and raw materials. Scientific and technological advances in Europe and North America allowed for the elaboration of modern organisational techniques in capitalist firms and sped the process of modern imperialism.

The application of science and technology to production took a firm base in the system as the concentration and centralisation of capital led to the creation of monopolies. The merging of bank capital and industrial capital to foreshadow the era of finance capital marked a new stage in capital accumulation. Capital was now endowed with international mobility and had new dimensions which altered the class struggle internationally.

Colonial workers who produced raw materials which were processed in Europe were at the bottom of a chain of exploitation, thus any analysis of the textile worker in Lancashire had to include the condition of the worker who planted and picked the cotton in far-flung corners of the earth, such as Sudan, Montserrat or Georgia.

This need for raw materials precipitated the partition of Africa among the major European powers, which was formalised at the Conference of Berlin in 1885 when Britain, France, Germany, Portugal, Belgium and Spain divided up the whole continent without regard or respect for the local or regional interests of the African nations. The economic gap which had developed between Europe and Africa was part of the trend within capitalism to polarise wealth and poverty at two opposite extremes.

After 400 years of slavery and depopulation, the European monopolists could reorganise the African societies to ensure that they provided the raw materials – copper, cotton, diamonds and rubber – in addition to producing tea, coffee and cocoa for Europe. The limited amount of capital expended in the process of incorporating African labour into the world system meant that naked force was the principal instrument in capturing and 'pacifying' the vast continent.

Europeans made a grab for whatever they thought spelled super profits, and they consciously acquired many areas, not for immediate exploitation, but for future expansion.

Europe was racially as well as economically motivated in the partitioning of Africa. In many parts of the world, capitalism in its imperialist form accepted that some measure of political sovereignty should be left in the hands of the local population. This was so in Eastern Europe, in Latin America and to a more limited extent in China.

However, European capitalists came to the decision that Africa should be directly colonised. The ideas of white superiority which had gained ground during the era of the slave trade accompanied the colonial project, and justified the political domination which was needed to firmly root capitalist economic values in Africa; for Africans did not willingly go to the mines to dig gold, copper, or diamonds for Europe. Extra economic coercion, forced labour and a whole host of coercive laws were the means by which the monopoly firms brought Africa fully into the world capitalist system.

The industrialists who now exploited the resources of Africa deployed missionaries, anthropologists and soldiers of the imperialist State to speed up the flow of wealth from Africa to Europe. Modern imperialism, which V. I. Lenin described as "the highest stage of capitalism", can be distinguished from all other forms of imperialism.

Unlike the imperialism of Rome, Greece, Carthage or Egypt, the technological changes at the capitalist centres had endowed capital with the military means to dominate the whole world. The technological and military capacity at the centres of capital accumulation could not be replicated at the periphery. In the heyday of the Roman Empire the levels of social development were such that when the dominated societies mastered the techniques of war and technology, they could break away from under the heel of Roman occupation.

Under the modern system of imperialism, economic development and underdevelopment were institutionalised as opposite sides of the same coin. The strengthening of the military apparatus of the imperialist State went hand in glove with the process of monopoly. The form of force which characterised the societies of France, Britain, Germany and the United States was the industrial army built around the weapon system. Armed forces were built around weapons such as tanks, battleships, aircraft and new means of command and communication.

The entry of capitalist industry into the arms market led to vast outlays of capital going into shipbuilding, heavy engineering and weapon systems as the products of modern industry were subject to the technological dynamic which was and is characteristic of the industrial environment.

The armaments industry also called for raw materials from Africa: chrome from Southern Africa, iron ore from West Africa, manganese and columbite from the Congo and Angola. These minerals were part of the needs of a society rapidly advancing with the weapons made from them, spreading the destruction of African skills. Metallurgical skills, mining skills and handicraft techniques which had been developed over the centuries were destroyed so that Africa could supply the raw material needs of the monopolists. This destruction of skills and the devastation of the societies has been graphically documented in Walter Rodney's *How Europe Underdeveloped Africa*.

There is no system of domination which does not develop a body of ideas to legitimise its plunder, and in Europe the ideas of racism which had festered during the period of slavery were circulated with vigour throughout the world. Never before in the history of humanity did the ruling class have the power to spread its ideas throughout the world as it did during the epoch of imperialism. When the motion picture industry emerged in the USA as another branch of capital, the whole world was bombarded with the images of white superiority which justified world domination.

By the turn of the century the United States had given notice of her imperialist intentions by muscling the weaker European capitalist nation, Spain, out of the Philippines and Cuba. Big American family firms, such as the Mellons, the Rockefellers, the Morgans and the du Ponts, who had made fortunes during the Civil War (1861-1865), organised monopoly firms in steel, petroleum, banking and chemical industries.

The expansion of capitalism within the US had consumed the indigenous Indian population, and the racists popularised the genocidal wars against the Indians through 'cowboy' movies. It was inside the USA that one of the most vicious forms of racial repression was practised. Europeans who practised outright racism outside their own borders found a unity with the American ruling class in their attempt to codify and consolidate the ideas of white supremacy.

Anthropologists have written volumes on the 'barbaric tribal customs' of Africa, and these writings have been supported by pseudo-scientific and biblical arguments. It was said that it was the unique and independent cultural heritage of whites which accounted for the greater material advancement of Western Europe and North America. This cultural chauvinism was vigorously promoted among the white workers who supported overseas expansion and compromised their own struggles by assisting the capitalists in military campaigns in Africa.

It is not insignificant that it was in this period that Edgar Rice Burroughs conceived the notion of Tarzan – the half-naked white man swinging through the jungle, pacifying Africans and animals alike – while behind Tarzan were the explorers and missionaries who saw their task being to 'civilise the darker races'.

The technological advances in the field of communications, which led to the development of the wireless, sound and television pictures, inculcated visual images of the 'cultured white' and the 'docile uncivilised black'. It was in response to this universal denigration of everything African that the New World blacks founded Pan-African organisations, culminating in one of the biggest movements of this century – the Universal Negro Improvement Association, founded by Marcus Garvey.

The ideas of race consciousness and African redemption, which Marcus Garvey forced into the international arena, expressed the challenge of the oppressed African. Marcus Garvey drew from the foundations of Ethiopianism and Pan-Africanism to centralise the idea of race in the struggle of oppressed Africans, and helped to lay the foundations of the ideology of Rastafari.

Ethiopianism

> *"Princes come out of Egypt, Ethiopia stretches forth her hands unto God."*
>
> *Psalm 68, v.31*

The Rastafarians of today are heirs to a tradition which searched for the glory of the African past in the midst of white western domination. Because of the totality of the experiences of slavery, racial discrimination and the partition of Africa, the slogan 'Africa for the Africans' had emerged as the song of freedom on the continent of Africa and among Africans in the New World.

Since the bible and biblical ideas were so prominent in the experience of domination, the thrust for self-determination and basic human rights was expressed in the biblical terms of redemption and deliverance. The usage of these terms had been most evident in the USA where the black church was the venue of solidarity and unity.[1]

Far from being an opiate, the religiosity of blacks was a complex phenomenon, with many church leaders standing at the forefront of the anti-slavery movement. During the 18th century a religious force had developed in the USA which looked to the biblical references to Ethiopia as a means of challenging the myth that blacks were destined to be 'beasts of burden'. These blacks were part of the Ethiopian movement.[1]

Ethiopia was a major centre in the biblical world, along with Jordan, Syria,

Palestine and Egypt, and for centuries Europeans referred to the whole of the continent of Africa as Ethiopia, while the region which today bears the name 'Ethiopia' was formerly the Kingdom of Abyssinia. The biblical references to Ethiopia were cherished by blacks, and when the Abyssinians defeated the Italians at Adowa in 1896, the black people in the US took the words of the psalm, "Princes come out of Egypt, Ethiopia stretches forth her hands unto God" to mean that the redemption of Africa was near at hand.

The news of this African State under a Christian King defeating a white army excited the blacks, and Jamaicans in their village communities told the stories of Solomon and Sheba with the same zest as they told Anancy stories. They declared that the present rulers of Abyssinia (Ethiopia) could trace their heritage to the union between Solomon and Sheba.

Many Jamaicans who had gone to the USA came into contact with the African Methodist Episcopalian (A.M.E.) Church, which was at the forefront of black church institutions adopting the name 'Africa' when other church leaders were preaching that blacks were afflicted with the curse of Ham. From the time of slavery the Ethiopian movement was a force in the black church movement and William Scott, who studied the impact of Ethiopianism on Afro-American thought, said that:

> *"Stimulated mainly by references to ancient Ethiopia in the Scriptures and Sermons, Afro-Americans often perceived that African territory, however defined, as the salvation of the race. Some thought that one day a black messiah would emerge from Ethiopia to redeem the African race religiously, socially and politically. So ingrained did these and related views become that New World Africans often thought of themselves as Ethiopians, using that term to describe themselves and their organisations."*[2]

In the midst of the European plunder of Africa, preachers of the African Episcopal Methodist Church were carrying the idea that Africa must be saved "for Ethiopia shall soon stretch forth her hands unto God". This expression of Pan-African unity was carried further by Martin R. Delany, who went to the heart of Africa and returned with the cry "Africa for the Africans".

This cry was spread in Southern Africa when the Independent Church Movement linked their religion to Ethiopia, and to the freedom of Africa. As soon as it was clear that the missionaries were as much a part of the colonising forces as were the explorers, traders and soldiers, the more patriotic Africans who had been trained in the church sought to break with the white church movement.

Many of the African preachers had come to literacy through the mission schools, but were torn between the traditions of African resistance and the cultural influence of Europe, which was embedded within the teachings of the missionaries. Quoting Ephesians – "Servants be obedient to your masters" – the white church stressed humility and docility and acceptance of the colonial order of the world, while equating African ancestral beliefs with the devil, who was depicted as black.

According to the European version of Christianity, God the Father was white, God the Son was white, God the Holy Ghost was white, and Lucifer, the devil, was black. Faced with the virulent racism of the Dutch Reformed Church in South Africa, an Independent Church Movement developed and spread rapidly.

This Ethiopianism was a particular brand of black nationalism which opposed white colonial rule and "has its origins in South Africa in the 1870s when colour prejudice had stung so many Africans to set up their own churches rather than face the segregation and humiliation of the white man's place of worship".[3]

Through the Africa of the labour reserves and settler plantations, from the white highlands of Kenya to the gold mines of Johannesburg, the Pan-African call of "Africa for the Africans" became the sermons of the Ethiopian Church Movement. Europeans could not understand the full force of this nationlism taking a religious form*, and they were even more alert when Bishop Turner of the US-based African Episcopal Methodist Church visited South Africa and made contact with the church leaders of the Ethiopian Movement.

White supremacists, who balked at any movement outside white control, cringed at the rapid growth of the movement and called it a "pernicious revolt against European guidance". Colonial officials saw Ethiopianism as a Pan-African conspiracy – a threat to white supremacy in Africa which seemed part of a deeply laid plan in which Negroes from the New World were heavily involved. What in the eyes of the South African whites made the Ethiopian Movement especially dangerous was that there were over eight hundred different churches, and no established leaders.

Similar to within the Rastafari, there was no hierarchy in the Ethiopian Movement; thus it was difficult for the colonial State to penetrate the movement. The Bambata Revolt of 1906, against the growing Apartheid, involved leaders of the Ethiopian Movement, for religion and politics tended to reinforce each other;[4] and in a situation where there was no clear political organisation, the Ethiopian Movement filled a political void, spreading the call "Africa for the Africans". It was only after the formation of the African National Congress in 1912 that the independent churches no longer took the leading role in the struggle.

The cry "Africa for the Africans" was not confined to South Africa, but was to be heard across the Rift Valley and the Congo Basin to as far away as West Africa. S.K.B. Asante, in his study of Ethiopianism in West Africa, remarked:

*The strong black nationalist sentiments of the rural areas of Jamaica manifested themselves in the religious protests of Alexander Bedward. Bedward had re-interpreted the bible to depict the whites in the society as the devil, and he lambasted the merry-go-round of the Governor and his entourage. The British military were deployed against Bedward; and when his idealism began to become legend, the colonial authorities declared that he was insane and committed him to a mental asylum. See Barry Chevanes, *Jamaican Lower Class Religion: Struggles Against Oppression*, M.A. Thesis, U.W.I., 1971.

"After the victory over Italy at Adowa in 1896, Ethiopia acquired a special importance in the eyes of Africans as the only surviving African State. After Adowa, Ethiopia became emblematic of African valour and resistance, the bastion of prestige and hope to thousands of Africans who were experiencing the full shock of European conquest, and were beginning to search for an answer to the myth of African inferiority ... To articulate West African nationalist intelligentsia of lawyers, merchants, journalists, doctors and clergymen who had since the turn of the century persistently sought to share political power with the colonial ruler, the role of Ethiopia or Ethiopianism in nationalist thought and politics was great and inspiring ... In separate African churches, Africans did and could protest imperial rule and build articulate leadership to oppose the domineering and discriminating actions of the colonial officials."[5]

The racial contradictions of Imperialism had given rise to a form of protest which was similar in the US, the Caribbean and Africa. Shorn of its religious and idealist underpinnings, the concept of *Africa for the Africans* was to become the cry of the Pan-African Movement.

Pan-Africanism and Garveyism

Bishop Harry Turner of the A.M.E. in the USA provided the link between the Independent Church Movement in South Africa and the nationalists of the Caribbean. Inside Jamaica, Dr. Robert Love was one of the foremost critics of the colonial order of things and he was associated with those Caribbean blacks who made comparisons between the social conditions in the Caribbean and those in Africa. These Caribbean nationals were in the main educated blacks who – partly because of their own confrontation with the arrogance of colonial officials, and partly because of the pressures from the black majority – voiced sentiments which were radical.

Edward Blyden, Sylvester Williams and Dr. Robert Love were among the blacks in the Caribbean who gave expression to the international black grievances against floggings, low wages and colonial bureaucratic commandism. Edward Blyden had migrated to Liberia as early as 1850, and he was an early proponent of the concept of the African personality. He travelled back and forth between the US and Africa, spreading the call of "Africa for the Africans".

Dr. Robert Love carried this cry from Jamaica and in 1901 wrote:

"Africa for the Africans is the new shape of an old cry ... This cry will waken the so called civilised world to a consciousness of the fact that others who are not accounted as civilised, think, with regard to natural rights, just as civilised people think."

Dr. Love printed a newspaper, the *Jamaica Advocate*, and provided the early inspiration for a young Marcus Garvey, when he arrived in Kingston as a youth. It was through Dr. Love that Marcus Garvey was first exposed to the international movement called Pan-Africanism. Dr. Love had collaborated with Henry Sylvester Williams in 1906 in setting up branches of the Pan-African Association in Jamaica, after this son of Trinidad called the first Pan-African Congress in London in 1900.

The first Pan-African Congress was convened soon after W. E. B. DuBois had declared that the "problem of the twentieth century is the problem of the colour line". W.E.B. DuBois was one of the architects of the Pan-African Congresses which were called between 1900 and 1945. Hitherto, the force of Pan-Africanism has been documented within the framework of the conferences; but the ideology of Pan-Africanism is far richer than the sum total of the conferences and resolutions passed.

These conferences grew out of the response of Africans to their oppression and served as a coordinating point for the different struggles which were going on among blacks. The Pan-Africanists who initiated the conferences and wrote tracts on Africa were carrying out an exercise in self-definition which was aimed at establishing a broader sense of self-esteem and worth than that which had been permitted by the ideologues of Western Capitalism. This was and is the essence of Pan-Africanism, but during the first fifty years of the twentieth century this task was undertaken by educated blacks.[6]

Pan-Africanists such as George Padmore, C.L.R. James and W.E.B. DuBois dug up the African past to show to the world the artistic and cultural contribution of the African to humanity. In order to use the historical knowledge and analysis of the contact between Europe and Africa as a weapon in the struggle for self-determination, DuBois and Padmore wrote critical tracts such as *The World And Africa* (DuBois, 1947) and *How Britain Rules Africa* (Padmore, 1936).

During World War I, W. E. B. DuBois stressed the significance of the rivalry among the imperialist powers over the division of Africa which led to the war. His little-known pamphlet *The African Roots of War* appeared in 1915, and there were points of coincidence between Lenin's work on *Imperialism: The Highest Stage of Capitalism* and DuBois' pamphlet, especially on how the aristocracy of labour in the West united the capitalist and the *working class against the coloured proletariat of the world.*[7]

In the main the Pan-Africanists of the inter-war period laid great emphasis on the past existence of African Kingdoms; but one of the problems of this body of literature was that there was a narrow concentration on the behaviour of kings and dynasties without an accompanying analysis of the day-to-day life of the millions of Africans who lived outside the States of Egypt, Mali, Songhai, Benin, Axum or Zimbabwe.

The concern with Kingdoms reflected a particular idealist world view which was in keeping with the class outlook of the principal movers behind the Pan-African Congresses. This is not to deny that during the period of colonialism the Pan-Africanists were progressive and anti-imperialist, but their strategy for African liberation was confined to sending petitions to the colonialists.

It was not until the riots, demonstrations and popular protests of the proletarianised majority that many saw the masses as having a central place in the process of liberation. The limitations of the early nationalists can now be analysed against the background of the historical record of leaders such as Jomo Kenyatta and Hastings Banda, who both stood at the forefront of the Pan-African Movement, but while in power supported those external forces who wanted to dominate the continent.

Pan-Africanists of the pre-independence era, who paid lip service to the idea of regional and continental unity, reneged on one of the cardinal principles of Pan-Africanism – viz., that the people of one part of Africa were responsible for the freedom of their brothers and sisters in other parts of Africa; and indeed that black people everywhere were to accept the same responsibility. This betrayal is characterised today by the operations of the Organisation of African Unity (OAU), whose very existence came from the momentum of Pan-Africanism.

The idea of Pan-Africanism had taken deep root and it had to be given expression, if only in the form of a constitutional international assembly. To fully understand the contradictions of the OAU and its concept of African Unity it is necessary to state that any nationalist movement which is not guided by working class ideas is bound to degenerate.[8]

Degenerate nationalism was most explicit in the politics of Chiang Kai Shek in China, but could not be complete in Africa, since the constant struggles against white rule in Southern Africa called for positive responses from the rest of Africa; even if at the level of the African leadership these responses were at the best grandstanding. Some of the leaders are stridently anti-communist and continue to follow the path of George Padmore, who posed the false dichotomy between Pan-Africanism and communism. Padmore's book, *Pan-Africanism Or Communism*, presented the ideas of Marxism as a danger to Africa and Africans, and Padmore's politics deteriorated to the point where he found himself on the side of American imperialism in Guyana.*

The political decline of Padmore, who once stood at the pivot of the international workers' movement, corresponded with the practice of the nationalists who were pushing the idea of *Negritude*. There was in the Negritude movement a conscious and deliberate pre-occupation with the destruction of the myths and stereotypes of the Negro, and this movement represented a firm protest against French colonialism. However, the spokespersons for this movement, like Padmore, allowed their personal experiences in the international communist movement to lead them to become hostile to the ideas of Marxism-Leninism.

Hence, shorn of its progressive and anti-colonial content, Negritude ceased to

*In Guyana Padmore supported the anti-communist Forbes Burnham at a time when the C.I.A. and the British moved against Cheddi Jagan. For an account of this episode see Philip Reno, *The Ordeal of Guyana*, Monthly Review Press, 1974.

be a legitimate form of rebellion and became shrouded in mysticism. Leopold Senghor's Negritude was the dogma of the alienated intellectual, and in Haiti, Francois Duvalier turned Negritude into a sinister mythology, while forcing the people to live on their knees.[9]

In dissecting the character of nationalist movements and ideas, there must be an effort to stress the dualism of positive and negative ideas, of spiritual beliefs and material needs and of the mystical and political beliefs which emerge in all notions such as Ethiopianism, Pan-Africanism and now Rastafarianism. These ideas forced themselves as the global expression of black peoples.

It was the Garveyites who were to give concrete political meaning to these ideas in the form of the largest black mass movement in modern history. Marcus Garvey, the product of the Jamaican countryside, joined the ranks of the international protest and placed in this movement the centrality of race consciousness in the struggle for freedom. It is this central place of *race* which provides the continuity between the Ethiopian movement and the present manifestations of the *Dreads*.

Garveyism and Racial Consciousness

> *"I know of no national boundary where the Negro is concerned. The whole world is my province until Africa is free."*
>
> *Marcus Garvey*

It was V.I. Lenin who made the observation that oppressed minorities often reflect the techniques of the bourgeoisie more brilliantly than sections of the bourgeoisie themselves. Black workers in the U.S.A. at the end of World War I, chafing under the crudest forms of exploitation, forged organisations to struggle to better their lot and through their cultural outpourings they contributed to the intellectual development of the U.S.A. in a period which is now known as the Harlem Renaissance. Blues, spirituals, work songs, jazz music and theatrical performances were developed as the expressions of an exploited race bent on beating back the myths of racial superiority, which were to explode in Europe as an appendage to fascism.

Black people in this period displayed a greater sense of freedom and initiative in pushing their claims upon humanity because they lacked the handicaps of false ambition. They thus had access to a wide social vision and deep social consciousness. This vision was manifest in a plethora of organisations.

One of the most prominent organisations of this period was the Universal Negro Improvement Association (U.N.I.A.) and African Communities League, which was founded by Marcus Garvey under the slogan "One God, One Aim, One Destiny!" The nomenclature *Universal* was no mean claim, for from the time of its inception the U.N.I.A.'s objective was to:

> *"establish a confraternity among the race; to promote the spirit of pride and love, to reclaim the fallen; to administer and assist the needy... to*

assist in the development of Independent Negro nation and communities; to establish a central nation for the race, to establish Commissionaries or agencies in the principal countries and cities of the world for the protection of all Negroes, to promote a conscientious spiritual worship among the native tribes of Africa, to establish universities, colleges, academies and schools for racial education and culture of the people and to work for better conditions among Negroes everywhere."[10]

Under this objective the U.N.I.A. became the largest mass movement among black people this century, with 996 branches in 43 countries and over five million members.

The moving spirit behind this vast organisation was Marcus Garvey, who was born in Jamaica on August 17, 1887,[11] into the section of Jamaican society where the ideas of "cleave to the black" and "colour for colour" reverberated in the hills and in the tenement yards.

His childhood in Jamaica was not very different from that of the vast majority of blacks whose rudimentary elementary education prepared them for the rigours of hard work; and at the age of fourteen he moved from the parish of St. Ann to the capital city, Kingston, to work as an apprentice. This apprenticeship system, which had been introduced at the end of slavery, was still the predominant form of socialising workers into skilled crafts, and by the time he was eighteen Garvey was working as a master printer.

Understanding the limited scope for self-expression offered to black people, he joined the trek of the 126,000 migrants who moved to Central America, only to find out that the conditions of exploitation and racial humiliation were not unique to Jamaica.[12] Utilising his skills as a printer, he began his long career as a radical journalist and organised workers wherever he worked, calling for better conditions and more pay.

From Central America Garvey returned briefly to Jamaica, and in the same year, 1912, he set out for England. It was in London that he was exposed to a set of systematic ideas on Africa through the medium of the foremost Pan-African journal at that time, the *African Times and Orient Review*, edited by the Egyptian Duse Mohammed.

In coming into contact with African seamen and students, Garvey learned of the day-to-day life of the broad masses and learned that the practice of direct rule, indirect rule, mandated territory or protectorate status all amounted to condemning blacks to be the *wretched of the earth*. Before the outbreak of World War I Garvey returned to Jamaica, where he set about organising the U.N.I.A.,[13] an organisation which hoped to embrace the purpose of black humanity, distinguishing itself from the local reformist pressure groups.

Marcus Garvey and the U.N.I.A. could not flourish in the Jamaica of 1914, for the colonial State did not allow blacks to have the basic democratic rights which were available to white workers in Europe and North America. He moved to the U.S.A. in March 1916 to raise funds for the organisation, but was engulfed in the battle for black dignity and African freedom which swept the U.S.A. during and immediately after the war.

When Marcus Garvey arrived in the U.S.A. the society was in the midst of the social upheavals generated by the war and the growing concentration of capital. The shortage of skilled labour, the military mobilisation campaign and the boom of war time production had a tremendous impact on the lives of black people, who had been confined to a very special form of exploitation - called sharecropping - in the South.

Capital requires cheap labour where it is most needed, and during the war the Northern manufacturers encouraged blacks to leave the South to migrate to the factories and steel mills of the Northern cities. Those who took the train journey to escape the lynch mobs of the South found that they moved to the low paid and unskilled jobs in the mass production industries - the meat packing plants, the foundries and the automobile plants.

Discrimination by the trade union leadership and rank and file forced the blacks into the middle of industrial strife as the capitalists used the newly arrived blacks as strike breakers. The blacks were eager to accept a job at any cost in order to escape the nightly marauding activities of the Ku Klux Klan.

The Ku Klux Klan was not a fringe political organisation; it was a national body of white supremacists, with a hierarchy, a code of conduct aimed at mutilating and killing blacks, and with millions of members penetrating at all levels of the Federal and State apparatus. So powerful was this proto-fascist club that in 1925 the Ku Klux Klan could mount a massive hooded march down Pennsylvania Avenue, in Washington D.C., the capital of the U.S.A.

The growth of the Klan corresponded with the popularisation in the universities of the ideas of black docility, and historians lent their academic authority to the side of the Klan. One of the widely read works of that period, *American Negro Slavery*, by Ulrich B. Phillips, presented an idyllic picture of the black man as the natural slave who simply delighted in being chained. This mythical picture was popularised through one of the most powerful mediums in the U.S. in the motion picture *Gone With The Wind*. The motion picture industry spread the idea of the inferior black throughout the world, and in 1915 the moguls of Hollywood popularised the activities of the Klan in the film *The Birth of A Nation*.

It was in this climate that the Klan embarked on an expanded campaign of lynching black people. Lynching was the most powerful form of racial repression and served the indispensable function of providing the ruling class with the means of reaffirming the collective sentiment of white dominance.[14]

Those blacks who moved to the Northern cities of Gary, Indiana; Detroit, Michigan; Chicago, Illinois; and Cleveland, Ohio, found that they were the tools by which the employers hoped to degrade labour as a whole.[15] Prior to World War I, Northern industry recruited cheap labour from Europe, and between 1870 and 1900 thirteen million immigrants crossed the Northern Atlantic Ocean from Europe.

One of the few things that united these immigrants, whether they came from Poland, Ireland or Italy, was that they soon adopted the American prejudice against black people. These workers who pushed their claims for basic industrial rights excluded black workers from the trade union movement and were hostile to the movement of black people from the South to the North.

The outstanding example of a trade union which rejected the racist principle of excluding blacks was the small but militant Industrial Workers of the World (I.W.W.) - known as the Wobblies. They attempted to champion the cause of all workers; but their radical vision of a worker state scared other trade union leaders, who assisted the capitalist class in destroying the I.W.W.[16]

Black workers bore the brunt of the social unrest and industrial strife of the post-war slump. Philip S. Foner, in his study of *Organised Labour and the Black Worker 1619–1973*, detailed how anti-black violence was actually instigated by the organised workers' movement. The most notorious example of this came after the Trade and Labour Council in East St. Louis, Illinois – an affiliate of the American Federation of Labour – circulated a letter calling upon the city council to retard the 'growing menace' created by the influx of undesirable Negroes, and also to devise a way to get rid of a certain portion of those who were already there.[17]

A small group of whites went about attacking black workers, and when they decided to defend themselves, a joint operation composed of the police and a white mob took to the streets shooting, lynching, and killing men, women and children. Hundreds of blacks were injured when the whites burnt out the black neighbourhood in one of the worst racial confrontations of the 20th century.

Segregated into overcrowded ghettoes, disenfranchised by the legal restrictions placed on black voters and attacked at night, the social and class consciousness of the black worker was expressed as *racial consciousness*. This racial consciousness was deepened by the exclusive black organisations which emerged in response to the violent thoughts and acts of white racist America.

Racial consciousness was an integral part of the class consciousness of the black working people in the U.S.A. and Marcus Garvey struck a responsive chord when he travelled through the society proclaiming: "Up you mighty race, you can accomplish what you will!" The U.N.I.A. inspired confidence and courage among blacks by telling them that "the best thing the Negro of all countries can do is to prepare to fight fire with fire."

Many blacks, especially from the ranks of the more than 300,000 demobilised black soldiers, decided to get up and stand up for their rights in the U.S.A., since they had just fought for democracy and freedom in France. These soldiers, organised by militant nationalists like the African Blood Brotherhood, fought political battles against white mobs, and when in Tulse, Oklahoma, the blacks repelled the white mob, the whites dropped bombs on the black neighbourhood.

It was in the context of these battles that Claude McKay wrote his poem:

"If we must die, let it not be like hogs
Hunted and penned in an inglorious spot
While round us bark the mad and hungry dogs
Making their mock at our cursed lot.
If we die let us nobly die
So that our precious blood may not be shed
In vain, then even the monsters we defy
Shall be constrained to honour us though dead.
Like men we'll face the murderous cowardly pack,
Pressed to the wall, dying but fighting back."[18]

This spirit of defiance was behind the energy and force of the black movement which is called the Harlem Renaissance, with the flourishing of organisations predicted on the push to uplift the oppressed blacks.

Marcus Garvey and the U.N.I.A. were part of this push and became pre-eminent among the organised resisters to racist attacks. The U.N.I.A. was one of the many organisations which out of conflict and cooperation cemented the bonds of racial consciousness. What distinguished the Garveyites was their ability to mobilise the poorest sections of the blacks, building branches of the U.N.I.A. in all corners of the society, and indeed all over the world. The indomitable energy and racial awareness of Garvey merged with the outpouring of black resistance, and the U.N.I.A. set up its headquarters at Liberty Hill, Harlem – then the centre of the black world.

Garveyism was a brand of militant nationalism which gave the black person a sense of identification with the whole of Africa while stressing self-reliance. While the educated blacks and the social climbers organised the Blue Vein Society and the Colonial Club, Garvey preached the need for an independent but powerful international organisation with his dictum: "A race without authority and power is a race without respect!"

Garvey and the Symbols of Racial Pride

The U.N.I.A. functioned as a mutual aid society and the branch headquarters of the movement served as cultural centres in the black communities throughout the Americas. Through the newspaper *Negro World*, the U.N.I.A. used selected episodes of the African past to instil confidence in all black people. The U.N.I.A. debunked the idea that black people were plagued with a biblical curse, and declared that if Europe is for the Europeans, then Africa must be for the African peoples.

Their programme of self-determination and anti-racism was enshrined in the *Declaration of the Rights of the Negro People*.[19] This declaration listed the main grievances of the race and demanded their resolution. Militant claims for self-determination tied the struggle for world-wide racial solidarity to the battles for the liberation of Africa.

It is this internationalist thrust which endeared the unorganised black people of the world to the U.N.I.A. There were U.N.I.A. branches in thirty-eight states in the US, and the U.N.I.A. was not only the organisation of the newly urbanised blacks but also the organisation of the mass of black workers and sharecroppers in the South.

Outside the USA, Cuba had the most branches – fifty-two – and the Greater Caribbean (including Central America and Northern South America) was the biggest Garveyite stronghold outside of the United States.[20] South Africa was the most thoroughly organised of the African countries, and no area of significant black population in the world was without a U.N.I.A. branch. This included Canada, Europe and Australia.

The U.N.I.A. branches in these far-flung corners of the capitalist world were kept together by the ideas of the *Negro World*. The success of the distribution of the *Negro World* showed that Garvey was sensitive to the need to combat the virulent ideas of the white film and publishing world. Black sailors and travellers saw it as their task to ensure that the newpaper, with its telling cartoons, reached the widest audience possible.

This newspaper attracted some of the most articulate writers of the Harlem scene, and Marcus Garvey was editor-in-chief of the paper while he was in the US. The paper was written in clear, simple language to reach the poorest black, and there were French, English and Spanish editions of the paper.

Similar to the present-day use of reggae by the Rasta to bind the racial pride of the blacks, the *Negro World* was a weapon which all racists feared, and in many colonial territories possession of the paper could lead to imprisonment or death.

It was through this paper and the network of branches that Garvey organised the massive conventions of the U.N.I.A., where the pageantry, dispensation of African titles, militant resolutions and cultural performances formed an integral part of the history of black nationalism. The first International Convention of the Negro Peoples of the World, in 1920, attracted delegates from five continents, and white America saw for the first time the full force of Garveyism when the Garveyites paraded through Harlem with their Royal Guards, Engineering Corps, Paramilitary Forces, the uniformed Black Cross Nurses, the Mounted Legionnaires and thousands of supporters chanting: *Down With Lynching, Join the Fight for Freedom* and *Africa Must Be Free*.

Numerous accounts of Garvey's political activities in the USA[21] have properly documented the impact of the U.N.I.A. on the black experience under imperialism. The U.N.I.A. brought together diverse black working people: members of church organisations, militant self-help groups, and black independent trade unions; pacifists, cultural nationalists, women's liberation fighters, socialists, and a whole host of unorganised black people.

All these forces were held together by the challenge of racial repression, and responded to the institutionalised racism of the imperial order by proposing a concept of nationhood, complete with the symbols of titles, flags and national

Garveyism was a brand of militant nationalism which gave the black person a sense of identification with the whole of Africa while stressing self-reliance.

anthems, and backed up by independent commercial enterprises, of which the most impressive was the attempt to build an international shipping company, the *Black Star Line*.

As the Rasta colours today provide the symbol of pride, the most widely known symbol of black nationalism was the flag of the U.N.I.A. – the Red, Black and Green – adopted at the 1920 Convention as the official colours of the race: "Red for the colour of the blood which must be shed for their redemption and liberty; Black for the colour of the noble and distinguished race to which we belong; and Green for the luxuriant vegetation of the Motherland".

These colours waved from the flagpoles of Liberty Hall in Harlem and in the divisional headquarters throughout the world, while in South Africa the Garveyites wore a red, black and green button.[22] The colours and the flag of the U.N.I.A. were important symbols, for prior to that period whites had heaped insults on the colonised condition of black people with the popular song: "Every Race Has a Flag But the Coon".

At the same historic Convention of 1920 the anthem "Ethiopia, Thou Land Of Our Fathers" was accepted:

> *"Ethiopia, thou land of our fathers,*
> *Thou land where the Gods love to be*
> *As storm clouds at night suddenly gather*
> *Our armies come rushing to thee.*
> *We must in the fight be victorious*
> *When swords are thrust outward to gleam;*
> *For us will the vict'ry be glorious*
> *When led by the red, black and green.*
>
> Chorus:
> *Advance, advance to victory*
> *Let Africa be free;*
> *Advance to meet the foe*
> *With the might of the red, black and green."*

In sharp contrast to the popular songs of the period, the anthem of the U.N.I.A. was a call for military preparations in anticipation of the inevitable struggle for black liberation. This call for military preparedness was phrased in religious terminology, for the Garveyites took great care to use every aspect of black life in the quest for racial pride. In this endeavour they went further than the Ethiopian movement; declaring that the black man should worship God in his own image, Garvey maintained that:

> *"If the white man has the idea of a white God, let him worship his God as he desires. If the yellow man's God is of his race let him worship his God as he sees fit. We, as Negroes, have found a new ideal. Whilst our God has no colour, yet it is human to see everything through one's own spectacles, and since the white people have seen their God through white spectacles, we have only now started out (late though it may be) to see our*

> *God through our own spectacles. The God of Isaac and the God of Jacob, let him exist for the race that believes in the God of Isaac and the God of Jacob. We Negroes believe in the God of Ethiopia, the everlasting God – God the Father, God the Son and God the Holy Ghost, the one God of all ages. That is the God in whom we believe, but we shall worship him through the spectacles of Ethiopia."*[23]

The U.N.I.A. went to great pains to fulfil the spiritual needs of its members and in the process helped to create an autonomous religious institution – the African Orthodox Church.[24] The dominant figure in this institution was George Alexander McGuire of Antigua, who had been ordained as a minister in the Church of England but who became an ardent nationalist in the face of the racism of the Church. Bishop McGuire, as he was known, was the Chaplain General of the U.N.I.A. and he wrote the catechism of the organisation. Bishop McGuire noted that:

> *"If God is the father of all he must have had black blood in his veins, and Jesus must have had black blood in his veins. So it is proper for the dark race to conceive of their Spiritual Saviour as a Negro."*

At the 1924 Convention the Garveyites unveiled a large oil painting of a Black Madonna and Child and the gathering implored blacks to worship God in their own image.[25]

Garveyism was however much more than symbols and imagery, though it cannot be denied that the painting of a Black Christ and the singing of the African National Anthem provided a tremendous uplift, when the whites were going to the movies to see *Gone With The Wind*, *Birth of a Nation* and *Tarzan*.

The Negro Factories Corporation was the business arm of the U.N.I.A. and this company had removal vans, publishing companies, laundries and restaurants throughout the USA. The U.N.I.A. set out to establish independent economic ventures which would break the hold of the white capitalists over the black communities and over Africa.

Probably the most ambitious venture which would have had far reaching consequences for imperialism was the *Black Star Line Shipping Company*. When the company actually launched four ships, giving notice that the organisational potential of the black masses was to be augmented by economic self-reliance, the capitalist class set out to sabotage the shipping company, and this they did with the assistance of unscrupulous blacks.

The Black Star Line was organised along cooperative lines, something akin to the 'partner', the informal banking system which existed (and still exists) among blacks in the Caribbean and the USA. Thousands of poor black people were willing to make amazing sacrifices to support a business venture which was conceived as part of a global strategy for African redemption.

The failure of the Black Star Line was a symbol of many of the weaknesses of the U.N.I.A. in general. The openness of the discussions regarding shares and the operation of the company exposed the limitations of the all-class notion of nationalism promoted by the U.N.I.A.

To blame unscrupulous and greedy elements for the failure is to minimise the fact that at that period the aspiring petty bourgeoisie, who wanted to advance within the system, were also a part of the U.N.I.A., though not the most important section of the organisation. Because the Garveyites were not guided by scientific principles, those elements whose struggle for dignity was based on becoming accumulators of capital moved in and out of the organisation.

The failure of the Black Star Line and frustrated efforts to secure a land base in Africa have served as the focus of a number of works on Garvey, portraying him as an egotist and a Zionist. These scholarly works incorporated the hostility of the white capitalists, the intelligentsia and their black imitators who opposed the full thrust of Garveyism.

While it should be stated firmly that it was the US capitalist class which hounded Marcus Garvey out of the USA after bringing a phoney charge against him, the hostility of the integrationists provided some of the ammunition to support the actions of the US government, especially those who involved themselves in the "Garvey Must Go" campaign of 1923. Marcus Garvey was indicted for using the United States mails to 'defraud investors' of the Black Star Line, and was imprisoned in Atlanta, Georgia.

The full threat of Garveyism to Western Imperialism was crystal clear, for the United States Government resorted to diplomatic pressures against Liberia to abort the U.N.I.A. settlement, and soon after the land earmarked by the U.N.I.A. engineers and surveyors was leased to the Firestone Rubber Company of Akron, Ohio.[26]

While the integrationists and liberals who promoted the theory of the American 'melting pot' denigrated Garveyism, those who exploited the labour and minerals of Africa understood the importance of the call *Africa for the Africans*. The colonialists concentrated on exploiting a narrow range of minerals and products, for the utilisation of the resources of Africa for the needs of the African people was never an objective within the colonial economy. Garveyism challenged the stunted growth of Africa and for this the colonial powers ensured that Marcus Garvey would never set foot on African soil. Indeed, the Colonial Office, for a time, dictated that no East African should go to the US for fear that they be 'contaminated' by the ideas of Garvey.

The persecution of Garvey by the imperialists was supported by his political rivals in the USA. The political differences between Garvey and his adversaries reached such depths that ultimately the movement of black people suffered. A close examination of the polemic exchange between Garvey and DuBois showed that neither could escape the pitfalls of individualism, and in the end it was the contradictions of a philosophy based on race which exposed the weaknesses of the Garvey programme.

Because the struggle against racism was fought on the rules established by the racists, the U.N.I.A. propagated a set of ideas which could ultimately be incorporated by the aspiring black middle class. However, at the time that

Garvey carried out his political activities, this stratum was too anti-black to positively identify with black nationalism.

Both black and white activists in the international socialist movement in the USA were opposed to Garveyism; they looked grudgingly at the conferences of the U.N.I.A., opportunistically hoping to 'bore from within'.

Marcus Garvey had mobilised the mass of black workers and farmers whom the communists and socialists had hoped to organise. These communists and socialists had never really appreciated the impact of racial repression, and had promoted the sterile notion of 'black and white unite and fight'.

Except for the black radicals, such as Cyril Briggs of the African Blood Brotherhood, who saw the progressive nature of Garveyism, by and large the white communists could not escape the virulent racism of their society. Blinded by their doctrinaire view of the struggle, they tended to effect a level of polarisation at the level of ideas between nationalism and socialism, which in practice turned away the black worker from the activities of the Communist Party. That these two ideas were not mutually exclusive was only realised in the era of Amilcar Cabral and Walter Rodney.[27]

Garveyism in Jamaica

When Marcus Garvey was deported from his Atlanta cell to Jamaica, he had hoped to keep the international movement alive, but it took him some time to fully appreciate the cultural depths of the colonial society. Unlike the United States where black workers in the North were in steady employment, the seasonal nature of Jamaican workers made it difficult for the producers of sugar cane and bananas to provide the kind of organisational support to keep an international movement of the importance of the U.N.I.A. going.

Moreover the colonial society did not allow black people the rudimentary bourgeois freedoms such as the right of assembly, the right to vote, the right to form trade unions and those basic rights which had become normative in the advanced capitalist countries. When Garvey had returned briefly to Jamaica in 1921, the British were sufficiently apprehensive to place battleships in the harbour.

Marcus Garvey returned to Jamaica to a tumultuous welcome by the poor. Len Nembhard, in his account of the *Trials and Triumphs of Garvey,* gave a vivid description of the speech delivered at the Ward Theatre in Kingston, and the expectations of the poor blacks. This book detailed the constant harassment by the State of Garvey, while the spokespersons for the dying planter class ridiculed the achievements of the U.N.I.A. F.M. Kerr Jarrett, the white planter of St. James, then head of the Jamaica Imperial Society, and H.G. DeLisser, the lead writer for the merchant's voice – *The Daily Gleaner* – vehemently denounced Garvey while calling upon the mulattoes to support British colonialism.

Garvey inserted himself into the Jamaica of the poor, bringing along with him the educated blacks who identified with the struggle for self-determination and redemption. He channelled the organisational reservoir of the society into a political party called The People's Political Party (P.P.P.).[28] This Party called for a minimum wage, guaranteed employment, social security, workers' compensation, the expropriation of private lands for public use, land reform, a Jamaican university, and the compulsory improvement of urban areas.

Amy Jacques Garvey's analysis of the political activities of Marcus Garvey in Jamaica emphasised the fact that the platform of the P.P.P. was anti-imperialist and anti-capitalist. The progressive nature of the P.P.P. can be measured by the fact that the neo-colonial society of Jamaica still cannot implement the programme of Garvey 52 years later, for the form of capitalism of the society could never guarantee full employment.

From the street corners of Kingston and from the lamp-lit shops and yards of rural Jamaica, Garvey brought his message to the poor. House servants denied knowing what Garvey preached in the homes of their employers, while at night on the stools outside their two-by-four structures, they told their children of the future liberation of Africa and sang the song "Ethiopia, Thou Land of Our Fathers".

The stratum which felt most threatened by the thrust of Garveyism was the Afro-Saxons, below the Imperial Society, who assisted the colonial Judiciary and Local Government Council to embroil Garvey in a number of legal problems.[29] The constant arrests of Garvey were meant to divert the attention of the poor from the inequalities of the society towards efforts to keep their leader out of St. Catherine District Prison.

So preoccupied were the masses with Garvey's freedom that in 1977 the reggae group *Culture* invoked the song "When The Two Sevens Clash" to remind the Jamaican people of the persecution of Garvey. A resurgence in the study of Garveyism and his international contributions has been imprinted in the minds of the young by *Burning Spear*, who proclaimed "Marcus Garvey's words come to pass, can't get no food to eat, no money to spend".

Reggae artists who speak in terms of Garvey's prophecy are reinforcing the view in Jamaican society that Garvey was a prophet. For many poor Jamaicans who interpreted the world in biblical and spiritual terms, Garvey was a prophet and they took his view of worshipping God through the spectacles of Ethiopia literally. The catechism of the U.N.I.A. had promised that "Princes come out of Egypt, Ethiopia shall stretch forth her hands to God" meant that a ruler would emerge in Africa to lead all black people to freedom. As a playwright Garvey had staged a play in Kingston depicting the crowning of an African King, so when in 1930 the newspapers carried pictures of the crowned Emperor of Ethiopia, many for whom the bible held all the answers were convinced that Emperor Haile Selassie was literally and biblically the 'King of Kings'.

The historic crowning of an African King was a welcome diversion from the constant reminder of the portrait of the white king and his wife, which graced the walls of all public buildings in Jamaica. Marcus Garvey had lit the fires of expectation with the following:

> *"We have great hopes of Abyssinia in the East – the country that has kept her tradition even back to the days of Solomon. Some of our peculiar sociologists when they discuss the intelligence of the Abyssinians try to make out that they are not Negroes, but everybody of ordinary ethnological intelligence knows that the Abyssinians are black people, that is it say, black in the sense of the interpretation of the Negro. They are part of the great African race that is to rise from its handicaps, environments and difficulties to repossess the Imperial Authority that is promised by God himself in the inspiration: Princes coming out of Egypt and Ethiopia stretching forth her hands."*[30]

The crowning of Haile Selassie was to provide a new deification, replacing the white God in heaven and the white representative at Buckingham Palace with the Coptic version of a God who was both divine and human. The beliefs of the first Rasta were a profound response to the sickness of the colonial society. Those who preached the divinity of Ras Tafari were rejecting the link between Christianity and whiteness, and were inexorably breaking with the philistine white Westindian society, thus linking their cultural and spiritual roots with Ethiopia and Africa. As a first step, this was progressive.

FOOTNOTES

1. George Shepperson has done the most thorough study of the Ethiopian movement in Africa and the New World. The major problem with his writing is that he tended to examine this nationalist response as a simplistic and idealist movement. See his article "Ethiopianism Past and Present" in C.G. Baeta, ed., *Christianity in Tropical Africa*, Oxford, 1968. For the specific development of Ethiopianism in 19th century black American thought see William Scott, "And Ethiopia Shall Stretch Forth Her Hands: The Origins of Ethiopianism in Afro-American Thought 1767-1896", Umoja, Spring, 1978.
2. W. Scott, ibid.
3. George Shepperson and Thomas Price, *Independent Africa*, Edinburgh University, Press, 1958.
4. The full impact of the Ethiopian movement on the Bambata Revolt of 1906, when more than 4000 Africans lost their lives in the struggle, is in doubt among scholars. The link between religion and politics found the most concrete expression in the armed uprising of John Chilembwe in Nyasaland in 1915. White missionaries and scholars blamed the Pan-African links between Chilembwe and the black American churches. This revolt was an armed protest against the unjust taxation and forced labour of the colonialists. See. G. Shepperson and T. Price, ibid., and B.G.M. Sandkler, *Bantu Prophets in South Africa*, London, 1964.
5. S.K.B. Asante, *Pan-African Protest: West Africa and the Italo-Ethiopia Crisis 1934-1941*, Longman, 1977. Asante discusses the political symbolism for West Africans in the turn of the century, p.11.
6. V.B. Thompson, *Africa and Unity*, Longmans, 1969.
7. W.E.B. DuBois, "The African Roots of War" – 1915, reprinted in DuBois, *On The Importance of Africa in World History*, Black Liberation Press, New York, 1978.
8. For a critical analysis of the compromises which led to the formation of the O.A.U. see Vincent B. Thompson, op. cit. See also H. Campbell, ed. *Pan-Africanism: The Struggle Against Neo-Colonialism and Imperialism*, Afro-Carib Publications, Toronto, 1975.
9. René Depestre, "Problems of Identity for the Black Man in Caribbean Literature" *Caribbean Quarterly*, Vol 19, No 3, 1973.
10. See Len Nembhard, *Trials and Triumphs of Marcus Garvey*, Gleaner Co., Kingston, 1940.
11. This is not meant to be a biography of Garvey but to locate his life in the process of the international struggle.

For a biographical account see *Philosophy and Opinions of Marcus Garvey*, compiled by Amy Jacques Garvey. See Garvey's own account of his youth, Vol II, pp 124-134.

12. Between 1902 and 1919, 126,000 Jamaicans migrated from the island.
13. For the origins of the U.N.I.A. see *Philosophy and Opinions of Marcus Garvey*, Vol II, pp 126-127.
14. Lynching was an integral part of controlling blacks, especially civil rights leaders, and the double crime of lynching and castration was used assiduously against black men, for the racist myth that black men were rapists was methodically conjured up when recurrent waves of violence and terror against the black community required a convincing explanation. Lynching was in turn complemented by the systematic rape of black women, and became an essential ingredient of the strategy of terror which guaranteed the exploitation of black labour and the political domination of black people as a whole. See Angela Davis, "Rape, Racism and the Capitalist Setting", *Black Scholar*, April, 1978, pp 24-30.
15. H. Braverman, *Labour and Monopoly Capital: The Degradation of Work in the Twentieth Century*, Monthly Review Press, 1976.
16. See Robert Allen, *Reluctant Reformers*, Anchor Books, 1975, pp 201-205.
17. Philip S. Foner, *Organised Labour and the Black Worker*, Praeger Publishers, New York, pp 137-139.
18. Claude McKay was one of the literary luminaries of the period, who moved in and out of the U.N.I.A. and other left organisations. In 1940 Winston Churchill used this poem to rally the British people against German fascism but he never acknowledged the authorship. See Claude McKay's autobiography, *A Long Way From Home*, 1937.
19. *Philosophy and Opinions of Marcus Garvey*, Vol II, pp 135-143. For an analysis of the continued significance of the demands of the Declaration see T. Vincent, *Black Power and the Garvey Movement*, Ramparts Press, 1971, pp 115-120.
20. For the number of branches see Tony Martin, *Race First: The Ideological and Organisational Struggles of Marcus Garvey and the Universal Negro Improvement Association*, Greenwood Press, 1976, pp 15-17.
21. Apart from the works by Amy Jacques Garvey, Theodore Vincent and Tony Martin cited above, the edited book by John Henrik Clarke, *Marcus Garvey and the Vision of Africa*, Random House, 1974, contains some useful speeches by Garvey. Prior to these works the most influential book was by David Cronon, *Black Moses: The Story of Marcus Garvey and the UNIA*, 1956. Cronon's work perpetuated a number of myths concerning Garvey. Cronon suggested that the U.N.I.A. had fascist characteristics and promulgated the view that the U.N.I.A. was a simplistic Back to Africa movement, but he did not understand the full impact of the partition of Africa on African people everywhere. The latter-day view, which derides Garvey's nationalism, misses the importance of racial consciousness in the struggle of black workers everywhere.
22. For an analysis of the Garveyites in Southern Africa see Tony Martin, op. cit., pp 119-121. See also "The Strange Career of Dr. Wellington – An African Garvey" by Bob Edgar, Institute of Commonwealth Studies Seminar Paper, London, 1975.
23. *Philosophy and Opinions of Marcus Garvey*, Vol I, pp 33-34.
24. The African Orthodox Church became a very influential movement in the Caribbean, especially among disgruntled trainees of Mico College in Jamaica and Antigua; while the Rasta was the poor people's response to colonialism, it would be safe to say that the A.D.C. in the Eastern Caribbean was a middle stratum form of religious nationalism. See Terry Thompson, *The History of the African Orthodox Church*, New York, Beacon Press, 1956.
25. The religious aspect of the U.N.I.A. was important. Bishop McGuire built upon the foundations of the Ethiopian movement. The catechism declared that the words of the Psalm "Princes come out of Egypt, Ethiopia stretch forth her hands" meant that Negroes will set up their own government in Africa, with rulers of their own race. For a religious interpretation of Garveyism see *Garveyism as a Religious Movement*, Randell Burkett, Scarecrow Press, N.J., 1978.
26. The Firestone Rubber Company was granted a 99-year lease for a million acres of rubber. The level of collusion between the British and US Governments and black lackies in preventing the establishment of a Garveyite community showed that the Imperialists understood the impact that such a community would have on the struggle for independence.
27. Karl Marx, writing at the height of the New York riots in 1863, had warned that "labour cannot emancipate itself in the white skin when in the black it is branded", but the socialists and communists never fully understood the significance of this statement. It was Lenin in the Soviet Union who precipitated the serious work by Marxists among blacks, for he penetrated the strategic importance of black labour in the U.S.A. After Lenin's admonition that the Communist Party should give direct support to the revolutionary movements among dependent nations and those without rights, the US Party sought to develop a programme for black people. However this programme was bereft of a full appreciation of the nature of white racism. For an analysis of Garvey and the communists in the USA see Tony Martin, op. cit., pp 221-272. See also H. Campbell, "The Communist Party and the Black Man in the USA, 1919-1928", Seminar Paper, Makerere University, November 1972. Some of the anti-communist statements of Garvey have been used as a weapon against the Rasta in Jamaica, but Garvey had the highest appreciation for the work of Lenin and the Bolshevik

Revolution. He was clear that he was against communism as practised in the USA.

28. Rupert Lewis, "Political Aspects of Garvey's Work in Jamaica 1929-35", *Jamaica Journal*.
29. Norman Manley, then an attorney for the United Fruit Company, was directly involved in one of the anti-Garvey legal wrangles. For an account of the anti-black outlook of the Manley household at that time see *Edna Manley* by Wayne Brown, André Deutsch, London, 1975. For an account of the personalities and politics of the period see J. Carnegie, "Some Aspects of Jamaica Politics 1918-1938", Institute of Jamaica, Kingston, 1975.
30. Editorial in the *Blackman*, 25 October, 1930.

Chapter Three

THE ORIGINS OF RASTA

Rasta and the Revolt of the Sufferers in Jamaica 1938

Introduction

This chapter properly locates the Rastafari as a class and racial movement within the context of colonialised Jamaica. The chapter begins with an analysis of how the race consciousness and political work of Garvey had sought to break the monopoly of the British over the society. For the rural poor, the crowning of an African King who could claim legitimacy from the bible and from the line of Solomon led to a new deification, replacing the white King of England with a black God and black King.

Jamaicans who spread the notion that Haile Selassie was divine and human had taken sides in a spiritual controversy which still rages between the Western Christian church and the Orthodox Christian religions.

The links between Jamaica and Ethiopia were strengthened after the Italian invasion of Abyssinia, for the Jamaican black people joined the international Pan-African movement which protested this form of fascism. Both Rastafari and non-Rastafari raised their voices against the Italian bombardment, but in Jamaica the individuals who were preaching that Haile Selassie was a Messiah found an outlet for their ideas through the Ethiopian World Federation.

This analysis of the origins of the Rasta links the first ideas of the movement to the writings of the *Voice of Ethiopia* to further stress the view that the ideas expressed by black people that Haile Selassie was the Lion of Judah was no mere millenarian escapism. The question which could be asked is what made Jamaicans who identified with Ethiopia millenarian, and those who walked around with pictures of the British King well-adjusted? The answer to this question is explored in the context of the idealism of the society, but more significantly within the realm of the response of the masses to colonialism.

The resistance of 1938 forms the central theme of this chapter, for this rebellion was an important point in Jamaican and Caribbean history.

In 1938 the sufferers accepted the 'brown man leadership' and for a while rejected the Bogle and Rastafari cry of "Colour for colour". The conditions of the poor and the results of the revolt are underlined to centralise the fact that the Rastafari developed in the absence of a materialist tradition in the society, especially after the massive population movements during the fifties.

After World War II the biggest movement of the population since the days of slavery took place, and it is from that period that the beliefs of the Rastafari in repatriation and the rejection of the leadership of the two-party system took form.

Because of the range of influences which came to bear on the origin of the Rastafari, this chapter seeks to illuminate the elements which were paramount, and does not seek to recount the history of Jamaica in this period. The richness of the period is captured by Ken Post in his book *Arise Ye Starvelings;* but his work represents the sufferers as Quashie and the Rasta as millenarian. The thrust of this chapter is to bring to life the rise and fall of the petty bourgeois nationalism of the two-party system.

The Origins of Rastafari

In 1930, in the region of Africa then known as Abyssinia, Ras Tafari, the great-grandson of King Sahela Selassie of Shoa and Son of Ras Makonnen, was crowned King Negus Negusta, after serving fourteen years as Prince Regent of this proud and independent African society. King Negus Negusta was crowned Emperor and assumed the throne name of Haile Selassie I on November 2, 1930, subsequent to the death of Empress Zawditu in April of the same year.

Between April and November, when the official coronation took place, Ras Tafari went to great lengths to let the world know that a black African leader was joining the international community of Kings and Princes. Arrays of princes and other powers attended the ceremony and the retinue of journalists recorded for history the pomp and colour as ras* after ras in full regalia bowed in homage before the imperial throne.

Colour pictures of the proceedings were reprinted in newspapers throughout the Western world and newsreels of the ceremonies for the first time gave many blacks a visual perception of Ethiopia. The pictures of this African King with an African army, along with the Duke of Gloucester – heir to the British throne – bowing before him sent a surge of pride through all Africans.

Black nationalists in Harlem, USA, celebrated the coronation, for they saw in Haile Selassie a powerful black man who possessed the capacity to restore to African peoples their respect, rights and dignity. Already in the period of the Harlem Renaissance one of the serious nationalist organisations was called the Abyssinians. Following the long tradition of the Ethiopian movement the Africans in America had declared that they were citizens of Ethiopia and that black people should take out citizenship under the flag of Abyssinia.

The Abyssinians had branches in Detroit, Chicago, Washington and New York, and their militant anti-capitalist language drew hostile attention, especially after they called upon the black people of the USA to burn the American flag[1] and sold the Abyssinian flag for one dollar (US), along with certificates of Abyssinian citizenship.

* Ras was the title used for a nobleman in Ethiopia.

The first Rastafari to appear in Jamaica came to the attention of the general population through incidents which were similar to those of the Abyssinians of the USA. Leonard Percival Howell began preaching to Jamaican black people that their loyalty should be to the Emperor of Ethiopia and not to the King of England. Howell, from St. Catherine, was one of those Jamaicans who had migrated overseas, returning to the island in December 1932. He moved between Kingston and St. Thomas, proclaiming his message that black people could not have two kings and that the only true king was Emperor Haile Selassie.

The *Daily Gleaner*, the voice of the planters and merchants which carried stories of Britain and the writings of the racist Rudyard Kipling, gave notice to the white cultural leaders of Jamaica of the true significance and potential of the doctrine of Howell by giving wide publicity to the charges of sedition which were being preferred against him because he sold pictures of a black Emperor. Within the space of one year Howell was holding meetings of more than 800 in the Pear Tree Grove and Leith Hall Districts of St. Thomas, the parish of Paul Bogle.

It was clear to the colonial authorities that the message of the Rastafari constituted a potent anti-colonial message, for the Gleaner reporter declared, on hearing Howell's message, that:

> *"devilish attacks are made at these meetings on government, both local and imperial, and the whole conduct of the meeting would tend to provoke an insurrection if taken seriously."*[2]

Police officers were taking the meetings seriously, for they watched with apprehension as the people placed their trust in Howell — so much so that they sang songs saying "Day by day I see what Leonard Howell is doing for my soul." Officers who tried to infiltrate the meeting at Seaford Town finally arrested Howell on charges of sedition, for in the words of the colonial State Howell abused the Sovereign and Governor of Jamaica:

> *"thereby intending to excite hatred and contempt for his majesty the King of England and of those responsible for the government of the island, and to create disaffection among the subjects of his majesty in this island and to disturb the public peace and tranquility of the island."*[3]

The colonial authorities were so conscious of the potential of a black man proclaiming Haile Selassie as the messiah that it was the Chief Justice of Jamaica at the time, Sir Robert Grant, who presided over the speedy trial of Howell and his Deputy, Robert Hinds. These two Rastafarians were sentenced to two years' hard labour and one year hard labour respectively, for selling pictures of Haile Selassie for one shilling and declaring that the newly crowned Emperor of Ethiopia was the King of black men – literally the returned messiah. Both leaders had defied the colonial State by telling black people that they should not pay taxes, for the island was theirs; and that they were part of the African nation.

The incarceration of Howell was the first attempt of many by the colonialists to crush the Rastafari. While they hounded Garvey out of Jamaica, there were thousands of poor blacks who were taking Garvey's promise of redemption literally and identifying the Emperor of Ethiopia as a principal force in this redemption.

This nationalist response to white imperialism which was to become the Rastafari movement developed independently in Jamaica, and the first teachers of the movement – Leonard Howell, Archibald Dunkley and Joseph Hibbert – were workers who had laboured both in Jamaica and in the USA. Howell was continually harassed by the State, to the point where they committed him to the mental asylum in Kingston.

The State was terrified that the Rastafarians were not only linking themselves to Ethiopia, but also called themselves Nya men – linking their ideas to the anti-colonial movement of Kigezi, Uganda – *Nyabingi* – which called for "Death to Black and White Oppressors."

One of the reliable ways of reconstructing the ideas of Rasta and the growth of the movement would be to look beyond the published accounts of the development of the Rastafari movement in Jamaica, which link the movement solely to Haile Selassie and Ethiopia. The ideas and beliefs which formed the basis of the movement developed over a fifty-year period and it is clear that when dealing with a social, cultural and religious movement like that of the Rastafari one must analyse the contradictions of the society which gave rise to Rasta, so that it becomes difficult to make definitive judgements about any one phase of the movement.

While those Garveyites who had some limited status in the society joined the Citizens Associations and were pressing for advancement within the colonial structure, African identity was basing itself within the working class and rural poor in the form of Rastafari.

The identification with Nyabingi showed a level of ideological advance over the limited religious expressions of the Bedwardites, who spoke of the "black wall and the white wall." Those Rastafarians who called themselves Nya men had understood, as the peasants of Uganda, that black agents of the colonialists, like the black slave drivers and the 'house niggers', could be just as brutal as the whites.

Up to the present the Nyabingi legacy in Kigezi, Uganda, is a legacy of anti-colonialism. For when Britain sought to extend the colonialism of forced labour, compulsory crops and unjust taxation on the peoples of the South West region of Uganda, the people resorted to armed struggle to resist British imperialism. Queen Muhumusa, who stood out as a valiant leader in resisting Britain, called upon all the resources of the society to fight the British, to the point where spirit mediums were incorporated in the struggle.

The battle between the peoples of Kigezi raged for more than 20 years, and despite the capture and banishment of the Queen, the armed confrontations continued. When the Europeans thought that they could impose indirect rule through the use of Buganda (African) agents, the people of Kigezi attacked the black District Commissioners so that there was an awareness among the people that oppression could wear a black skin as well as a white one.

This awareness found sympathy in Jamaica where the Rastafari, who proclaimed that Haile Selassie was crowned Emperor to redeem black people, read in local newspapers about the Nyabingi movement. Ken Post, in his book *Arise Ye Starvelings,* asserts that a contributor to a local Jamaican newspaper – *Plain Talk* – had written in 1935 that the leadership of the Nyabingi movement was taken over by Haile Selassie.[5] The writer had proclaimed that Haile Selassie would lead a revolt of the blacks against the whites; and the words of the article seemed prophetic as the news of the Italian invasion of Ethiopia was splashed across the front pages of the newspapers in Jamaica.

Rastafari, the Black World and the Italian Invasion of Abyssinia

The spiritual, political and cultural bonds between Jamaican workers, including the Rastafarians, and Africa and Ethiopia were increased subsequent to the fascist invasion of Abyssinia in 1935. Jamaican newspapers printed front page stories of the atrocities which were being carried out by Italy, who tested the latest instruments of death in Africa. Poisonous gas, aerial bombardment, the creation of concentration camps and those barbarous fascist practices which were to become commonplace during World War II were tested on Africans in Ethiopia between 1935-41.

Black people throughout the world interpreted the war as a racial war in so far as the European powers of the League of Nations supplied equipment and spare parts for the Italian war machine, while they were refusing to deliver arms to the Emperor of Ethiopia to defend the mass of African people.

The progress of the war was discussed as eagerly in the villages of the world as it was debated in the press and parliaments of Europe. Africans throughout the colonial world showed such an eagerness to fight in Abyssinia that the British were genuinely afraid that the reporting of the war could lead to anti-colonial revolts. From St. Lucia to Johannesburg, from Chicago to Ghana, from Kingston to London, black men and women offered to go to fight in Abyssinia.[6]

As far as the mass of black people in the world were concerned, the defence of Ethiopia was the defence of black dignity, and George Padmore, writing in *Crisis* magazine in 1935, summed it up correctly when he declared that it was the "duty of every black man and woman to render maximum moral and material support to the Ethiopian people in their singlehanded struggle against Italian fascism and not too friendly world".[7]

Black workers rioted in the streets of New York and there were pitched battles between Italians and blacks in New York City.[8] Black newspapers in

America exposed the duplicity of the European governments and in 1935 black people throughout the world were in the vanguard of the fight against fascism. This was certainly the view of a massive anti-fascist demonstration in Montego Bay, Jamaica, reported in the Gleaner on October 15, 1935.

At packed meetings black people called upon Britain to repeal the Foreign Enlistment Act and 1,400 signed a petition to allow Jamaicans to enlist in the Ethiopian army "to fight to preserve the glories of our ancient and beloved empire". Garveyites took the lead in calling mass meetings to denounce the Italian aggression. Mrs Amy Jacques Garvey addressed a packed meeting at the Ward Theatre on 13th October, 1935, and at the end of the meeting the Kingston Division of the U.N.I.A. called upon the British to allow ex-servicemen to volunteer to fight in Ethiopia.[9]

Meanwhile in South Africa, black workers who were organised under the ideas of Garveyism began a march up the continent to assist their African brothers in Abyssinia. They were turned back a few hundred miles by the British, who disarmed them.[10]

Britain took the protest in the Caribbean very seriously, for when the U.N.I.A. petitioned the Jamaican Governor, Sir Edward Denham, to be allowed to go to fight, this petition was forwarded to the Colonial Office. The criticisms of British collusion by blacks in the Caribbean were circulated to British governors in Africa with the advice to the governors that the criticisms were unfounded and that the war was not a racial war.[11]

To counter the militant anti-colonial sentiments which were developing in the islands, the British called upon loyal colonials to pass resolutions placing on record the "dignified efforts of the government of Great Britain to secure peace". The mulattoes and Afro-Saxons of the Kingston and St. Andrew Council did pass such a resolution, but the broad mass of black people deepened their identification with the Ethiopian Emperor; while the fact of the war was deliberately used as a device to strengthen the resolve to oppose the onerous conditions of the plantation society.

While Ethiopia featured as an external reference point for those who were in the forefront of the riots, the Rastafarians spread their theory that the Emperor was invincible, and one of the most prized pictures of the Rasta in Jamaica was that of the caped Emperor inspecting troops with his foot on an unexploded bomb.

Rasta identified the colonial state and the church as the principal agents of oppression to such an extent that zealous brethren could shout "fire and brimstone" as they passed the established churches of the colonial society. These sentiments were not unique to the Rastafarians: in West Africa young nationalists equated the church with oppression in the midst of the war, for the Pope in Rome had given his blessing to the fascist adventures of Benito Mussolini.

Identifying the League of Nations as the League of European Brotherhood, these nationalists declared:

"The means whereby the Africans, particularly those of West Africa, have been kept in subjection under the European nations is religion and Christianity. The Italo-Ethiopian war is destined to prove to the African masses that Europe with all its civilisation is still enshrined in barbarism and that Western civilisation is sheer mockery. It is also destined to prove to the African masses that religion, especially Christianity as it has been introduced by the whiteman to the Blackman is a heinous mass of deception. We must worship God according to our conviction, not according to the whiteman's Christianity. We must see Christ as a Blackman and all the Holy Angels as negroes. As for Western civilisation, it has to be properly sifted. Take what is good from it and throw the rest in the dustbin."[12]

These sentiments, which were articulated by the Pan-Africanist Wallace Johnson, in Ghana, were being echoed in Jamaica by the Rastafari as the aggression against Ethiopia spurred on fresh interest in the Garveyite conception of a black God. But in the midst of the war, Marcus Garvey castigated the Ethiopian monarch for his lack of preparedness for battle. When Haile Selassie had to flee from his kingdom and took refuge in London, Marcus Garvey, who was in London at the time, separated support for Haile Selassie from support for the people of Abyssinia. Garvey was aware of the callous neglect of the poor peasantry in Ethiopia and he castigated the Emperor for not unleashing the potential of his people to attempt to lift the living standards of the masses. Writing in the *Blackman* in 1936 Garvey maintained that:

"Mussolini of Italy has conquered Haile Selassie, but he has not conquered the Abyssinians or Abyssinia. The Emperor of Abyssinia allowed himself to be conquered by playing white, by trusting white advisers and by relying on white governments, including the white League of Nations ... If Haile Selassie had educated thousands of his countrymen and women, and raised them to the status of culture and general knowledge necessary to civilisation, the Italians never could have dared an offensive against Abyssinia, because Abyssinia could have found leaders on the spot competent and ready to throw back the invader. But that is not all. If Haile Selassie had negotiated the proper relationship with the hundreds of millions of Africans outside Abyssinia, in South and Central America, in the United States, in Canada, in the West Indies, in Australia, he could have had an organisation of men and women ready for service, not only in the development of Abyssinia as a great Negro nation, but on the spur of the moment to protect it from any foreign foe. But he had no diplomatic agents among Negroes anywhere and the few that he did appoint were to the courts of white nations and they were chiefly white men or Abyssinians who were married to Italians and had great leanings towards whites whom they tried to ape."[13]

Garvey's correct analysis of the dependence of the Abyssinian ruling class on

Europe did not dissuade those Jamaicans who interpreted the world in biblical terms. This biblical interpretation of the events in Abyssinia deepened as Haile Selassie in exile sought to mobilise the favourable international response among blacks through an organisation called the Ethiopian World Federation.[14]

Rastafari and the Ethiopian World Federation

A great deal of the support for the Abyssinians can be explained in terms of the search for an ethnic and racial identity amongst Afro-Americans and Westindians within the context of the massive exploitation and oppression they faced in the midst of the capitalist depression of the thirties. This period of assertive identification with Ethiopia, which had been characteristic of the individual Rastafari brethren in Jamaica, took an organisational form in the U.S.A. as Haile Selassie sent his cousin to New York to try to bring some cohesion to the many groups which were campaigning for the cause of Ethiopia.

Dr. Malaku Bayen, the official representative and the cousin of Haile Selassie, founded the Ethiopian World Federation in 1937 in New York City, out of the ranks of Garveyites, Communists and religious leaders; and within a short time he had established branches throughout the major black centres of the U.S.A. and the Caribbean. The programme of the Ethiopian World Federation (E.W.F.) was based on eight principles:
(1) the unity of blacks in all parts of the world;
(2) financial and moral support of Ethiopia and Ethiopian refugees;
(3) definite action as a united whole against wrongs perpetrated against members of the race in any part of the world;
(4) demand for the continental independence and full sovereignity of Ethiopia;
(5) Ethiopia for Ethiopians at home and abroad;
(6) no surrender to Italian aggression in Ethiopia;
(7) to aid Ethiopians in their determined and never failing campaign to expel Italians from Ethiopia; and
(8) to prepare our people to take their rightful place among the nations of the earth.[15]

Through their newspaper, the *Voice of Ethiopia*, the Ethiopian World Federation promoted support for Ethiopia and Haile Selassie under the slogan *One God, One Brotherhood*, in a conscious attempt to counter criticism of the Emperor's exile in London. The *Voice of Ethiopia* attempted to follow the tradition of the Garvey newspaper, the *Negro World*, and it was clear from the correspondents of the newspaper that the former branches of the U.N.I.A. in Africa and the Caribbean were recipients of the paper.

Under the masthead "It is better to die free than to live in slavery" and the slogan "Ethiopia Must be Free, Blackman Must be Free", this paper and the E.W.F. linked the future of Ethiopia to the freedom of blacks everywhere.

In Jamaica the paper was read with interest, and within a year the first branch of the E.W.F., Local 17, was established in Kingston. L.F.C. Mantle, the prolific writer of *Plain Talk* who had organised the Ethiopian Medical Aid

Fund, was the first president. From that date until the birth of the Twelve Tribes all the dispersed and heterogeneous individuals who preached that Haile Selassie was the messiah became organised under one international body, and the *Rastafari Movement* began to take shape in the Jamaican society.

Many of the beliefs and teachings of the present Rasta were taken from the *Voice of Ethiopia*; for example, the E.W.F. called upon all black people

> *"to learn Amharic, the history and culture of Ethiopia, and to learn about their own church – the Ethiopian Orthodox Church – which dates back to the 4th century and was founded by St. Mark".*

Rastafari in Jamaica, whose only link with Africa was through *The Voice of Africa* and Garvey's *Blackman,* were not to know that the linguistic and cultural diversity of Ethiopia was richer than Amharic, and that the promotion of Amharic as opposed to other Ethiopian languages was part of the cultural chauvinism of the Ethiopian ruling class.

Thus Rastas, in their communities, studied Amharic as an African language and tried to establish a system of spiritual and religious expression in keeping with Ethiopian Orthodoxy.* At their Sunday night meetings the brethren waved the black, red and green flag of Garvey, beat their drums and sang with fervour that "the Lion of Judah shall break every chain and bring us the victory again and again".

These adherents of black nationalism accepted literally the claim of the Ethiopian World Federation that Haile Selassie was the Elect of God and Light of the World. When the *Voice of Ethiopia* added that the true Israelites were black and that Africans formed the *Twelve Tribes of Israel*, giving an historical account of the Falashas who, it claimed, had carried the Ark of the Covenant back to Ethiopia,[16] many Rastas believed that blacks were indeed the children of Israel.

The influence of the E.W.F. waned during World War II, especially after the death of Dr. Malaku Bayen in 1940; but more significantly because the ideas of the Rasta by themselves could not carry the people forward in the anti-colonial struggle. The movement was revived during the fifties when the divisive nature of Jamaican two-party politics led to scepticism among many workers. In 1955 the New York branch of the E.W.F. sent Mamie Richardson, the singer, to Jamaica to popularise the work of the E.W.F., and within a short time the E.W.F. expanded to over 18 branches.

It was at this time that the ideas of repatriation began to become an important set of ideas among the Rasta. These ideas of going back to Africa were given currency by the black nationalist paper of New York – *The African Opinion* – which carried on the work of the *Voice of Ethiopia* in deifying the Emperor of

*The Rastafari had introduced into Jamaican society the orthodox version of Christianity in which God was human and divine. This theory – the dyophysite – is the thrust of one of the beliefs of the Rasta and is different from the Western belief – the monophysite theory – which holds that Christ has one nature. The Ethiopian monarch promoted these ideas as a variant of the divine rights of kings in such a way that the Ethiopian Orthodox Church was a pillar of the Ethiopian State. For an analysis of the differences between the monophysite and the dyophysite theory see *The Church of Ethiopia,* published by the Ethiopian Orthodox Church, Addis Ababa.

Ethiopia, declaring that the victory over Italy and the return of the Emperor showed that he was the *Conquering Lion of Judah*.[17]

The full essence of Rasta doctrine, while expressing a sense of racial solidarity among the Jamaican poor, could not and did not concentrate on social transformation within Jamaica or the Caribbean; hence, while the surge of interest in Africa served as an external reference point, the conditions of poverty and exploitation in the Caribbean demanded direct political action.

The fact that the Ethiopian masses had taken to arms was deliberately used as a device to strengthen the resolve of the blacks in the Caribbean to oppose colonialism. This resolve led to the violent confrontations which shook the Caribbean – beginning in St. Vincent and Guyana in 1935, spreading like bush fire to Trinidad and Antigua, and erupting in Jamaica in 1938.[18]

The Capitalist Depression in Jamaica

The theological questions of whether Haile Selassie was divine and human or simply a messiah and redeemer paled into insignificance as the conditions of the capitalist depression threatened the whole livelihood of the working poor. So wretched were the conditions of unemployment and underemployment that the threat of force and the use of force remained central to the process of alienating labour in Jamaica.

The majority of workers (except for those artisans who had registered under the 1919 trade union ordinance) were not organised in their own organisations. The planter monopoly over most of the arable land and over the reward for work meant that the working people of Jamaica, like the majority of colonised workers, suffered from a special type of super exploitation. Civil disputes between employers and employees were placed under the sanction of criminal law, according to the Masters and Servants Ordinance, and it was not until 1940 that the penal sanctions of the Masters and Servants Law were abolished.[19]

The fact that the working people in the colonies had no political rights meant that the legal protection afforded to trade unions in capitalist countries under the Trade Union Law of 1919 was not extended to them. There was no Workers' Compensation Law, no factory legislation which provided for the minimum safety regulations in the sugar mills, no minimum wage, and the militarist notion of industrial relations was evident from the fact that the Commissioner appointed by the Colonial Office to investigate *Labour Conditions in the West Indies* was a major in the British Armed Forces.[20]

Without the right to fight for better wages and without the ability to vote, the political deprivation of the broad masses ensured that in 1938, one hundred years after the emancipation of slavery, the same rate of 1/- (one shilling) per day for cutting cane was being paid as in 1838. Rates for particular tasks were not fixed by general agreement or collective bargaining, but usually on the spot. In 1937 the day rates for the back breaking tasks of weeding and cutting cane on the plantations ranged from nine pence (9d) to ten and a half pence a day.[21]

The tasks of cutting sugar cane, loading bananas, of digging and breaking rockstones with handtools, and the general tasks of the underdeveloped economy were particularly labour intensive. Banana loaders who worked in tattered rags throughout the night, balancing two or three bunches of bananas on their heads, had to make worksongs to alleviate the degrading conditions of supplying bananas for consumption in Europe and America.[22]

Allan G. St. Claver Coombs, in giving testimony before the Royal Commission in 1939, told how banana loaders had to run and walk while loading the boats, and how the loaders, who worked in a line, were whipped if they broke the line.

It was the conjunction of low pay, poor housing and the absence of political rights and rampant coercion which led the poor people to call themselves *sufferers*. This characterisation of the poor as sufferers was the people's attempt to define their location in the international system. Efforts to unduly separate the urban poor from the rural poor and small farmers in recent scholarship overshadow the unique characteristics of the proletarianised masses in the Caribbean. The vast outmigration of poor people from the society was such that many of the one hundred and seventy-four thousand who returned to Jamaica returned to the rural areas, hoping to survive as small farmers, but hiring themselves out as seasonal labourers.

There was always overlap between the position of small farmers and workers, while the incomplete crystallisation of the class structure meant that many workers were not completely separated from their means of subsistence.

So unique was the character of the labouring masses that the total wage earning population of 269,000 in 1937 was not significantly higher than the numbers who had been migrant workers in Central America and the USA. Thousands of those who were forced to leave Central America during the depression returned to their village communities or joined the ranks of the unemployed.[23]

The existence of a large pool of unskilled labour and the high rates of unemployment meant that the ratio of labour to capital was always high; and the presence of the large army of reserve labour acted as a social sanction which was as effective as direct State coercion in the control of the working people.

Not only did the existence of the large numbers of unemployed depress the wages of those toiling under the sun, but the low wages meant that the labourer had to bring his whole family into the web of exploitation. Many of those in the rural areas depended on family labour to provide food from the provision grounds and the disposable income went to buy clothes and occasionally codfish and mackerel.

Workers in the urban areas were hardest hit by the capitalist depression: wages actually fell between 1935 and 1937. Working class families were further humiliated by the fact that the mothers had to hire themselves out as domestic servants, working from 6 a.m to 10 p.m. for between two shillings and six pence to six shillings per week. On top of this they had to feed themselves out of this wage. There was no legislation to regulate the number of hours worked and the call for a mimimum wage was never considered in the society.

The objective deterioration of living standards was clear to the colonisers, who in their attempts to compile a cost of living index showed by their own calculations that it would take a worker 6 days to be able to afford a loaf of bread.[24] Constant surveys by the State reported that it was impossible to balance the family budget.[25]

Report followed report in tragi-comic succession, commenting on the appalling conditions of the people, the undernourishment and malnutrition of children and the absence of rudimentary social services. Hookworm, yaws, beri-beri, scurvy and rickets accounted for a considerable measure of disability, and the absence of clean running water led to numerous bowel diseases.

The low standards of sanitation helped to stunt the general state of health of the sufferers. From time to time the whites drew attention to the poor state of dwellings, the overcrowding, the presence of rats and the precarious structures with earthen floors which the poor called homes. The Moyne Commission had this to say of the notorious Smith's Village in Kingston:

> *"In parts of Smith's Villages, on the outskirts of Kingston in Jamaica, we found large areas covered by ruinous shacks none of which could have escaped condemnation in this country even under standards long since abandoned."*[26]

The conditions of squalor were accentuated by overcrowding, and the names given to these slums were most appropriate, e.g. Swine Lane in Montego Bay, and Dungle, i.e. Dung Hill, in Kingston.

The living conditions of the people and the absolute impoverishment of the society was one clear indicator of the inadequate technique and general backwardness of this underdeveloped capitalism.[27] The political power of the planters ensured that production was limited to the production of export crops – bananas, sugar, coffee – and there was actual hostility to the exploitation of other productive resources.

It necessitated the entrance of US capital after the war to exploit the vast bauxite resources – with negative results for the society. The depression in Europe sent the price of sugar down from £16.15/- per ton in 1927 to £9.19/- and ten pence in 1937. So abysmally low were the prices of colonial products that in 1936 the price of a ton of raw sugar and the price of a ton of hay were the same.

Hence, after the society planted the cane, weeded the land, reaped the cane, transported it to the factory and ground it, the price was the same as for a Sussex farmer cutting a ton of hay to store for the winter. It was this complete domination of the colonial society which precipiated the mass resistance of the sufferers in 1938; and as in 1865, the leadership came from the ranks of the poor.

And The People Rise Up in 1938

The revolt of the poor in Jamaica formed an important turning point in the history of the society and is significant in the study of the Rastafari; for though the Rastas did not play a central role in the rebellion, the ideas of black consciousness which were taught by Garvey and carried forward by the Rastas helped to instil the confidence necessary to confront the British State.

It is not insignificant that the 100th anniversary of the abolition of slavery began with a workers' revolt in the parish of Paul Bogle and of the Bongo men; and in the area with the largest concentration of Rastafarians.

At Serge Island in St. Thomas, 1,400 workers armed with machetes and sticks went on strike for higher wages on the fifth of January. They forthrightly demanded higher wages, stopped carts and wagons from entering or leaving the estate and practically shut down the parish of St. Thomas. The colonial State, which always supported the planters, brought police reinforcements from Kingston. In the resulting attack by the police on the sufferers, 34 strikers were injured and 60 were arrested.[28]

The rebellion in St. Thomas set a pattern which was replicated throughout the length and breadth of Jamaica. In every parish the workers and small farmers blocked roads, cut telephone wires, broke down bridges, burnt cane fields, destroyed banana trees, ambushed the police with sticks and stones, and stood up to demand an end to the semi-slavery conditions of the society. This revolt heralded the return to history of the proletarianised masses; and the protests were distinguished by the organisation, mobilisation and self-expression of the workers and their leaders.

The self-expression of the Jamaican sufferers had developed considerably during the depression, and the activities of the Garveyites and Rastafari had imbued a deep sense of race consciousness and confidence among the poor.[29]

During 1937 there were hunger marches organised by the Jamaica Workers and Tradesman Union (J.W.T.U.), the trade union which was formed and organised by the workers themselves. The Headquarters of the J.W.T.U. was at 39 Barnett Street in Montego Bay, where Marcus Garvey had spoken on his visit to Western Jamaica in 1929. Allan George Coombs, the ex-serviceman who started the union, worked tirelessly to establish branches throughout Jamaica and it was Coombs and the ex-Garveyites, like Tom Tom, who welcomed Alexander Bustamante to the organisation of the workers.[30]

The militant and direct action of Coombs on behalf of the sufferers could be distinguished from the plethora of Citizens' Associations and Welfare Groups which were the main organisations of the burgeoning petty bourgeoisie (usually called the middle class). This stratum simmered under the crude degradation of colonialism, but they did not link their protest to that of the masses, for they had internalised the disparaging attitudes of the whites towards black people. Their protests consisted of writing letters to the newspapers and to the Colonial Office. It was not until after the violent and spontaneous protest of the poor that this stratum joined the push for self-determination and political rights.

While the Jamaican middle class remained equivocal and hesitant in their protest, the sufferers embarked on the making of a statement of their deprivation. *This statement was written in blood.*

Construction workers at Frome Sugar Estate in Westmoreland confronted the big conglomerate Tate and Lyle, demanding four shillings per day and rejecting the two shillings and six pence which was offered. Among the ranks of these skilled workers were returned migrants who were aware of the vast profits of companies such as Tate and Lyle, and through their experiences in Central America understood the gains of increased wages as a consequence of unionisation and organised protests.

Coombs had been active in Westmoreland, but the crucial leadership during the strike of April 29, 1938, came out of the ranks of the workers themselves. When the employers tried to use scab labour from the vast reserve of men who had assembled to seek work, one of the workers' leaders rallied the more than one thousand strikers, saying:

> *"It will be death. We have three days' pay to get from the Company. Let them pay us now. It is going to be serious here today. I have read that the Company wanted 1000 men at 4/- per day and the best accommodation. I have heard it said that if we accept 2/6 per day we will be paid: but I want to tell you that if any men accept 2/6 per day, if it is even my father, I will bear the gallows for him."*[31]

This uncompromising spirit guided the actions of the poor, who defended themselves when the manager fired shots to scare them and called in the police to disperse the strikers instead of paying them. Armed policemen were rushed in to intimidate the workers, and when the police decided to stand their ground the police opened fire, killing four sufferers, among them an expectant mother. Thirteen others were injured and 105 were arrested; calm only returned when the mobile appeaser, Alexander Bustamante, arrived from Kingston to offer to mediate on behalf of the workers.

Bustamante endeared himself to the sufferers by siding with them against the police, and since this was very unusual for a 'brown man' to do, the reputation of Bustamante as a defender of the rights of the poor increased, especially after the prolonged strikes and takeover of the streets of Kingston by the dockers and their allies.

In Kingston the news of the police violence against the strikers led to a new sense of solidarity. Mass meetings in the capital raised the question of poor wages and linked the events in Frome to the ongoing strike by the dockers.

These workers at the docks in Kingston had demonstrated a level of class consciousness and sensitivity towards the world economy which they serviced, for they were closely tied to the import/export functions of the economy. The strike by the dockers was supported by the unemployed of Kingston, who on May 23, 1938 moved to take over the city of Kingston. The colonial report recorded that:

"Persons of all classes going to business were set upon, public property was destroyed, streets blocked and train cars attacked. A hostile mob entered the Sewage Pumping Station and drove out the staff and another took possession of the Gold Street Power Station of the Jamaica Public Service Company. Several thousand people collected in Harbour Street, where Bustamante and Grant were endeavouring to hold a public meeting, and refused to disperse at the request of the police. They were eventually dislodged by a baton charge undertaken by 60 officers and men who were subjected to a rain of stones and brickbats."[32]

All the elements of the rebellion could be gathered from the report, for the people would not move until their demands for better wages were met and until Bustamante and St. William Grant (who had emerged as leaders) were released from detention. In forthright solidarity with Bustamante and Grant the workers and their allies refused to listen to Norman Washington Manley, who had offered himself as a mediator.

Manley, who had built up a career as an attorney for the big local and foreign capitalists, had urged the workers to go back to work; but the workers held out even after the police had been reinforced by the British army of occupation, the Sherwood Foresters.

Marching under homemade banners and singing the songs of war and resistance, "Onward Christian Soldiers Marching Unto War", the heritage of cultural resistance was being translated into armed revolts. This revolt in Kingston called forth a positive response from the weak-hearted middle class, who threw their organisational skills behind the workers, hoping to channel rebellion into narrow constitutional struggles.

Herein lay the essence of the emergence of Norman Washington Manley as a political leader.[33] But the project of the middle stratum was not destined to succeed until after the smoke of the rifles had cleared and the leaders of the workers were put in jail.

During May and June every parish was convulsed by armed resistance as groups of poor people confronted the forces of the Colonial State with their lives From May 28 to June 8 banana loaders who had been whipped, cane cutters who wanted more pay, domestic servants who wanted better working conditions, small farmers who wanted to end the monopoly of white sugar barons and the unemployed who wanted work took over towns and plantations and stood up for their rights.

Faced with the clear determination of the poor the police responded with simple brutality. The Colonial State's own inquiry stated:

"A number of witnesses were heard before the Commission whose evidence was directed to show that the police were not justified in firing on the crowd on the morning of June 3rd at Islington, St Mary. They went further and said that there was no crowd and that the police deliberately picked out persons and shot them."[34]

Eight persons were killed and 32 wounded by gunshot, and more than 139 received injuries from the police, the army and the hastily recruited special constables; but this tool only gave notice to the white planter class that their period of political hegemony was now coming to an end.

The year 1938 was historic, for it showed that all sections of the proletarianised masses were organised and that direct action was the only way to bring about change. The ferocity of the rebellion only subsided after the employers decided to increase wages and the colonial authorities enacted labour legislation which legalised the activities of trade unions, amended the Masters and Servants Law, passed a Workmen's Compensation Law and provided for inspection and enforcement of safety regulations in the sugar factories.

These limited gains of the masses provided the stepping-stone for the aspiring petty bourgeoisie who desired to participate more fully in the perverse capitalism which colonialism had introduced.[35] The political concessions of the society began in 1938 and ended with the granting of political independence in 1962.

Numerous accounts of the rebellion and its aftermath have centralised the personalities of Norman Manley and Alexander Bustamante, two cousins who were jockeying for a place in the planter society. It took some time for Manley, Bustamante and their supporters to understand that the revolt had fundamentally changed the social order. Writing to Robert Kirkwood, his class ally and director of the sugar conglomerate Tate and Lyle, Norman Manley reassured him in June 1938 that "in spite of the disturbances there is much to laugh about."

The colonialists welcomed the intervention of Manley, who acted as a force to restrain the thrust of the rebellion. Praising him, they declared:

> *"Perhaps no man on the island did more to re-establish confidence and restrict the growth of the disorders than Mr. N.W. Manley, K.C., who came forward immediately after the beginning of the disturbances, placed himself unreservedly at the disposal of the working class and undertook to submit, on their behalf, their claims for better pay and working conditions to the proper authorities. He appreciated that what was desired could only be obtained by constitutional means and that if the disturbances were to continue, the chief sufferers would be the labouring classes themselves. Both sides were gainers by his intervention: employers had someone with whom to negotiate, who understood conditions in the island and who knew what demands could be reasonably made and what could not. Mr. Manley toiled unceasingly for almost a month, addressing meetings throughout the island, negotiating with employers, conferring with various groups on the subject of their demands and finally representing them before the Board of Conciliation. We think that his services to the community as a whole were invaluable."*

It would be a historical fallacy to deny that at that time the Jamaican nationalism of Manley, Nethersole and those who founded the People's National Party (P.N.P.) was progressive. These elements had internalised the positive and negative ideas of bourgeois democracy and with their organisational skills were able to take over the leadership of the struggle for independence.

For a short period of the history of Jamaica, black people were willing to allow the black nationalism and race consciousness of Garveyism and Rasta to take second place to the strident Jamaican nationalism of the P.N.P. Out of the bonds on conflict and cooperation the organisation of the middle class emerged in the form of two principal parties, both with mass working class support.

A great deal of ink has rightly flowed to record the contributions of both Bustamante and Manley to the formation of the pluralistic society which was channelled in the form of competition between two political parties. However, not enough critical work has yet been done to analyse how their competition spread divisions among the poor workers, escalating into street violence in 1949 and developing to become internecine warfare in the era of neo-colonialism.

Bustamante imprinted his authoritarian stamp on the workers' movement in the formation of the Bustamante Industrial Trade Union (B.I.T.U.), and it was from this trade union base that he launched the Jamaica Labour Party (J.L.P.) in 1943, when Britain decided to grant universal adult suffrage.[38]

Initially the People's National Party escaped the authoritarianism of the J.L.P and the B.I.T.U., since it was a coalition of ex-Garveyites, educated mulattoes, elements from the active New York Jamaica Progressive League who had returned home, and young Jamaicans who linked their ideas to the Marxist tradition.

It was the organisational and educational work of this core of Marxists which gave the P.N.P. some credibility among the poor, such that the P.N.P. eventually became a mass party in 1949. For a short period, the work of Hugh Buchanan, Richard Hart and Arthur Henry promised to uplift the general cultural level of the society beyond the stunted mediocrity of the colonial order.

The strength of the left as a force in the P.N.P. led the party to declare a platform of 'Democratic Socialism' in 1940, but after the electoral reverses of 1945 and 1949 and with the McCarthyite anti-communist hysteria of the post-war era, Norman Manley expelled the Marxists from the P.N.P.[39] Manley then brought back his son, Michael Manley, from abroad to organise the P.N.P.'s faction of the working class under the National Workers' Union.[40]

Nepotism, political violence and victimisation became entrenched as part of the Jamaican political culture in the transition from colonialism to neo-colonialism. Even before the British flag was lowered on August 6, 1962, the black masses were becoming cynical about the myth of racial harmony which lay at the centre of the national motto – *Out of Many One People*.Many had begun to look to the ideas of Rastafari as the promise of the Jamaican nationalists became a sell-out to the U.S. and Canada.

The Transition from Colonialism to Neo-Colonialism*

Jamaica limped from formal colonialism to constitutional independence during a period of international decolonisation. Constitutional independence was not an end to the struggle of the poor, but was simply an important step in a process which had been accelerated in 1938 – a process which forced British overrule to reconsider the local arrangements for supervising the colonial economy.

In the period leading up to 1962, the competing elements of both parties were socialised in the rules of the game to such an extent that the continuities between the pre-independence and the post-independence period in the area of economic policies led to workers adopting defensive measures to retain the rights of collective bargaining and the right to strike.

The decade before independence was characterised by an unprecedented movement of population consequent upon the penetration of foreign capital. This penetration was supported by the myth that the society was developing – the myth clothed in glowing statistics which recorded increases in productivity.

The glowing figures published by the State belied the lopsidedness of the economy and the unequal division of the social product. United States and Canadian capital replaced weaker British capital, exploiting the vast reserves of bauxite, setting up hotels and establishing import substitution industries to exploit the 'unlimited labour'.

Between 1950 and 1957 Jamaica became the world's largest producer of bauxite after the high grade of the ore was acquired by Canadian and US companies (Alcan, Reynolds, Kaiser Bauxite; later they were joined by Alpart, Revere and Alcoa). The mining and processing section of the bauxite industry replaced sugar as the central pivot of the economy such that the bauxite alumina complex represented 15 per cent of the Gross Domestic Product and two thirds of all exports.[41]

Though the exploration of open pit mining of bauxite never employed more than 10,000 workers at any one time, it displaced thousands from the rural areas and increased the burden of unemployment on the society.[42]

The acute land shortage of the society was further aggravated by the expansion of the bauxite multi-nationals; for as the companies bought up the land of the small farmers the foreign capitalists became owners of over 191,000 acres of land, or 7% of the land area of Jamaica, in 1976. Most of the land was purchased from small farmers, to the point where the activities of the transnationals displaced *560,000* rural Jamaicans from the countryside between 1943 and 1970.

Small farmers, skilled and unskilled labourers, tradesmen and craftsmen left the parishes of St. Ann, Clarendon, St. Elizabeth and Manchester on boats and

* Kwame Nkrumah defined neo-colonialism as the stage in which a state has all the trappings of political independence, but is still economically dependent. See his book, *Neo-colonialism, The Last Stage of Imperialism*, Heineman Books, 1965.

planes for the United Kingdom, as they were pressured off their land. Before the British imposed immigration controls, 163,000 Jamaicans left their homeland for the cold and pollution of Manchester and Birmingham, Bristol, Brixton and Nottingham.[43] Between 1950 and 1968 an equal number migrated to the United States and Canada, the real numbers being in dispute, for there were large numbers of farm workers who broke contract and remained in North America without the knowledge of the relevant authorities.[44]

This massive outmigration, along with the migration to the urban areas of Kingston and Montego Bay, must be seen within the context of the pressures placed on the people to sell their land. A corollary of this massive movement of population was that the total acreage under cultivation dropped by 18 per cent between 1945 and 1968, and the society became more dependent on foreign food supplies.

This massive movement of population had an unsettling effect on the cohesiveness and organisation of the working class movement precisely at the time when the clarity of purpose of the working class movement was needed to critically comment on the direction of public policy. In this situation of deepening dependence, the consciousness of the poor was manifest more and more in the race consciousness of the Rastafari; such that when thousands were being packed on the boats like bananas, the idea of repatriation became central to the ideology of the Rastafari and became epitomised in the slogan *Africa Yes, England, No.*

The Jamaican nationalism of the petty bourgeoisie was essentially a narrow project which included cutting off the mass of the Jamaican people from the West Indian Federation, while the State became a prop to foreign capital by guaranteeing infrastructural support for industrial enterprises, and permitting the unlimited remittance of profits to corporate headquarters in Europe and America.

Norman Girvan, in his study of *Foreign Capital and Economic Underdevelopment,* exposed how the transnationals perpetuated the underdevelopment of the society. Jamaican society exhibited the outward appearance of prosperity with the traffic jams, the chains of supermarkets and resort hotels; but at the same time the units of housing for the vast majority of the population had been decreasing, the water supply for the poor was inadequate and more and more people were going without proper clothing. The decrease in agricultural production opened the festering sores of unemployment as the young people left the craggy hills for the slums and tenement yards of Kingston.

On top of the unevenness between town and country, the "Out Of Many One People" nationalists perpetuated the racial stereotypes consistent with their image of the black poor. Racist stereotypes of a happy-go-lucky people were reproduced on glossy tourist brochures in the hothouse effort to organise recreation for the international bourgeoisie. Public policy was influenced by the desire to provide the proper economic infrastructure and the proper hospitality – a smiling, docile population to provide the proper welcome for the Errol

Flynns, John Connollys and Ian Flemings.

Incredible images, complete with romanticisation of the poverty, were supported by advertisements in the *New York Times* – "Rent a Villa, Rent a Car, Rent a Nanny." North American investors were courted with incentive legislation so that they could exploit the expropriated small farmers; and the continuities between slavery and neo-colonialism were expressed in the operations of Rose Hall Great House in St. James, which was taken over by a Chicago investor.

It was not accidental that one of the most important interventions of the Rastafari brethren took place at Rose Hall in April, 1963, as a protest against the segregation on the North Coast of Jamaica. In the failure of the promise of 1938 the Rastafari movement began to grow and take shape in Jamaica. The cultural resistance of the Rastafari marked a new stage in the struggle, even though the Rastafari never escaped the idealism and mysticism of the society.

Idealism and Materialism in Jamaica

At the ideological level, the economic project of the political leadership exhibited a level of idealism bordering on naivety in their explicit view that the development of the society could be built on economic dependence and export of the population. The idealism was also expressed in the motto – "Out of Many One People" – for this motto promoted the myth of racial harmony, a myth which was given intellectual credence under the rubric of cultural pluralism.[45]

This ideological smokescreen was increasingly being used to obscure the interplay between race and class in the society. The idea of the multi-racial society suggested that power was distributed among all groups equally, but at the core of the ideas of cultural pluralism was an acceptance of the superiority of white cultural values. In a society where 91 per cent of the population was African and a small white minority dominated the State, the motto "Out of Many One People" was a sham. It was not surprising therefore that those who would give a lavish welcome to the Queen of England and hold up Britain as the barometer of civilisation should call the Rastafari millenarian and escapist.[46]

The Rastafari, who identified with an African king, were manifesting a component of the idealism which was central to the character of Jamaican society. The belief in the supernatural, the centrality of the spirit world and the religious belief that all contradictions could be solved by a supreme being were dominant features of the society. While the church and religious institutions had a large following among the sufferers, the established church was careful not to excite the masses with ideas of equality before God. But the Rasta represented a section of the downtrodden blacks who were intent on pushing their claims on society that black men were equal, to the point where black men should have their own king and God.

This was a positive feature of a growing but eclectic movement, for one would not fault the Rastas in a society where the spiritual world was treated as prior to nature, and where the existence of a spiritual entity explained and conditioned the world.

There had never been in Jamaican history a tradition of materialist and scientific inquiry. Individual Jamaicans who were attracted to the ideas of socialism and those Marxists who published the *Labour Weekly* in 1938 raised questions about the path of development of the society, but these individuals were never a force which could shape the intellectual development of the society. Though resolute, they did not have the organisational base nor material resources to shape the reproduction of ideas, though they made a significant impact on the society.[47]

The dominant ideas in the society were the ideas of bourgeois reformism and reliance on the private entrepreneur. These ideas were disseminated through various mediums and at the cultural institutions of learning the ideas took shape with the Arthur Lewis theory of 'unlimited supplies of labour', the M.G. Smith theory of 'cultural pluralism' and the American modernisation theories of David Apter, Lucien Pye and Walt Rostow. The differing variants of the idealists were to reinforce the dependence of the society.

For a crucial period when the population was being displaced there were no organisations which sought to imprint a materialist tradition – a tradition which sought to understand scientifically the real process of development in the material world, in culture and society. It was not until after the Abeng period, 1968, and the eventual formation of the Workers Liberation League in 1974, that a bold effort was made in the direction of breaking the idealist traditions.

Rastafari represented one variant of the idealism of the society, but it was distinguishable in that it was the movement which was vehemently opposed to the festering sores of racial injustice. These poor Jamaicans, over the period 1930 to 1950, developed a set of beliefs which sought to build upon the foundations of the race consciousness of Marcus Garvey. The Rastaman started from the point of view that black people should never forget their African heritage, and in this they linked their future to the redemption of Africa.

The idealism of the Rasta was an idealism which was pregnant with criticism of the social order, and more importantly over the period they developed symbols of resistance. The symbols of the Rasta were interlinked with the beliefs, and it needs to be re-asserted that none of these symbols or beliefs emerged spontaneously.[48] They emerged in relationship to the changes which were going on in the society. For example, the idea of repatriation never developed as a full force among the Rastafari until the massive out-migration of the fifties. And it is important to underline the fact that this pressure towards repatriation developed in conjunction with the land grant of Haile Selassie to Africans in the West.

The symbols of the flag, the lion, the drum, the chalice, the locks, and the distinctive language were reflections of a style of resistance. The Rasta were neither crazy nor millenarian, for they were part of the sufferers who were making their own protest against the sickness of the colonial society.

Their beliefs developed out of their experiences with a positive identification with Africa, and it was only after the State realised the full power of Rasta that the dimension of religious deification of Haile Selassie was centralised, and theorists in Jamaica began to speak of the 'Potential of Rastafarianism as a Modern National Religion'.[49]

In the process of becoming a central part of the Jamaican society the Rastafari did not seek to lay any claim to religion. They identified with the Nyabingi, King Ja Ja of Opobo, Marcus Garvey, Kwame Nkrumah and Patrice Lumumba, and filled the ideological vacuum with the amalgam of their political, cultural and idealist ideas.

The Dreadlocks of the hills were making their imprint on the consciousness of the poor and it is to the evolution of the movement which we now turn. The Rastafari were creating the musical forms to strengthen the people to meet the violence and thuggery of neo-colonialism.

FOOTNOTES

1. Grover Cleveland Redding, the leader of the Abyssinians, was arrested following a gun battle with the police and was declared insane for his unrepentant attitude towards white America. See T. Vincent, *Black Power and the Garvey Movement*, Ramparts Press, California, pp 85-87.
2. *Daily Gleaner*, 16 December, 1933.
3. *Daily Gleaner*, March 14, 1934. The trial which was reported in the press presents one of the most complete expressions of the orientation of Howell and the first Rastafari.
4. When the British found that they could not defeat the Nyabingi militarily, they banned it under the Witchcraft Ordinance of 1919. On doing this the British decided to promote a cult of rain-making and fortune-telling, for in the words of the British "Since purely military efforts have proven useless against the Nyabingi, it would appear that a considerable influence might be enlisted for European administration by a more sympathetic handling of a conservative cult and the powerful but innocuous local fortune telling relating to an institution which enters so deeply into the lives of these people." See Elizabeth Hopkins, "The Nyabingi Cult of Southwestern Uganda" in Robert Rotberg and Ali Mazrui, eds. *Protest and Power in Black Africa*.
5. Ken Post, *Arise Ye Starvelings*, Martin Nijhoff, The Hague, 1978. Post quotes extensively from the newspaper *Plain Talk*. This author could not trace copies of this periodical either in Britain or in the Caribbean. Post declared that it was through this article that the concept of Nyabingi became part of the Rasta doctrine.
6. Public Records Office FO/371/20154. For an analysis of the varying responses in the English-speaking Caribbean see Robert G. Weisbrod "British West Indian Reaction to the Italian-Ethiopian War: An Episode in Pan-Africanism", *Caribbean Studies*, April, 1970.
7. Robert Weisbrod, "British West Indian Reaction to the Italian-Ethiopian War: An Episode In Pan-Africanism" *Caribbean Studies*, April, 1970.
8. Herbert Julien, the black airman from Trinidad, had volunteered his services to the Ethiopians but left in the middle of the war very critical of the class nature of Ethiopia. See his biography, *The Black Eagle*, Jarrolds, London, 1964.
9. Blacks in the USA spearheaded the fundraising activities to assist the fighters of the Abyssinian army. One black pilot enlisted in the airforce and actually helped to build up the foundations of the Ethiopian airforce. For a full analysis of the impact of the war on black America see William Scott, *A Study of Afro-American and Ethiopian Relations 1896-1941*, Ph.D. Princeton, 1971.
10. Bob Edgar, *Garveyism in Africa:* Dr. Wellington and the American Movement in the Transkei 1925-1940, Institute of Commonwealth Studies Seminar Paper, 1975, p. 108.
11. Public Records Office FO 371/20154.
12. S.K.B. Asante, *Pan African Protest: West Africa and the Italo-Ethiopian Crisis 1934-1941*, Longman, 1977, p. 87.
13. *The Blackman*, July/August 1936. London was the centre of the Pan-African opposition to fascism. C.L.R. James had founded an organisation called the International African Friends of Abyssinia, but it evolved into the International African Service Bureau. The IASB attracted to its ranks the foremost Pan-Africanists of the era. George Padmore was the Chairman and Wallace Johnson was the General Secretary. Other notable

officers were R.T. Makonnen, Louis Mbanefo, N. Azikiwe, Jomo Kenyatta. These nationalists used the conflict in Ethiopia to enlighten British workers as to the true conditions of colonialism, child labour and colour bar. It was within this context that George Padmore wrote his book, *How Britain Rules Africa.*

14. For a full account of the history of the Ethiopian World Federation see William Scott's thesis, op. cit.
15. *Voice of Ethiopia*, May 1938.
16. The Falashas are the only ethnic group in Ethiopia which practises Judaism as their religion. Despite efforts by various Emperors to convert them to the Christianity of the Ethiopian Orthodox Church the Falashas have clung to their brand of Judaism. See Edward Ullendorf, *The Ethiopians*, Oxford University Press, 1960, pp 110-112.

    In Jamaica many Rastas took on Ethiopian names which were prominent at this time. Mortimer Planno, the long-standing Rasta teacher, called himself Togo Desta and one of the most influential Rasta organs today calls itself the Twelve Tribes of Israel.
17. In 1954 Haile Selassie paid an official visit to the United States of America where he presented awards to the leaders of the EWF. At a mass rally in New York Reverend Adam Clayton-Powell said to the Emperor: "We honour you because you are the symbol around which we place our prayers". *African Opinion*, October-November, 1954.
18. In the Eastern Caribbean and Jamaica the identification with the resistance in Africa was linked to the struggle for better conditions. Disturbances had already begun before the outbreak of the first attack on Africa – beginning in the sugar estates in Trinidad in May to July 1934. In January there were disturbances in St. Kitts, May 1935; in Jamaica, Falmouth, September to October 1935; struggles at various estates in Guyana, October 1935; St. Vincent, June 1937; the massive revolt of Trinidad led by Uriah Butler, June 1937; Barbados, 1937; and general disturbances in Jamaica, May-June 1938. See Fitzroy L. Ambursley, "The Working Class in the Third World: A Study in Class Consciousness and Class Action in Jamaica 1919-1952", *Working Papers on Caribbean Society*, Dept. of Sociology, U.W.I., 1978.

    The best account of the 1938 struggles has been documented by Ken Post in *Arise Ye Starvelings*, op. cit., though many readers may react negatively to his concept of Quashie and the false dichotomy between Garveyism and communism. This work of Post was the development of his earlier published piece "The Politics of Protest in Jamaica 1938" in *Social and Economic Studies*, UWI, December 1956. See also O.W. Phelps, "Rise of the Labour Movement in Jamaica" in *Social and Economic Studies*, Vol 9, No. 4.
19. The Masters and Servants Law No. 27 of 1940 was amended to allow for labour organisations and trade unions, for under the first trade union law of 1919 unions were liable for damages as a result of strikes and peaceful picketing.
20. Major G. St. J. Orde Browne, *Labour Conditions in the West Indies*, Cmd 6070, July 1939. This major had been the Labour Commissioner in East Africa where he was vehemently opposed to the ILO plea for the unionisation of labour. See *The African Labourer*, Frank Cass, London, 1967.
21. The Orde Browne report gives the rates as 2/6 maximum and 1/6 minimum, but these figures related to the post-1938 increases. See Table of Wages, pp 94-98.
22. One of these songs was popularised by Harry Belafonte, "Day De Light Come An Me Wan Go Home". A.G.S. Coombs gave a vivid account of the conditions of these workers in his testimony before the Moyne Commission.
23. Unemployment remained above 25 per cent of the labour force during the period under review. It was very difficult for the colonial authorities to estimate the number of unemployed because many sufferers refused to register, suspecting that the registration was a play to conscript them for the British army.
24. *Annual Report of the Social and Economic Progress of the People of Jamaica 1933*, p. 34.
25. The table tabulated by the British was that the minimum needs of an urban family to pay for codfish, salt, flour, crackers, yam, cocoa, sugar, mackerel and herring would be 17/6 per week, while the weekly wage ranged from 6/- per week for domestic servants to 5/- per week for cane cutters and longshoremen, who earned 6d per day. It is noticeable that the calculations did not include fish, meat, eggs or those elements of a balanced diet which were considered normal. It is a credit to the resilience of the poor that out of the ackee and codfish, mackerel and bananas, yam and bananas, they created dishes which have become part of the standard diet of working people.
26. *West Indian Royal Commission Report*, p. 174
27. The Royal Commission Report said that "the general level of agriculture in these colonies is low in technical knowledge, business organisation and managerial efficiency. Systematic farming on a plan suited to the inherent circumstances of the area is unknown", op. cit p. 37.
28. O.W. Phelps, op. cit., p. 422.
29. There were a number of black nationalist organisations which were active in 1938. These included Howell's Rastafari brethren, Joseph Hibbert's Ethiopian Coptic Faith, H.A. Dunkley's King of Kings Mission and African Black Ironsides led by "Slave Boy" Evans. See Post, *Arise Ye Starvelings*, op. cit., p. 239.
30. Coombs worked tirelessly to establish branches of the union all over the country. In 1937 Coombs appointed

Bustamante treasurer of the union but within a year Bustamante had outpaced Coombs with his financial resources and organisational skills to place his authoritarian stamp on the workers' movement in Jamaica.

31. *Daily Gleaner*, May 3, 1938. For the colonial version of the Frome Uprising see *Commission Appointed to Enquire into the Disturbances Which Occurred in Frome Estate in Westmoreland, 2 May, 1938,* Government Printing Office, Jamaica, 1938.
32. *Report of the Commission Appointed to Enquire into the Disturbances Which Occurred in Jamaica Between 23 May and 8th June 1938*, G.P.O., L938, pp 4-5.
33. Norman Manley and Alexander Bustamante dominated Jamaican politics for thirty years after the rebellion of the people. For a critical analysis of the role of Norman Manley see Louis Lindsay "The Myth of Independence, Middle Class Politics and Non-Mobilisation in Jamaica", Working Paper, Institute of Social and Economic Research, UWI, 1975.
34. *Report of the Commission 1938*, op. cit., p. 2. The report went on to criticise the behaviour of the special constables who were hastily called up for service. Of the 4,729 specials, 3,194 were called upon to help the police and army put down the rebellion.
35. Ken Post documents the different aspirations of the middle class in his book, op. cit. pp 349-385.
36. From a letter written by Norman Manley to Robert Kirkwood CO 137/827.
37. *Report of the Commission*, p. 3. Before that month the concern of Norman Manley was how to represent the big capitalists. For an analysis of his world see Wayne Brown, *Edna Manley*, 1975. For a sympathetic analysis of Manley see Rex Nettleford, *Norman Manley And The New Jamaica*, Selected Speeches and Writings, 1938-1968, Longmans, 1971.
38. For a sympathetic analysis of Bustamante's role in the workers' movement see George Eaton, *Alexander Bustamante and Modern Jamaica*, Kingston Publishers, Kingston, 1975. For a critical appraisal see Ken Post, op. cit. p. 414.
39. See Louis Lindsay, "The Myth of Independence", ISER, op. cit.
40. The role of Michael Manley as a trade union organiser and his dependence on the anti-communist ICFTU and the British TUC is documented by Jeffrey Harrod in *Trade Union Foreign Policy*, A Study of British and American Trade Union Activities in Jamaica, McMillan, 1972.
41. On the role of bauxite in Jamaica's economic and political life see "Caribbean Conflict: Jamaica and the US", *NACLA Report on the Americas*, Vol. XII, No. 3, May-June, 1978. Also see *Alcan, Jamaica and Cabora Bassa*, Liberation Support Movement, Canada, 1971.
42. Norman Girvan, "Impact of Multinational Enterprises on Employment and Income in Jamaica", ILO Working Paper, Geneva, 1976.
43. "Going Foreign – Causes of Jamaican Migration", *NACLA Report of the Americas*, Jan.-Feb. 1981, pp 2-8.
44. Between 1963 and 1976 148,028 Jamaicans were recruited as cheap labour to do agricultural work in the US under Section H-2 of the US Immigration and Nationality Act. One estimate placed the number of contract workers going off to become illegal immigrants at approximately 100 per month.
45. The chief exponent of this idea was M.G. Smith, see *Plural Society in the British West Indies*, Berkeley, 1965.
46. M.G. Smith's influence on the study of the Rastafari has been considerable. He was one of the authors of the first study of the Rasta which was commissioned by Norman Manley in 1960. This study perpetrated a number of falsehoods about the movement which have been reproduced internationally. The number one untruth was that the 'Rasta was a violent cult'. See *The Rastafari Movement in Kingston, Jamaica*, 1960, Smith, Augier, Nettleford.
47. Rupert Lewis, "Hugh Buchanan" in *Socialism,* Kingston, W.L.L. Jamaica. See also Trevor Munroe *The Marxist Left in Jamaica 1945-1950*, I.S.E.R., Kingston, 1977. Jamaica was represented at the *First Internation Congress of Negro Workers,* held in Hamburg, Germany, July 1930. This conference was held before the period when support for socialism was equated with support for the Soviet Union.
48. Leonard Barrett who wrote on the Rasta has repeated the Smith, Augier, Nettleford conception that the Rastafari believed that the white person was inferior to the black person. This writer could not find in the writings or expressions of the Rastafari ideas to justify this claim. See L. Barrett, *The Rastafarians,* Heinemann, 1977, chapter 4.
49. George E. Cupmer, *The Potential of Rastafarianism as a Modern National Religion*, Recorder Press, 1979.

Chapter Four

MAN IN THE HILLS: Rasta, the Jamaican State and the Ganja Trade

Long before the British flag was lowered in Jamaica on August 6, 1962, the Rastafarians were among the far-sighted ones who had perceived the neo-colonial movement of the society. At this time, despite the wanton waste and dislocation wrought by the foreign companies, the working poor continued to support the two-party political/trade union centre, hoping that the elementary concessions wrung in 1938 would be preserved; and the voices of the Rasta were like shouts in the wilderness.

Many small farmers from St. Elizabeth and St. Ann, who had been uprooted by the bauxite companies, watched helplessly as the transnational bauxite companies bulldozed their homes and their small provision grounds to take out the red dirt from the ground, sending this dirt to the sea on conveyor belts, where ships could carry it to provide jobs in the aluminium industry in Europe and North America.

The transnational corporations (TNCs) were only part of the global strategy of imperialism which allowed the international capitalists to continue to exploit the labour of the poor of the periphery, while adjusting to the new constitutional charges of self-government and independence.

One of the most significant contradictions of this period was the rush by the intermediate classes in the society to accumulate and consume. Leading politicians openly flouted basic principles of government and the system of victimisation and political violence was becoming part of the political culture of Jamaica: much more so after the battle for the control of the streets of Kingston in 1949 – a battle between Wills O. Isaacs and Alexander Bustamante which reinforced leaderism and personality politics among the people.

The Rastafarians were the first to comprehend the limitations of constitutional decolonisation and soon after the 1938 revolt a small group had sought to set up their own communal form of existence in the hills of St. Catherine. A few of the Rastas had thrown their lot in with the struggles, and one of the brethren became a chauffeur for Norman Manley. The colonial State knew that although the Rastas were not part of the trade union movement, they played a role in the strikes – so much so that the 1938 Report spoke of "ganja smokers who strike for better conditions."[1]

Leonard Howell, one of the first spokespersons for the movement, used his considerable material resources to organise a commune in St. Catherine in 1940. Howell had used his skills as an organiser for the *Ethiopian Salvation Society*, an anti-fascist organisation, using the money to provide for the poor of the society.

For his uncompromising call for racial awareness and support for the African king who was fighting in fascist Italy, Howell was placed in a mental asylum in colonial Jamaica; for in the eyes of the colonial State any black man who told black people to turn their backs on the white imperial King of England must have been a *mad man*.

On his release from the mental institution Howell participated in the general mobilisation of the poor by joining the UNIA to stage a 'Jubilee', forthrightly proclaiming the promise of the rise of Rastafari in the society.[2] Leonard Howell took with him the spirit of enterprise and cooperation when he set up the first Rasta commune at *Pinnacle* in the hills of St. Catherine. As a literate and ardent student of the history of slavery and resistance, Howell was not unaware of the symbolic significance of his move away from the competition between Manley and Bustamante to the rural areas.

The effort to set up a communal settlement was not without precedent, for immediately after the emancipation of slavery the Baptists had followed the movement of the ex-slaves from the plantations to the free villages of the hillside. These Baptists came out of a long anti-slavery tradition, and they bought land in Sligoville to set up independent communities.

That the free villages represented a threat to the labour supply of the plantation was clear from the frenzied opposition by the planters to these communities. Because sugar cane had to be reaped quite soon after maturing, the possibility that these villagers could be independent of the income of the planters meant that they could effectively withdraw their labour when it was most needed.[3]

Village residence and the growing of ground provisions became an established form of strengthening the bargaining power of the rural poor in Jamaica, and it is to this form of existence that Howell and his fellow Rastas returned in 1940. The choice of St. Catherine was significant, for at that time this parish had the largest number of sugar plantations – six out of a total of the twenty-six which were still functioning: the notorious Worthy Park, Inns Wood, Caymanas, Sevens, Bernard Lodge and United Estates.[4]

These sugar estates owned an inordinate amount of land, and right throughout their history the planters represented less than one per cent of the population but occupied more than fifty-six per cent of the total land acreage.[5]

It was into this situation that Howell inserted his movement with over 1,600 fellow Rasta, hoping to set up a cooperative enterprise outside of the exploitative relations of the society. The historical record of this experiment remains unclear, for most of the reports on the commune have followed the colonial lead of labelling the Rastafari as violent cultists who harassed their neighbours.[6]

The colonial State showed such unrelenting opposition to the settlement that with hindsight it is now possible to assert that they wanted to kill the seed of cooperation and open love for Africa before it blossomed in the society.

But despite the harassment and arrest this seed grew, even after the colonial State scattered some of the followers of Howell by arresting them on ganja charges in July 1941. Extra powers had been given to the police under the Defence Regulations and more than 173 armed policemen, under the direction of the Commissioner of Police, were deployed to break up Pinnacle. The description of the raids in the press showed that the whole exercise was conceived as a military operation against those who told the poor not to pay taxes to the colonial State.

Leonard Howell was again put in prison by the colonialists along with 28 others, who were charged with growing ganja. It was from this time that the State began to use the charge of cultivating ganja as a weapon against the sufferers.

When Howell was released from prison in 1943 he returned to this cooperative settlement, and it was in this period that some of the overt characteristics of the Rasta began to appear. Although there were different groups which preached the Coptic version of divinity and humanity, it was in the Pinnacle settlement that symbols of resistance which characterise the Rastafari began to take shape.

Today when one speaks of the Rastafari it is usual to refer to the symbols of locks; the ites (red), green and gold; the symbol of the lion; the distinctive use of the Jamaican language; and the use of ganja. Each of these symbols developed over a period and were not simply an outward mark of identifying the Rasta, but a reflection of a form of resistance, linking these symbols to some concrete struggle among African peoples.

Characteristically, the complex of negative and positive ideas which have characterised the movement from its inception was also present at Pinnacle; for though the Pinnacle settlement was based on communal principles where work was done in common and goods equally shared, Howell was pre-eminent among the brethren and sistren. It was Howell who owned the property and who organised the administration of the experiment.

From all accounts this ownership had its own manifestations in the relations in the settlement, but it showed some sense of opposition to the idea of private property, for Howell did not seek to profit from the labour of his followers. Unlike the host of jinnals and sam fie men (smart men) who used their knowledge to exploit their fellow men, the Pinnacle settlement was attempting to restore to the society some of the spirit of communalism and collective work.

Locksmen

After the constant police raids the administration at Pinnacle made greater efforts towards protecting the commune, and the guards at the gate were referred to as *Ethiopian* Warriors. When the struggle of the Land and Freedom Army (called Mau Mau) in Kenya exploded, and the Rastas saw pictures of the freedom fighters with their natural hair, long and matted, the Rasta positively identified with these fighters and began to wear their hair in 'locks'.

The appearance of the Rastas with their locks threw greater fear into the hearts of the ruling class, for the popular version of beauty at that time suggested that a black person who wore their hair long and in its natural form was ugly and offensive. Parents would sometimes curse their children as 'nattie head pickney'. Some black people, both men and women, went to great lengths to process and straighten their hair so that it would look European.

The locksmen found biblical justification for the growing of their hair and beard.* Because of the opposition of the wider society to the appearance of these bearded black men who called their beard 'precepts', there was a sense of solidarity among the Rastas; for the State, in their effort to humiliate the brethren, attempted to shave their locks.

The more the police tried to humiliate the Rastas, the more they were determined to keep their appearance, which was called 'Dread'. It was in this period that the concept of 'Natty Dread' became part of the vocabulary of resistance.

The symbol of the dreadlocks became a lasting sign of black pride in Jamaica, a symbol which was to gain international significance after reggae artists took on the physical appearance of the Dreads and exposed this culture of the hills to the saloons of London, Frankfurt and Amsterdam, to the big musical centres of Los Angeles and New York, and ultimately to the Independence Celebration in Zimbabwe.

The first pictures of the freedom fighters in Kenya had appeared in 1953 in the local press, and by 1954 the chief external organ of the Rastafari ideas – *African Opinion*, which was published in Harlem, New York, but widely distributed among the small Rasta communes – carried stories of the Burning Spear and Dedan Kimathi. But when the authorities saw this manifestation of African nationalism in Jamaica, they were determined that Howell and his followers must be mad. So the police raided the Pinnacle commune in 1954, arrested followers of the Rasta doctrine, and again placed Howell in a mental asylum in Kingston.

At that time the three weapons the State used against the Dreadlocks were: (1) the Dangerous Drugs Law, arresting them for the possession of ganja; (2) the Vagrancy Act; and (3) placing them in the mental hospital at Bellevue in Kingston. Leonard Howell, the first major leader among the locksmen, was charged with the possession of ganja and also placed in a mental asylum.

One may wonder why the State felt so threatened by the Pinnacle experiment. The fact that the Rastafarians were building a new sense of solidarity and self-reliance among the rural poor posed long-term problems for the planters and their police guardians.

The Rastafarians were breaking some of the old capitalist habits which had become ingrained in the rural areas. The petty malice and covetousness which had been bred as one component of the individualism of the society was being transcended with a new spirit of *peace* and *love*. The State could not tolerate this; hence the Rastas of Pinnacle were dispersed to the ranks of the growing unemployed in Kingston.

Leonard Howell spent some time in Bellevue, and despite the inaccurate report that he had died there, Howell – known as 'Uncle Percy', the 'Bard of

*This biblical justification can be found in Numbers 6:5. The locks were formed simply by washing the hair and allowing it to dry without combing, brushing or treating it in any way, and because real dreadlocks could only be grown by African descendants, the Rastas found that this physical identification with the Kenyan freedom fighters was one way of distinguishing them from their Caucasian Jamaican overlords.

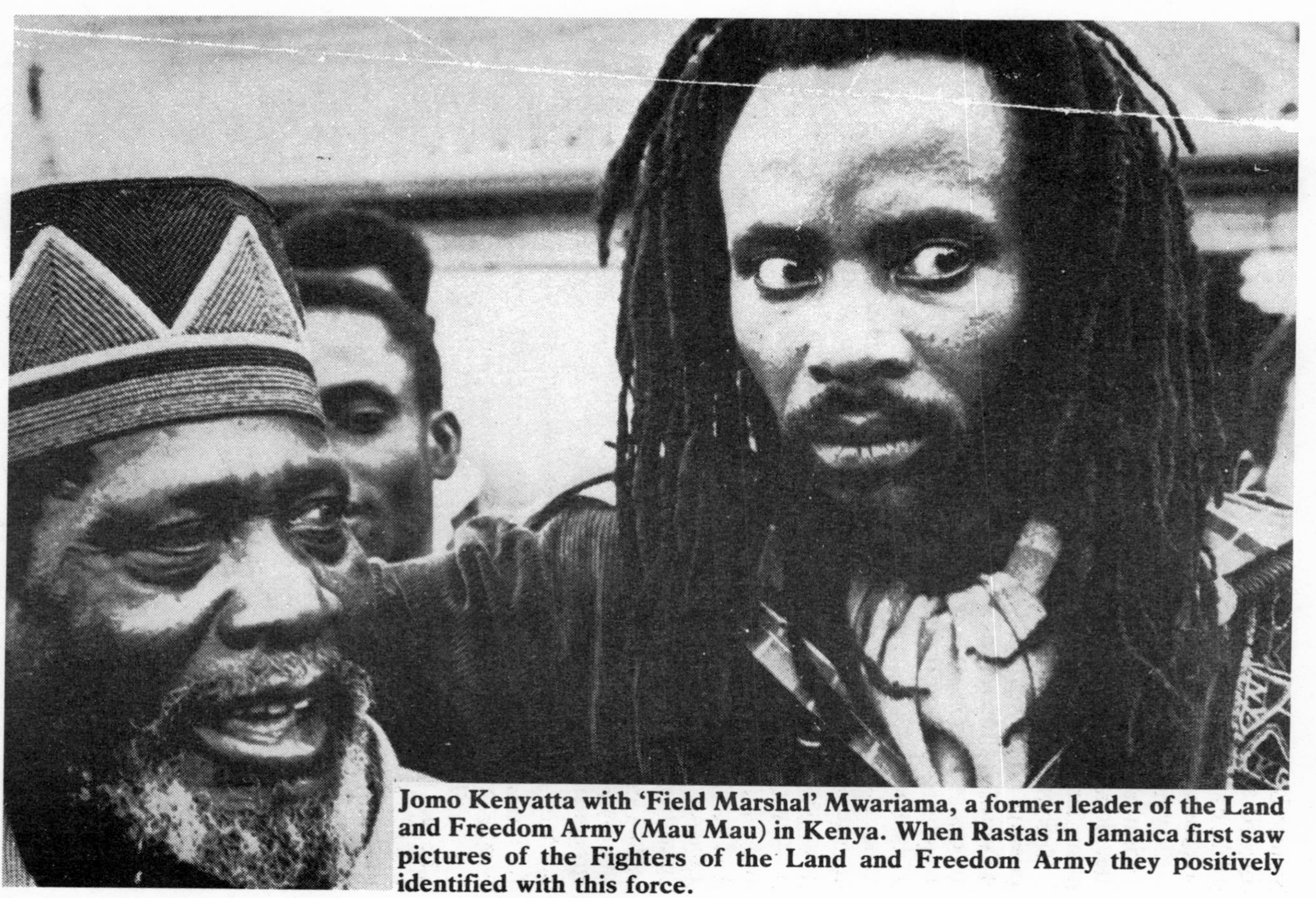

Jomo Kenyatta with 'Field Marshal' Mwariama, a former leader of the Land and Freedom Army (Mau Mau) in Kenya. When Rastas in Jamaica first saw pictures of the Fighters of the Land and Freedom Army they positively identified with this force.

Pinnacle' and 'The Gong' – thrived to the healthy age of 90. The last report of Howell at Pinnacle was when the Jamaica *Daily News* reported on May 23, 1979, that the camp had been robbed by armed men.

Locksmen in Kingston and the other urban areas posed new problems for a society not accustomed to black people overtly identifying with Africa. Yet not all Rastas wore locks, for as the police took to harassment, some Rastas shaved their locks, choosing the biblical justification that after seven years the Rasta can shave his locks.

The problem of locks also became urgent for the Rastas as the neo-colonial crisis of unemployment deepened, for lumpen elements whose lives had been distorted by the violence and thuggery of the society took on the physical trappings of locks, tam and Rasta language such that Rastas had to go to great lengths to distinguish themselves from these criminal elements.

The existence of 'false Dreads' did not dissuade Rastas from bringing up their children with locks. This posed a major problem for the society, since the State institutions could not countenance Rasta children having the freedom to wear their hair in the manner that their parents preferred. As young Rasta children became of school age, the issue came to public attention, especially when Rastas asserted their right to attend Secondary Schools.

At Cornwall College in Montego Bay, the State was forced to present a *Code of Conduct* after the school was closed when Rasta youths insisted that they should have the right to wear their hair in dreadlocks.[7] The Ministry of Education issued a code of conduct requiring students to dress "according to conventional standards of neatness, and their hair should be washed clean and well groomed." The code further stipulated that:

> *"whatever conflicts about the interpretation of what constitutes 'proper and accepted standards of hygiene, neatness and good grooming' occur, this should be settled first by the principal, failing that by the Board and failing that by the Ministry."*

This code of conduct gave broad discretionary powers to headmasters and headmistresses. Though the code of conduct stated that "if a student adopts the Rastafari religion, the parents or guardian would be required to approve if the student is below the age of 18," many teachers who harboured anti-Rasta sentiments harassed young Rasta children: so that the fact of the Rasta child in school was not an accepted feature of the society. In fact, this problem of being harassed because of their locks faces locksmen, women and children all over the world of Dreads.

'Rastaman A Lion' – From Quashie to Lion

The symbolic assertion of identification with the Mau Mau and the Burning Spear, which began in the hills of St. Catherine, also carried with it a sense of dignity and black pride which was consistent with the new image of self-respect. For in the hills, because the Rastas were independent craftsmen, making their own handicrafts, cooking their own food and unleashing a certain sense of self-reliance, they were dropping the shuffling Quashie traits which had been developed by the slave as a weapon for survival. Rastas held their heads high as they walked the streets of their communities, and while spreading peace and love combined the confidence and strength of the *lion* among the poor.

Quashie and Anancy were two legacies from the period of slavery which thrived in Jamaica, legacies which had reduced the black person to minimise his strength and intelligence in the face of the insecure slave masters and afterwards the planter class.

The trait of Quashie became intertwined with the personality of many Jamaicans, though this seeming docility was in many cases accompanied by the Anancy trait. Anancy was the archetype of the jinnal* in Jamaican society, and this jinnalship was, most times, at the expense of other oppressed sections of the society.

Rastafari in Jamaica believed that it was time that black people should drop these character traits of the adaptable hustler and be straightforward with their fellow men and women. This was a major challenge in a society where racism, which had spawned the era of slavery and colonialism, had left its mark on the self-esteem of the black person.

To begin to repair this psychological damage the Rastas declared their identification with the *lion* – in its roar, its hair, its body strength, intelligence and total movements. The mane of the lion's hair was compared favourably with the locks of the brethren, and while ordinary Jamaicans were reading about Tarzan and Phantom pacifying lions and Africans, the Rastas emerged in Jamaican society as 'lions'.

Dennis Forsyte, recapturing the symbolism that this invoked, said in his analysis of Rastafari and the revival of African Lionism that:

> *"The African lion symbolises some of the same black ideals and hope that Brer Anancy symbolised in our 'ancient' consciousness, but the lion is more of a fitting ideal for a people bent on a militant march forward towards their own maximum and ultimate self-realisation and self-discovery.*
>
> *"The African lion expresses more of the natural and ideal spirit and ideal strivings of the enslaved Africans. The lion image offers a more universal and wholesome definition of how man ought to organise himself outwardly and how he should feel inwardly. It represents the Brethrens' supreme symbolic yearning for wholesomeness and power to compensate for their powerlessness and their alienated existence. As such they have gone well forward of the mass of the working class people in becoming conscious of the need to develop an independent philosophy of life, in ways more appropriate to and reflective of our experiences, needs and*

*A *jinnal* in the Jamaican language is someone who is a tricky or crafty person. He could also be a rogue who is dishonest, but such persons are usually called sam fie men. See *Jamaican Talk*, Frederick Cassidy, MacMillan, London, 1961, pp 215–216.

> *vibrations as Africans. Rastas express a vision of life radiating from the ancient memories of our deepest longings."*[8]

This identification was made easier by the fact that the Ethiopian monarch had tame lions in his household and that he himself had acquired the title – the *Lion of Judah*. Throughout the world monarchs had used the lion as a symbol of strength and even the British, who denigrated everything African, have used this symbol to adorn important public buildings and sites of national importance, such as the Wellington Statue at Trafalgar Square, London, and the southern entrance to Westminister Bridge, adjacent to the Houses of Parliament.

Rastafari now claimed the lion as their symbol and in the rural areas one of the most popular sayings was "Rastaman a lion," for the Dreadlocks were supposed to be a "symbolic reincarnation or imitation of the lion in man form, both in face and body, as well as in the spirit structure." The picture of the lion began to appear on Rasta dwellings, on their meeting halls, on their push carts, and on their stalls or snowball carts. These carts, painted in the colours of Marcus Garvey – red, black and green – with the roaring lion, began to replace the images of Hollywood stars which were heretofore painted by the poor.

It is this kind of art which gave rise to the work of Ras Daniel Hartman, a gifted artist whose painting of the Dreadlock surrounded by five lions became universally famous. Ras Daniel Hartman's depiction of the Dread trinity became a Jamaican masterpiece, and the Rasta paintings, sculptures, ceramics and other artistic talents were unearthed for the first time.

When the Pinnacle settlement was broken up by the State, the Rastafari brethren and sistren were dispersed to other parts of the island. Most had congregated in Kingston, and it was this general increase of the number of locksmen proudly identifying themselves as lionsmen which drew the attention of sociologists and anthropologists. It is significant that the first piece of scholarship on the Rastas, by George E. Simpson, spoke of "Political Cultism in Western Kingston."[9]

At this period the Rastas were an expressed Pan-African force, and the intelligentsia could not help but notice this, even though they placed the stamp of cultism on the movement. However, the State did not take a dispassionate attitude to the appearance of black men and women wearing those locks, similar to the dreaded Mau Mau who were being shown on the British newsreels. Hence, the police intimidated Rasta, and the Afro-Saxon leadership, along with their white overlords, applauded. The scope for police harassment was circumscribed by the fact that most of the followers of this new movement were skilled men and women, fishermen and farmers, who spoke of peace and love.

The author's own memory of this early period was of the Rastas of his community being cabinet makers who did a thriving business, supplying cheap but well finished furniture to poor people, undercutting those hire purchase stores which were charging high interest rates. These Rastas were patient and hardworking and they were looked upon with respect in the community.

On Sunday evenings, they would congregate at Charles Square – now called Sam Sharpe Square – and have meetings. These gatherings were of a religio-political nature, but many youths were attracted to the stirring tales of Africa, to the intense drumming, the frenzied waving of the flag and the singing of "The Lion of Judah shall break every chain and give us a victory again and again."

But the police did not allow the gatherings to continue in peace. The deep spiritualism and love for Africa which were expressed posed a challenge to the ruling class and the challenge became urgent when large numbers of Rastas came together. The first major gathering of Rastafari in Kingston, called Nyabingi, precipitated a hostile response from the State and laid the basis for future relations until the University intervened with their report in 1960.

Hail Jah Rastafari

As outlined in the last chapter, the struggle between the transnational bauxite companies and the small farmers had led to the dispersal of thousands from the craggy hills of St. Elizabeth and the red clay dirt of Manchester and St. Ann. This dispersal coincided with the massive emigration to the United Kingdom, but the more black conscious among the population flocked to Kingston saying: "*Africa Yes, England No!*"

The presence of these black people in Kingston coincided with the efforts by Prince Emanuel, one of the Rasta leaders in Kingston, to hold a *Groundation* in March 1958, where the people chanted to the intense drumming of the *Burra* drums and sang:

> "*By the Rivers of Babylon, there we sat down*
> *And there we wept, when we remembered Zion.*
> *For the wicked carried us away in captivity*
> *Required from us a song,*
> *But how can we sing King Alpha's song*
> *In a strange land.*"

Rastas had used the words of the Psalms to depict their condition and in the minds of poor people the name *Babylon* became a symbol of oppression. The name Babylon was linked to all oppressive forces, whether it was the imperialist states, the local black oppressors or the police who carried out the wishes of the State.

This *Groundation* or *Nyabingi* attracted thousands of locksmen to the curiosity of the State, even the governor, and the assembly had come after a spate of organisational activity among those who were linked to the New York-based Ethiopian World Federation. Members of the New York branch had visited Jamaica to carry the news that Haile Selassie had given a land grant of 5 gasha (500 acres) to Africans in the West who wanted to settle in Ethiopia.

Correspondents for the widely read *African Opinion* had listed very persuasive reasons why black people should return to Africa and from Jamaica one of the leaders of the Rastas, Mortimer Planno, wrote that "Repatriation to Africa was a *Human Right*."[10]

Among the reasons for returning to Africa given by *African Opinion* was the need to join the anti-colonial struggle, and it was significant that these burning reasons were articulated in the same year that the French and British invaded Africa at the Suez Canal. It is in this context that appeals were made for volunteers to return to Africa and for money to be collected to help the Mau Mau and other anti-colonial struggles.

Rastas in Jamaica were part of those Pan-Africanists who felt strongly about the freedom of Africa and the Groundations of Prince Emanuel in Kingston coincided with rallies held in New York, where Carlos Cooke, the most ardent US-based Garveyite of the period, held meetings calling on black people to return to Africa.

The fact that there were external reference points for the doctrines of the Rasta was not lost on the colonial authorities, who in the thirties had shown apprehension about the attempts by black people to coordinate a struggle to defend the Kingdom of Abyssinia. At the Nyabingi in Kingston in 1958 the full-length photograph of the Emperor standing with his right foot on an unexploded Italian bomb was used as a symbol of defiance and invincibility.

While using the name of this invincible monarch – Ras Tafari – black men in Jamaica were wearing their hair in locks and looking to African liberation, participating in an exercise of self-definition which was aimed at establishing a broader re-definition of themselves than that which had so far been permitted by those in power.

The body of ideas and beliefs which guided Rastafari at that time was deeper than simply a deification and glorification of Haile Selassie. His Imperial Majesty (H.I.M) stood for African independence in an uncompromising manner and the existence of Ethiopian Orthodoxy enabled Rastas to speak of the divinity of Haile Selassie, a conception quite consistent with the Coptic and dyophysite thinking.

But this African king was only one of the leaders of Africa with whom the Rastafarians identified, for at this time the Burning Spear (Jomo Kenyatta), Patrice Lumumba and Kwame Nkrumah were on the same plane as Haile Selassie. The fact that Haile Selassie was linked to other African leaders was also evident from the fact that Rastas attached the name *Jah* to the common name of H.I.M.

Undoubtedly, Nathaniel Hibbert and Leonard Howell would have heard of King *Ja Ja* of Opobo, the African king from West Africa who was deported to the Caribbean in 1887. King Ja Ja had valiantly fought the European traders in the Qua Ibo River region of West Africa, but when the Europeans divided Africa at the Conference of Berlin, the British were afraid of the independence of this important African king, who was an erstwhile trader and whose navy was invincible on the inland rivers.

When Britain found that they could not defeat this king they offered him a treaty of friendship, took him out to the open sea, and then kidnapped him, since they knew his boats were no match for the British Navy in the Atlantic Ocean. King Ja Ja was taken to Ghana, tried, and deported to the Caribbean.[11]

He was first taken to Grenada, but the British were afraid of the long history of rebellion among the Grenadians, so they placed him in St. Vincent.[12] King Ja Ja never relented: he continued to speak out for African independence, writing letters to the Foreign Office demanding that he be returned to his Kingdom. The people of the Caribbean were attracted to King Ja Ja and they made songs about his marital and martial exploits.

Rastafarians who were searching for levers of identification beyond the white Queen and the British Governor looked to the bible and found the name of Jah. The Psalmists had declared "Sing unto God" sing praises to his name, extol him that rideth upon the heavens by his name Jah and rejoice before him".[13] In extolling the name of their preferred king the Rastas linked it with the name of King Ja Ja, such that today at Rasta concerts, meetings and cultural groundations there is the chant "Jah Rastafari".

The beliefs of the Rastafari took shape within the context of the colonised society and what scared that State was how such a sense of unity and community could persist among the brethren and sistren despite the lack of central organisation and fixed lines of communication.

Are Rastas Violent Cultists?

After the successful Nyabingi held by Prince Emanuel in 1985, the State saw that the movement was growing and they intensified the harassment of the Rastas. This was especially so after the Cuban Revolution, when on January 1, 1959, Fidel Castro came to power after years of fighting the Batista dictatorship.

Rastas positively identified with the new Cuban regime and the 1960 Report recognised that for the brethren:

> *"The Communist system is far more preferable to the capitalist system of the white and brown Babylonians. Dr. Fidel Castro is showing what can be done in Cuba, but for sixteen years Jamaicans have used their control of government merely to perpetuate and intensify slavery."*[14]

Consequent to this identification with social change in Cuba and Africa, the police stepped up acts of *provocation* leading to two altercations in Kingston in 1959, one at Coronation Market and another at Rosalie Avenue, where Claudius Henry figured prominently. Claudius Henry, like so many other black Jamaicans – such as Claude McKay and Marcus Garvey – had gone to the USA to escape the racial discrimination of the educational system and to avail himself of opportunities for self-achievement.

While training as a religious leader in New York, Henry was exposed to the activities of the Ethiopian World Federation, to the ideas articulated in the *African Opinion*; and was present when Adam Clayton Powell paid a glowing tribute to Haile Selassie when he visited the US.

On Henry's return to Jamaica in 1957 he noted that the Rastafarians were the most forthright of those in the society asserting Pan-Africanism and black consciousness, and he joined the ranks of the Rastas, setting up his African Reform Church and calling himself Repairer of the Breach.*

Though space does not permit full investigation of the projects of the Repairer of the Breach, especially with respect to his programme of repatriation,[15] Henry's place in the history of Jamaica and of Rastafari was written in the blood of his son, Ronald Henry, who was murdered by the (British) Royal Hampshire Regiment subsequent to his call for Jamaicans to rise up against PNP/JLP manipulation.

In 1960, this call by Ronald Henry and his followers, who had declared for armed struggle in Jamaica one year after the Cuban revolution, was a call by a section of the black population which wanted to move rapidly towards political and economic emancipation. But the revolt of Ronald Henry, Gabidon and their supporters came to grief: the social conditions then did not lend themselves to a solution by armed struggles, since the working poor had not yet exhausted all the possible gains by the bourgeois democratic struggle.

Jamaican workers and small farmers had given their allegiance to a trade union and political party machine which they hoped would preserve the concessions won, to ensure that Jamaica did not become another Haiti or Ecuador. This partly explains why even third parties, like that of Millard Johnson, which carried forth a Garveyite platform, did not gain ground in 1962.[16]

Such an hysteria was whipped up in the planter press over the 'boy scout' revolt of Ronald Henry that the State intensified the harassment of the Rasta, for in the minds of the white Jamaicans the Rastafari were in the vanguard of a revolutionary conspiracy.[17] Increased powers in the hands of the military led to the Detention Powers Bill, which provided for the detention of a suspected person without trial.

Cooler heads in the society were cautious about labelling all Rasta violent and criminal, and the Rastafari themselves defended their right to their political and religious beliefs, calling on sympathetic members of the community to carry out a study of the movement in order to calm the hysteria that all Rasta were violent and out to 'kill whitey'.

The University Report

Norman Manley had agreed to the requests by the Rastafarians and later in 1960 Rex Nettleford, Roy Augier and M.G. Smith presented their *Report on the Rastafari Movement in Kingston*, the first scholarly treatment of the Rastas in Jamaica. At that time the report was useful in that it intervened when the white racist elements were calling for draconian measures against the Rastas, but it is ironical that this report, which was supposed to be sympathetic to Rastas, laid the basis for so many distortions and so much confusion on the history of the

*Henry was known in Jamaica as Claudius Henry R.B. He was quite aware of the drive in the US to raise funds for Africa and it was in this period that he sold 15,000 tickets at 1/- each for those who wanted to go to Africa. There were doctrinal differences between Henry and some of the older Rastas and in New York the EWF warned Henry that they were the only ones who could organise for blacks to return to Ethiopia. See *New York Age*, October 3, 1959. Henry was an activist who used the techniques of US store front preachers to gain adherents to his ranks. His activities in Kingston in this period are described by A. Barrington Chevannes, *Claudius Henry and Jamaican Society*. After Henry's release from prison in the late sixties he became an ardent supporter of Michael Manley and the People's National Party, endorsing the 1972 electoral campaign and in the process enlisting strong ecclesiastical discussion on the role of religion and politics in Jamaica.

movement. One reviewer of the Report called it "crisis writing", but even if the Report was written in a hurry there should have been no excuse for the lack of original research into the development of the Rasta.

Instead, apart from the ideological flap of structural functionalism, the Report borrows heavily from George Simpson's observations and reinforces the anti-black sentiments of Simpson. J. Owens himself, in revising Simpson's work had said that:

> *"One might question the emphasis Simpson places on racialism in listing the key doctrines. In each list, at least three of the six points are concerned with black superiority, white inferiority, and the revenge that blacks will eventually visit upon whites. One cannot help but feel that Simpson was too much influenced by subjective feelings. Certainly, it is somewhat traumatic for a white man to confront such a black orientated cult, but he should also be aware that his presence will naturally prompt many comments concerning race. This reviewer found that his initial contacts frequently stimulated racial comments, but later and prolonged contacts gave no evidence of any inordinate racialism."*[18]

J. Owens, himself of European stock, continued by saying that:

> *"He does not go deeply into the inner coherence of the Rastas' position, with the result that others reading his exposition and having no direct knowledge of the Rastas would perceive them as another sect."*

These two positions, that of a fanatical sect and a group of millenarians who preached black racism, have become the lasting legacies of the 1960 Report, to the point where subsequent books on the Rastas went to great lengths to argue that Rastas believe the white person is inferior to the black person.[19]

If the authors of this Report had done some basic research into the history of the development of the movement instead of relying on the clearly anti-black *Gleaner* reports on the Howell commune, then it would have been clear that the burst of the Rasta phenomenon developed within the context of a Caribbean response to the Italian invasion of Abyssinia, and the unity of this historic event to the Garveyite promise of an African King who would speed the process of redemption. In my own research and contact with Rastas over thirty years, I have never come into contact with any section of Rastafari ideas which speaks of revenge upon whites.

The Report on the Rastafari reinforced popular misconceptions on ganja; centralised the personality of Haile Selassie, spoke of the group fantasy or millenarian cultism, distorted the history of the movement and in the end warned the State about the potential of links between the Rastafari and Marxists.*

*For a full account of the context and controversy surrounding the Report on the Rastafari Movement, see Rex Nettleford, *Mirror Mirror*, Sangsters 1970, pp 52-64.

> *"In our survey we encountered certain groups among which the Marxist interpretation and terminology predominated over the racial and religious. Events in Cuba, China, Egypt and elsewhere endow the Marxist analysis with a pragmatic validity and power. In so far as this political philosophy employs the ideology of Rastafari racisms its spread throughout the bulk of the population is assured unless the government takes positive steps to meet legitimate needs of the lower classes including the Rastafari group."*[20]

Anti-Marxism was always a big thing in the ideology of oppression of the colonial State and on two significant counts the Report suited the needs of the State, for not only did it promote the religious and metaphysical aspects of the movement, but it gave ammunition to the authorities to be used against Rastas – such that twenty years later in the UK the British Home Office could quote select sections of the Report in guiding the police and Prison Officers on how to mistreat young Rastafarians.[21]

This promotion of idealism meant that many young Rastas had no knowledge of the development of Rasta beyond Garvey and Haile Selassie; they could not, therefore, understand the importance of Bogle's call "Cleave to the Black", nor the Pan-African ideals of the slaves who left the strong love for Africa in Jamaica.

Finally, because of the incorrect information on the origins of Rasta, one sociologist writing on the Rasta in England has gone so far as to compare the Howell commune to Charles Manson's criminal activities in California, because for that writer, ganja had the same effect on the human mind as LSD, while reggae music stimulated Rastas to violence.[23]

Rasta, Ganja and the State

The links between Rasta, ganja and violence were once again fervently discussed in the Jamaican press after the Coral Gardens rebellion in 1963. Easter weekend 1963 witnessed an important intervention by the Rastas because they asserted their right to walk across the Rose Hall land to their small lot of ground provisions. Rose Hall at that time was being developed as a tourist attraction, and the whole area was being built up by real estate developers to be renamed Coral Gardens.

Young Rastas such as Felix Waldron – a promising mathematician – had turned their backs on the miseducation of Cornwall College and had spent their time out in the hills behind Rose Hall and in the gullies preaching about Lumumba, the Congo, Nasser and Haile Selassie. They had defended their right to walk across the area (regardless of whether their presence horrified tourists) and in the altercation that followed one incident on Holy Thursday, a petrol station was burnt and the policeman who had come to prosecute the Rastas was attacked with a spear.

The State called out the army, and after the deaths of eight persons, the military and the police carried out mass arrests of Rastafarian women, men and children. Not since the Sam Sharpe revolt, in the same region, had there been such a mass arrest of black people. The prisons were full, and when the heat of the sun caused uncomfortable conditions in the detention centres where the Rastas were held, the police turned water hoses on those arrested.

On top of the arrests the *Gleaner* carried stories that the defendants were under the influence of ganja. There was no question of their rights as citizens of independent Jamaica, for the response of the politicians was "de bwoy dem lazy and dem no wan wuk, dem only wan fe smoke ganja". Such a simplistic analysis called for simplistic answers – the brutal force of the State – and so the war on Rastas and the war on ganja became one.

This was an escalation of the war which was launched in 1938 when the planters had declared ganja a pest. It was after the 1938 revolt that the use of cannabis went on the statute books under the *Dangerous Drugs Law*, and since then this law has been used against Rasta by the colonial and neo-colonial State. In the words of Dr. Lambos Comitas:

> *"Outlawing a popular custom is also a very convenient control device. The ganja legislation in Jamaica is very clearly like the legislation against illegitimate children or against obeah, a particular form of lower class religion. It can be used by the elite to control the lower classes with no loss in world opinion."*[24]

Outlawing a Popular Custom

From the outset of the formation of Rasta camps, communes and settlements in Jamaica, it was noted that the smoking of the chillum pipe occurred frequently, and those who lived close to the settlements would notice from time to time a familiar billowing of smoke and hear the 'puck, puck' of the chillum pipe.

The pipe and the ganja, which were incorporated as part of the culture of Rasta and working class Jamaica, had been imported into Jamaica from India. As in India, ganja, which is the Jamaican name for the plant *cannabis sativa*, was used for many purposes. Also known as Indian hemp – used to make twine and rope – cannabis, marijuana, iley, calley, bangi, and other names, it was "a household remedy in India from ancient times". Large-scale use of ganja in Jamaica and the Caribbean in the most recent history (because there is no record of whether it was used by the Arawaks) dated from the importation of indentured Indians into Jamaica.

Ganja has been and continues to be used widely by the working people of Jamaica. It is smoked, brewed as medicinal tea and tonic, cooked in food and applied externally. The climate of Jamaica is particularly hospitable to the crop, of which there are two harvests per year; and this plant has an advantage over perishable crops in that it can be stored without deterioration.

However, because the usage of this crop was predominantly a working class phenomenon in the Caribbean, Britain did not raise a whimper but acceded at the League of Nations in 1924 when the Egyptian delegate pressed for cannabis (ganja) to be added to the list of dangerous drugs to be regulated. *Before that, the British brought ganja to the Caribbean on a regular basis and sold it to the Indian indentured workers, especially in Trinidad.*

The law prohibited the cultivation of the plant and regulated the sale and possession of it such that anyone who sold or dealt with ganja had to take out a *licence*, paying a duty of ten pounds to the Treasurer or sub-Treasurer of the colonial State.

After the League of Nations Conference (a conference which Garvey termed 'a League of White Nations') the British authorised the use of Indian hemp for scientific and medicinal purposes, but declared that:

> *"the raw resin however which is extracted from the female tops of cannabis sativa, together with the various preparations, of which it forms the basis, not being utilised for medicinal purposes and only being susceptible for harmful purposes, in the same manner as other narcotics, may not be produced, sold, traded under any circumstances whatever".*[25]

This law lay dormant on the British statute books in Jamaica until after 1938 when the planters associated ganja, Rastas and the revolt, leading to a revision of the Dangerous Drugs Law as a weapon against poor blacks, especially the Rastafari who suffered periodic raids.

The 1941 Amendment (just when Pinnacle was being raided) for the first time in the history of Jamaican law incorporated the principle of mandatory imprisonment, precisely what the planters had called for after the rebellion.

> *"No longer did a judge have the option of jailing or not jailing a convicted ganja offender; conviction automatically meant imprisonment. In addition, possession of any amount of ganja, no matter how small, was taken to imply possible intent to sell. Even if a man had just a* spliff *(a cigarette), he was liable to a lesser penalty for smoking, but if he had not yet lit it, he was liable to the much heavier penalty for possession."*

The police had discretionary powers over the type of arrest and thousands of Rastas and youths were branded as criminals, and imprisoned for possession of a herb which was part of the popular culture. After the resistance at Coral Gardens in 1964, the law was strengthened so that Rastas could be sent to prison for five years. A Rasta or worker would be imprisoned for up to one year, and fined up to £100, on a first conviction.[26]

The figures from the paper of H. Aubrey Fraser, on "The Law and Cannabis in the West Indies", * showed how the number of arrests escalated as the crisis

*The middle class person who was arrested for possession had the family connections to ensure that charges would be dropped. If they were charged, then their lawyers would argue that only the female part of the plant, cannabis sativa, was declared to be part of the Dangerous Drugs Law. This loophole was subsequently closed. The court affirmed that a person could be charged for both the male and female part. For full details see H. Aubrey Fraser, *The Law and Cannabis in the West Indies*, pp 374-375.

Jamaica intensified, especially during the years of increased political violence, 1967 and 1968. Arrests for unlawful possession went up by 300%, and it was not until the Rastas helped to defeat the Jamaica Labour Party regime (the one they termed Pharaoh) that the PNP amended the provisions for mandatory imprisonment, so that now there was a fine for those arrested for possession for the first time.[27]

This amendment had come partly because many of the children of the petty bourgeoisie and political careerists were now being attracted to the power of Rasta, including the spiritual use of ganja. Michael Manley's administration understood that they could not deal so repressively with a popular custom, but they continued to use the anti-democratic and anti-people law.[28]

One of the most serious indictments of the State is that even if they have been constrained by international agreements on the question of legalising ganja – freeing up the herb – they have not generated the kind of scientific research which would help the society to understand the long-term medicinal use of this herb. Dr. Vera Rubin and Dr. Lambos Comitas, in their work on *Ganja in Jamaica*, listed some thirty ailments which were susceptible to cure by ganja (marijuana), including asthma, colds, stomach disorders, fever, rheumatism, glaucoma and others.

These researchers have come from a tradition of scholarship in Jamaica and the United States which has debunked the idea that ganja acts as a stimulant towards crime, and at the end of their study the Chairman of the National Commission on Marijuana and Drug Abuse of the USA said that:

> *"There is little correlation between ganja and crime, except insofar as the possession and cultivation of ganja are technically crimes."*[29]

No comparable study has been done in Jamaica by the State, and the pressure of the State to outlaw this popular custom led to a level of cooperation between the United States security apparatus and the Manley regime, such that the later claims of Michael Manley that the CIA were out to remove him were most ironic.

Kola Nuts and Ganja

The use of ganja for spiritual purposes among African peoples is not without precedent. In West Africa, before the advent of the Europeans, the *Kola Nut* played a similarly important multifaceted role in the culture of the people. The *Kola* trade was part regional and long distance trade along the coast of West Africa. Walter Rodney, in his reconstruction of the history of the Upper Guinea Coast while the area was still free of profound European influence, made references to the Kola trade and the use of the Kola nut among the people. He wrote:

> *"The value of Kola in West Africa can scarcely be overstressed.*
>
> *The Kola nut is associated with religious rites, initiation ceremonies and property rights; it is used as a stimulant, a yellow dye, for medicinal*

purposes, as a symbol of hospitality and in diplomatic relations between rulers, and it was particularly highly regarded among Islamicised peoples."

Continuing by outlining the trade routes of this important commodity among the people, Rodney then went on to show how the Portuguese and Afro-Portuguese traders had taken over the production and distribution of Kola nut and how:

"All exchanges in which the Afro-Portuguese had a hand ultimately promoted the Atlantic trade, which too often meant the trade in slaves."[10]

These slaves took the Kola nut to the New World, but the centrality of this multi-purpose nut subsided among the slaves, especially because the plantation society frowned upon authentic African religious practices. Further research in this area would shed light on why the religious and spiritual uses of Kola did not persist, for in Jamaica the Kola nut is still used in the rural areas, especially as an antidote for poison. In Jamaica the Kola nut is known by its Twi name – bisé – and bisé, or bizzy tea, is still brewed for medicinal purposes.

By the end of the 19th century the Kola nut in Jamaica had been replaced by ganja as a herb associated with healing and spiritual reflection. Ganja was grown for personal consumption and the privatisation and secrecy surrounding the uses of the herb developed after the anti-people laws were invoked to stamp out its use.

What little trade occurred took place outside of the government controlled shops and commercial outlets, and ganja cultivation was carried out to subsidise the income of the small farmer, especially after the invasion of the rural areas by the bauxite tractors and heavy equipment. The evidence at Pinnacle, St. Elizabeth and St. Thomas was that the Rastafarian settlements were self-sufficient, but that this self-sufficiency was disrupted by the police raids against the camps.

The dispersal of the Rastas, along with other uprooted small farmers, led to a small trade in ganja in the late fifties and early sixties. Police raids and repression forced the ganja trade into the realm of 'criminal activities', such that secrecy and suspicion began to replace the old spirit of trust and cooperation between users.

A new stratum of 'traders' – called 'dealers' – emerged in Jamaican society, aping the behaviour of the Afro-Portuguese who had intervened in the Kola nut trade. Rural farmers who grew the plant became secretive, and the traditional concept of sharing a reciprocal day's work was effectively abandoned by young farmers who had to protect their ganja fields. If the trade in ganja had this effect on the rural areas, it would have an even more profound effect on the whole society.

The incipient trade in ganja to provide for the needs of the urban users was gradually changing as the lumpen elements found an alliance with capitalists in the United States of America to export ganja to the United States mainland.

Similar to the way in which the Afro-Portuguese had begun large-scale planting of Kola trees and selling the nut in bulk, a stratum of big cultivators emerged in the hills of Jamaica to supply the US market.

By the middle of the sixties the export of ganja to the US was a multi-million dollar a year business, highly organised, with capitalist and potential get-rich-quick individuals from the US arriving in Jamaica in sailboats, motorboats, yachts and aircraft to take out tons of ganja.

Makeshift airstrips and a capital intensive coordination – involving two-way radios and contacts at customs and immigration – meant that this new export boom was out of the hands of the small farmers and Rastas. Small capitalists, furniture exporters, law enforcement officers, senior civil servants, big landlords, and minor political careerists all joined in this trade as the contradiction between the law and the people led to a tremendous criminal and violent apparatus to protect the ganja fields and to ensure that large-scale supplies were not hijacked.

The most destructive aspect of this link with the US was the speed with which a guns/ganja organised crime nexus emerged. Guns of all sorts proliferated in the society, consistent with the increase in trade, so that a gun culture began to emerge in the society. This coincided with the growth of a stratum of lumpens in the urban areas who terrorised poor communities.[31]

Between 1964 and 1967 a subculture of angry youths developed in the society. Answering to the pseudonym *Rude Bwoy* and searching for avenues of self-expression and recognition, these unemployed youths were quickly integrated into the export trade, many of them as enforcers.

Gangs going by names such as Skull, Sprangler, Zulu, Phantom, Pigeon, Vikings, Dirty Dozen and Phoenix battled with each other for the control of neighbourhoods. The very names of these gangs showed how they had internalised the ideas of the Hollywood bad men like Dillinger and Clint Eastwood, for these youths had been attracted to the ideology of consumerism. Without the discipline and training of workers or small farmers, these young people created terror among working people, such that they were feared by both citizens and police.

The myth that the Rastafarians were violent deepened as some of these lumpen thugs took on the physical appearance of locksmen to further their work of intimidation. Both political parties used these youths for intimidation, and political warfare became part of the culture of guns/ganja and violence.[32]

Terry Lacey, in *Violence and Politics in Jamaica 1960-1970*, did not simply outline the statistics of guns, clashes and arrests, but showed how the political warfare and state of emergency was linked to industrial disputes. Both Michael Manley and Pearnel Charles, in separate studies – *A Voice in the Workplace* and *Detained* – have attested to the role that violence played in their trade union activities. Both surrounded themselves with 'bad men' recruited from the ranks of the unemployed, and in the end the scourge of *unemployment* acted as a social sanction which was as effective as direct coercion in brutalising the working class movement.

Operation Buccaneer

When Michael Manley and the PNP were supported by the youths and Rastas in 1972 in the electoral struggle against the JLP, progressive elements in the society expected a programme which would lead to the decriminalisation of ganja and the use of the State to disarm the Rude Bwoys. Instead, Manley concentrated on a level of populism and partisanship which did not seriously alleviate the problem of party-retained gunmen. The period after the election led to a boom in the ganja trade, and as the competition for the big export deals began to involve top functionaries of the society, this struggle took its toll in the physical elimination of public figures.

It was during this new phase of violence that the PNP regime set up the undemocratic *Gun Court* in order to curb the levels of gun violence. Manley and his then Security Minister, Eli Matalon, brushed aside the norms of bourgeois law so that one could be incarcerated in this 'concentration camp' structure for the possession of a spent shell. On top of this, the PNP gave the US government unprecedented powers to operate in Jamaica, under the guise of stamping out the ganja trade.

By 1974 the ganja trade was such an important aspect of capital accumulation that it became part of the circuit of transnational capital, even reaching the pages of the *New York Times* and the *Financial Times* in Europe.[33] These organs of capitalism had recognised that Jamaica had become the most important exporter of this herb to the US – about US$400 million per year – such that this illicit traffic was becoming the number one export from Jamaica. (In 1980 the Prime Minister, Edward Seaga, said that the trade was up to US$2 billion per year.)

Similar to the export of other commodities, the value added accrued to foreign operators, for in 1974 one pound of cured weed bought in Jamaica for US$8-10 was sold on the streets of New York for US$200 per pound; and the United States Drug Enforcement Agency* estimated that two million pounds were smuggled into the US in 1974.[34]

To curb this trade, which sections of its ruling class perceived as a threat to 'National Security', the US embarked on a programme to *eradicate* large-scale ganja cultivation. With the active cooperation of the PNP administration and without consulting the people of Jamaica, the United States embarked on an operation which was unparalleled in its scope in a foreign country. With

*The Drug Enforcement Agency was the super drug agency created by Richard Nixon as part of the "all-out global war on the drug menace". The new drug agency incorporated the Bureau of Narcotics and Dangerous Drugs, the Office of Drug Abuse and Law Enforcement, the Office of National Narcotics Intelligence, those sections of the US Customs Service involved with drug investigation and the drug enforcement related functions of the Office of Science and Technology. When this organisation was unveiled in March 1973, its first administrator was John R. Bartels whose first job as an attorney had been defending cigarette companies against lawsuits from lung cancer victims. See *High Times*, December-January 1976/7, pp 78.

hindsight one wonders why Michael Manley handed over the entire operation to a branch of the US State, involving the activities of all kinds of intelligence agents.

Boasting of the scale of the activities of this operation – called Buccaneer – the Drug Enforcement Agency outlined to a Senate Hearing the deployment of resources in this invasion of Jamaica. The following lengthy quote gives some indication of the scale and nature of the operation:

> *"Operation Buccaneer was the largest, most successful, most diversified foreign task force ever undertaken by the US Narcotic enforcement organisation. The basic objectives of Buccaneer, as requested by the Jamaican Government, were to disrupt the unabated marijuana cultivation in Jamaica and to disrupt the hard drug and marijuana trafficking in the United States. In accomplishing the goals we drew from the wealth of expertise available within and without the DEA. DEA personnel served on Operation Buccaneer as pilots, undercover agents, boat operators, radio and radar technicians, secretaries, general 1811 investigators, and intelligence analysts. Other personnel functioned in the areas of administration, supervision and logistical support. This operation was successful from objective and subjective points of view. Buccaneer was the first task force requested by a foreign government that encompassed the full range of law enforcement functions, coupled with military and para-military activities. The development and implementation of Buccaneer represented many 'firsts' for us:*
>
> *(1) Our first attempt at transporting, setting up, and operating a fixed-base sea and air unit in a foreign country.*
>
> *(2) The first time we have contracted for the purchase, transported, installed, maintained and operated an entire communications system, not only provided compatibility between DEA and Jamaican equipment, but provided a 24-hour communications link between the command post in Jamaica, DEA bases in the United States, and the US Coast Guard cutter assigned in the Windward Passage.*
>
> *(3) Buccaneer was the first narcotic interdiction program in which the US Coast Guard participated by totally dedicating cutters for a sustained period. For five months 182 or 378 foot Coast Guard cutters, with DEA agents on board, patrolled the Windward Passage, performing intelligence and interdiction functions.*
>
> *(4) This was the first occasion on which a foreign government has requested such a multifarious task force, and at the same time fully dedicated elements of its own military and police forces.*
>
> *(5) With coordination from DEA, this was the first time a single foreign narcotics task force had the interrelated cooperation and participation of several US government agencies: Department of State, Agency for International Development (AID), American Embassy Kingston, Department of Agriculture, Coast Guards, Customs Service, Army,*

Navy and Air Force. Within DEA all domestic regions contributed with TDY personnel, and at Headquarters there was participation or input from the Officers of the Chief Counsel, Liaison, Public Affairs, Training, Science and Technology, Intelligence, Enforcement and Administration."[35]

The task force, under the guise of eradicating ganja, carried out full-scale military manoeuvres in the rural areas, and the search and destroy methods used were like the military tactics of the abortive Vietnam campaign. Listing the helicopters, aircraft and specialist personnel in this programme the news sheet of the DEA – *Drug Enforcement Agency* – later showed how, after the ganja farmers resorted to premature harvesting to save part of their crop,

"*to counter this tactic, some of the troops remained above the helicopters, which then went off to sweep the surrounding areas for caches of drying ganja, usually spread out on tarpaulins in the sun. Containers of kerosene were carried to speed the burning process. By late November it was becoming difficult to find fields of sufficient size visible from the air, and emphasis shifted to a search for seabeds and the pursuit of an aggressive search-and-destroy campaign on the ground.*"[36]

At the end of this programme, which undermined the sovereignty of Jamaica, the trade still flourished, despite the proud claim by the DEA that they seized 730,000 pounds of ganja, 8,083 pounds of ganja seeds, 20 pounds of cocaine, 11 weapons, 17 boats, and confiscated US$143,000.[37]

What began as a campaign against the Rastafarians in 1954 led to a reinforcement of the US military over security operations in Jamaica, such that Michael Manley's later protestation about the Central Intelligence Agency sounded hollow as Rastas said "Don't involve Rasta in a de *Rat Race*".[38] These brethren had long called on the State to *Legalise It*, or free up the weed, for they were bearing part of the blame for the violence and thuggery which had been unleashed. The Dangerous Drugs Law had developed a tremendous criminal apparatus and despite the clear implications of the escalating trade, poor smokers and cultivators were bound together with the big dealers in their defiance of the law.

It was difficult to later mobilise against genuine CIA efforts at subversion, for the people had looked on as Matalon and intelligence agents from the US placed innocent youths in the Gun Court, while the big capitalist traders continued the trade – at the same time exporting the capital to their accounts in North America and Switzerland.

Jamaica became the centre of international attention during the 1976 electoral struggle, after the Manley regime vociferously claimed that the CIA was intent on destabilising Jamaica. Unprecedented levels of violence and a crude anti-communist campaign had been the signs that in the struggle for political power in Jamaica there was intense outside intervention – similar to the activities of the CIA. The then US Secretary of State, Henry Kissinger, flew to Jamaica to tell the people of the Caribbean not to support the war of African freedom fighters in Angola. Cuba had taken up the challenge and had decisively intervened in Angola to drive back the South African invasion.

The Rastafari movement had been at the forefront of the Pan-African support for African liberation, holding African Liberation Day rallies and through the medium of *reggae* sang songs on the *Tales of Mozambique, MPLA, Africa Must Be Free* and *War*. These songs of freedom were joined by the active campaign of a small Left, which published pamphlets on the CIA subversion. So that when the Jamaican people were mobilised to defend their sovereignty and to defend African freedom fighters, the United States imposed a pseudo-Rasta group to promote confusion in the ranks of the Rastas. This campaign by the US took the organisational form of the Ethiopian Zion Coptic Church.

Coptics and the New Subversion

It is a strange twist of history that in the same month that the United States supported the South African invasion of Angola, the Ethiopian Zion Coptic Church was incorporated in Jamaica,

> *"for the teaching and spreading of belief in the Bible, the Moral Laws of God, the Fatherhood of God and the Brotherhood of Man to safeguard and transmit to posterity the purity and righteousness of the precepts and teachings as taught by them".*[39]

The Ethiopian Zion Coptic Church, which claimed to be Rastafari, has come to international attention for its passionate defence of the right to smoke and use ganja, as it was a 'holy sacrament', and in the process has endeared many young Rastas to the ideas which they promote.

The Coptics have, in the process of linking themselves with local blacks, introduced the concept that 'White Americans' could be Rastas, calling into question one of the fundamental tenets of Rastafari that *'the Rasta is one who never forgets that he is an African'*. From their headquarters in *Star Island*, in Florida, USA, these capitalists, who have found it convenient to wear the cover of Rasta, set out to acquire land and followers in Jamaica so that they could further their accumulation.

Following the tradition of the planters of old slavery days who organised a system of planter/overseer relations, the white Coptics cooperated with a local Rasta – called 'Elder Keith Gordon' – to set up a capitalist organisation involving the ownership of vast land holdings and farms, cattle, rice fields, deep sea fishing boats and other assets.[40]

During the years when the Jamaican leader was protesting to the world that "Jamaica is not for sale", the Coptics bought up land to such an extent that apart from the bauxite conglomerates, the Coptics are the biggest single landowners in Jamaica, owning over 10,000 acres of land worth more than Ja $20 million.

From time to time poor farmers appealed to the regime to stop the Coptics from monopolising the land and rural infrastructure.[41] But these appeals were ignored, until in 1981 the *Daily Gleaner* could speak of the Coptics as "a country within Jamaica".

For during the five years of expansion, the Coptics added to their rural properties a container haulage company, *Coptic Containers* – a wrecker service, hiring out forklifts,

> *"they own a gas station, a supermarket, a furniture store, an aircraft, deep sea fishing boats, and heavy duty equipment, including tractors and front end loaders which they hire out. In all, the Coptics own some 400 motor units. Besides they own choice properties in Beverley Hills and other exclusive areas in Kingston, Mandeville and elsewhere."*

As capitalists they lived a life commensurate with their exploitation of labour, and press reports told the population that there were no lack of video sets, telephones or two-way radios; and:

> *"contributing to their Mafia-image are their fleet of sleek cars, equipped with two-way radios and with tinted windows and windscreens"*.

These so-called Rastas were featured on US television – CBS 60 Minutes – and television pictures showed the palatial house of the leader, Brother Louv – a house worth US$270,000 in 1975, paid for in cash.[42]

Few doubt that the acquisition of this form of obscene opulence comes from the cultivation, export and trade in ganja, for the word 'coptic' spawns images of ganja, and the leadership actively promote an international campaign ostensibly in support of the legislation of its 'holy sacrament'. Through its newpaper – *Coptic Times* – this pseudo-Rasta religious formation has been promoting the use of ganja while promoting anti-communist ideas and distorting the lessons of Marcus Garvey.

Because the coptics and their advisers perceived the importance of Garvey to the ideology of Rasta, they embarked on a programme to popularise a notion of Garvey as an anarchist and rabid anti-communist. Hiding behind an international and popular campaign to legalise cannabis, the *Coptic Times*, one of the few newspapers distributed free internationally, has, instead of presenting thoughts on those tobacco and alcohol companies who lobby the UN to ensure that cannabis remains a narcotic, carried out a virulent anti-communist campaign among Rastafari and youths in Jamaica.

During the 1980 bloody election campaign, when a new kind of terror was unleashed against the Jamaican people, *Coptic Times* told the youths in one page not to be involved in politics, while on another page told them to fight against communism. This newspaper had earlier actively opposed the visit of Michael Manley to the Soviet Union, at a time when the people of Jamaica and their elected government went on a State visit to the USSR.

At the end of a violent election campaign where 500 persons, including a junior minister, died, the Coptics boasted to the *Washington Post* that "Ganja saved Jamaica from Communism". (No-one doubted the very close connections between the coptics and State and Federal officials, since more than once charges have been dropped when the leaders of this new trade were arrested.)

So organised were these white Rastas that they could employ Ramsey Clark, a former US Attorney General, as their legal representative. With such connections the purveyors of a new kind of confusion among youths openly violate the laws of Jamaica, and this was amply demonstrated in 1980 when one of their aircraft was seized by the Jamaican police at an airstrip in St. Elizabeth. The coptics arrived in another aircraft, fired at the police and rescued the captured plane.[43] Only an organisation with the support of another State could brazenly violate Jamaican airspace in that manner.

In 1979 members of the Coptic organisation were held with US$80 million worth of ganja destined for the US market, but as of this date of writing, none of the leadership had been charged for smuggling the weed.[44]

Not only has this capitalist organisation infiltrated all branches of the Jamaican State, but its campaign has been to bind young people to the ideas of capitalism through fetishising ganja. Because of the indiscriminate nature of the present smokers of the herb, contrary to the former communal use by the Rastas, the coptics have used this to promote commodity fetishism among young people, and in the process tied them closer to imperialism. Everywhere in the West the capitalist class understood that this was the way to undermine the anti-capitalist appeal of Rasta, so that from New York to Kingston, from Grenada to Birmingham, police officers are involved in the ganja trade, using the trade to drive a wedge between progressive Rastas, anti-imperialist elements and those Rastas who were seduced by the TV sets, video equipment and stereo equipment which are dangled before them.

This contradiction reached its apogee in Grenada in 1980 when pro-capitalist elements mobilised Rastas around the cultivation of ganja as part of a campaign against the Grenada Revolution.

The presence of coptics marked a new stage in the contention of the culture of oppression and the culture of resistance. Undoubtedly, because of the very nature of police repression against Rastas in the past, genuine brethren have been cautious in distinguishing themselves from a formation which passionately defends the herb. However, in the face of the vital need for deliverance and redemption, it will become clearer that it is not in the interest of the brethren to make a fetish out of smoking the weed; for just as the use of the Kola nut subsided because the trade was taken over by slavers, conscious Rasta elements are shunning the anti-Rasta of the Ethiopian Zion Coptic Church.[45]

More and more it is becoming clear that the words of Cabral need to be invoked among the Rastafari:

> "*In the face of the vital need for progress, the following attitudes or behaviours will be no less harmful to Africa: indiscriminate compliments; systematic exaltation of virtues without condemning faults; blind acceptance of the values of culture,* without considering what presently or politically regressive elements it contains; *confusion between what*

is the expression of an objective and material historic reality and what appears to be a creation of the mind or the product of a peculiar temperament; absurd linking of artistic creations, whether good or not, with supposed racial characteristics; and finally, the non-scientific or scientific critical appreciation of the cultural phenomenon."[46] (My *emphasis)*

Imperialism from the outset had wanted to reinforce the regressive elements ot Rasta, for through the work of their anthropologists and sociologists they had understood very well the dialectic of negative and positive influences of the history of black people and Rastafari. While those aspiring for a scientific and progressive orientation had no time for insights which seemed to depart from models in Western Europe, imperialism, knowing ıhe full force and potential of Rasta, did not ignore the search for an African identity by the Rastas, but rather took care to foster its most negative aspects: the reinforcement of individualism – and the alienation from the revolutionary features of Marxism.

Through a bevy of researchers the international capitalists have sought to promote the particularly metaphysical and idealistic aspects of the movement, while relying on the original distortions of Simpson that Rastas were black 'supremacists'. This project continues, so that many young Rastas who did not have the original foundation have simply accepted the wearing of the locks as a religious phenomenon, and invoke backward ideas on the role of women and the place of the Rasta in the struggle for liberation.

The challenge of imperialism to Rasta has meant that the movement has had to fall back on all the resources of resistance which had been handed down from the slaves. To remedy the promotion of false Dreads, the Rastas have embarked on a quiet programme of cultural resistance; while at the ideological level Walter Rodney pointed to a possible path for the Rasta with his materialist interpretation of African history, which was aimed at liberating the Rastas from the preoccupation with Haile Selassie.

Rodney's *Groundings* were part of a project to explain that black people in the West could not support anti-people regimes in Africa, even if at a moment in history this regime had been at the forefront of the struggle for African liberation. After the 1972 Pan-African Congress and his own return to the Caribbean, Rodney warned that there will be more disillusionment; for

> *"we have shared romantic visions about the African continent. We have allowed illusions to take the place of serious analysis of what actual struggles are taking place in the African continent; what social forces are represented in the government and what is the actual shape of society".*[47]

This statement, made in reference to the changes in Tanzania, could very well have been a preparation for the Rastas for what was taking place in Ethiopia.

It is to the conjunction of the *Groundings* of Walter Rodney with the cultural resistance of Rasta and the international explosion of reggae that we now turn.

FOOTNOTES

1. The owner of Worthy Park Estate suggested that the organisers of the strike at his estate were under the influence of ganja. It was beyond his understanding that black people would be revolting because of low pay, backward technology and unhealthy working conditions. After the 1938 revolt the colonial State, in its general drive against the people, decided that "ganja is a pest to the community and should be exterminated: We suggest that persons convicted of cultivating, selling or otherwise dealing in it should be sentenced to imprisonment without the option of a fine, instead of as at present where a fine may be imposed without imprisonment". *Report of the Commission appointed to Enquire into the Disturbances Which Occurred in Jamaica in 1938*, p. 3.
2. Ken Post, *Arise Ye Starvelings*, p. 418.
3. Philip Curtin in his study of post-emancipation Jamaica demonstrated how these villagers acted as wage earners in their confrontation with the planters. See his *Two Jamaicas*. Walter Rodney in his study of the *History of the Guyanese Working People*, John Hopkins Press, Baltimore, 1981, debunked the theory that these villagers were any pre-capitalist independent peasantry. He elaborated the idea of how these villagers acted as wage earners and small farmers because of the inadequate crystallisation of the major classes under colonial capitalism.
4. *Report of the Sugar Commission 1944-5*.
5. George Beckford, *Persistent Poverty*, Oxford University Press, 1972, p. 23.
6. This colonial attitude was given historical validity in the *Report of the Rastafari Movement in Kingston, Jamaica*, 1960. The references to this report are from the reprinted version in *Caribbean Quarterly*, Sept. 1967, p. 8.
7. *Daily Gleaner*, March 9, 1978.
8. Dennis Forsyte, *West Indian Culture Through the Prism of Rastafarianism*, Mimeo, UWI, Dept. of Sociology, Mona, 1979, p. 47.
9. George E. Simpson, "Political Cultism in Western Kingston", *Social and Economic Studies*, Vol. 4, Nov. 1955. This title is significant in that the first observers were aware of the overt political content of Rastafari before they stamped the religious notion on the movement.
10. *African Opinion*, Jan.-Feb. 1956.
11. There is a complete file on King Ja Ja at the Public Records Office under the Foreign Office File, FO 403. For his activities in West Africa see D.O. Dike, *Trade and Politics in the Niger Delta*, Oxford University Press.
12. Older residents of the island of St. Vincent still remember the calypsos made about King Ja Ja.
13. Psalm 68, Vs. 4. *Jamaica Talk* by Frederick Cassidy, Macmillan, London, 1968, also said that Jah was the Maroon name for God. See p. 237.
14. *Report on the Rastafari Movement in Kingston*, p. 21.
15. Leonard Barrett, *The Rastafarians*, Heinemann Books, London, 1977, pp 94-98.
16. Millard Johnson was a major force in the Jamaican Black Consciousness movement in the period leading up to independence, 1962. He was linked to the UNIA and campaigned under the platform of the Garveyite programme, calling his party the same name as that of Garvey – the People's Political Party. As of now there has not been a major study on the failure of the PPP in Jamaica. In the United States one study which was carried out in the tradition of modernisation and cultural pluralism looked in some detail into the PPP. See John C. Gannon, *The Origin and Development of Jamaica's Two Party System 1930-1975*, Ph.D. Thesis, Washington University, 1976.
17. Rex Nettleford, *Mirror Mirror*, Sangsters, Jamaica, 1970, p. 86.
18. J.V. Owens, "Literature on Rastafari", *New Community*, Journal of the Commission of Racial Equality, London, Vol. VI Nos 1 & 2, Winter 1977/78, p. 151. This review is a useful and sympathetic treatment of most of the literature on Rasta.
19. This distortion is repeated in Barrett's work, see pp 113-115.
20. *Report On Rasta*, p. 28.
21. *British Home Office Circular to all Prison Department Establishments*, Circular 66/76, July 1976, London. Prison officers cut the locks of Rastas, and refused the legitimate demands of special dietary considerations for Rastas in prison.
22. Nettleford, op. cit., p. 57.
23. Ernest Cashmore, *The Rastaman, The Rastafari in Britain*, George Allen & Unwin, London, 1979, p. 26. Cashmore used the code words, the 'Spell of Africa', as a future justification for the forced repatriation of blacks from Britain.
24. Interview with Dr. Lambros Comitas, *High Times*, No. 32, 1978, p. 33.
25. H. Aubrey Fraser, "The Law and Cannabis in the West Indies", *Social and Economic Studies*, No. 5, 1974, pp

361-385. For an analysis of the extensive use of *Ganja in Jamaica* see book by the same name by Vera Rubin and Lambros Comitas, Anchor Books, 1976. In my research into the scientific studies of ganja I have found the library of the Institute for the Study of Drug Dependence, London, to be the most comprehensive, with all the UN meetings and relevant declarations. They are located at Kingsbury House, 3 Blackburn Road, London. Because of the number of studies in the metropoles which called for the Legalisation of Cannabis, the UWI Extra Mural Dept. came out with a pamphlet in 1978 which reinforced the colonial view of the narcotic properties of ganja. See *Ganja*, by John W. Commissiong, UWI, Mona, 1978.

26. *Ganja in Jamaica*, p. 26.
27. See Amendment to the Dangerous Drugs Law, *Laws of Jamaica*, April, 1974.
28. Michael Manley was fully conscious of how the laws created a criminal sub-culture. See "Manley and Marijuana", *High Times*, No. 4, 1978.
29. *Ganja in Jamaica*, foreword by Raymond P. Shafer.
30. Walter Rodney, *History of the Upper Guinea Coast 1545-1800*, Clarendon Press, 1970, pp 206-208.
31. Horace Campbell, "Commandist Politics and Political Violence", *Third World Forum*, Montreal, 1977.
32. Terry Lacey, *Violence and Politics in Jamaica 1960-1970*, Manchester University Press, 1977, pp 87-94.
33. *Financial Times*, September 5, 1974.
34. *Drug Enforcement*, Journal of the Drug Enforcement Agency, Fall, 1974. See story on Operation Panhandle, p. 29. According to the United Nations Statistics the amount of cannabis seized was: 1971, 575 kg; 1972, 15,822 kg; 1973, 62,521 kg; plants: 1971, 91,647; 1972, 401,000; 1973, 395,000,000; seeds: 1971, 8,973,104; 1972, 402,500,000; 1973, 397,500,000.
35. "The Marijuana-Hashish Epidemic and Its Impact on United States Security – the Continuing Escalation", Hearings before the Subcommittee to Investigate the Administration of Internal Security Act and other Laws, *United States Senate*, Washington, May, 1975, p. 441. The evidence had shown that Manley cooperated with the most conservative and racist elements in the US at that time.
36. *Drug Enforcement*, Winter, 1975, p. 15. This issue devoted considerable space to the way in which Operation Buccaneer was conceived, planned, prepared and executed.
37. See *Drug Enforcement*, Winter, 1975 For a critical account of the whole DEA see *High Times*, Dec.-Jan. 1976.
38. Single released by Bob Marley in early 1976 when Michael Manley claimed that the CIA was destabilising Jamaica. This record was banned from the airwaves in Jamaica.
39. *Jamaican Gazette Extraordinary*, July 24, 1975.
40. In their expansion in Jamaica the coptics have infiltrated all levels of the State and society, and despite the dangers posed for the future sovereignty of the country, the press continue to write glowing reports of their activities. See *Daily Gleaner*, April 26, 1981.
41. *Jamaica Daily News*, January 14, 1980.
    In St. Thomas the coptics set up their headquarters at Creighton Hall, a former slave estate near White Horses. They exploited the local farmers though a system similar to the sharecropping which was and is practised in the United States. See "Coptics in St. Thomas", *Jamaica Daily News*, August 15, 1980.
42. *CBS Television Network*, "60 Minutes", Vol. XII, Number 7, as broadcast on Sunday October 28, 1979, 7:11-8:11 EST. This programme told the story of the leader of the coptics – Thomas Reilly – who moved from Boston to set up the headquarters in Miami, calling himself Brother Louv. The coptics have diversified business interests, including land in Colombia. Members of the 'Church' have been involved in very large drug busts, involving 13 tons, and 20 tons, but the charges were later dropped because of lack of evidence.
43. *Jamaica Daily News*, Sept. 18, 1980.
44. *Jamaica Daily News*, Nov. 23, 1979.
45. *Jamaica Daily News*, Sept. 14, 1980.
46. Amilcar Cabral, *Return To The Source*, Monthly Review Press, 1973, p. 51.
47. Walter Rodney, Interview in *Black Scholar*, November, 1974.

Chapter Five

RASTA, REGGAE AND CULTURAL RESISTANCE

"Since music, art and literature play an important part in our society, we must learn to serve the masses in a progressive manner. We must not only take part in non-political developments, but we must use our talent to influence the entire world with the greatest force."

Ainsley Vaughan

"Get up. Stand up for your rights."

The Wailers

"In our epoch the Rastafari have represented the leading force of this expression of racial consciousness."

Walter Rodney

Rasta and the Rediscovery of the Cultural Heritage of the Slave

Rastafarians in Jamaica were in the process of creating a popular culture which was based on the spirit of resistance, combined with the good humour and spirit of joy which had become part of the disposition of black peoples of the world. As capitalist relations in the society deepened, and the people had the distinct feeling that capitalism was destroying their personality, the Rastas were a section of the working poor who wanted to break the spirit of competition and individualism which permeated the society and its main institutions.

Already in the hills of Sligoville, the Rastas had repaired the breach of envy and malice with an openness and honesty which scared the planters. The spectre of another village community which could breed the germs of black resistance, similar to the free villages of Paul Bogle at Stony Gut, sent chills down the spines of the planters.

Dispersed and despised, the Rastas moved to the urban areas to face humiliation, arrest and hostility. But the quiet campaign of the hills was taken to the city and the spirit of sharing, cooperation, self-reliance and solidarity which guided Pinnacle went to the tenement yards of Kingston and the rubbish heaps called 'Dungle', where they were forced to live.

One of the early manifestations of the new spirit was in the very preparation of food and meals – in the making of ital food. Forced to live at the barest minimum, the Rastas sought a diet which would ensure a healthy existence, since they knew that the medical infrastructure of the society was prejudiced against the poor and Rastas. Instead of relying on the old custom of consulting obeah men or women, the Rastas took care to learn about those herbs and plants which had medicinal value, and took greater care to prepare the kind of food which guaranteed good health.

Long before the high levels of chemicals and preservatives in food processing had caused concern for the *Food and Drug Administration* in the United States, the Rastafari had denounced the high content of drugs in the locally imported food, and were teaching their neighbours the value of local food crops in the making of ital food.

Rastafari were at the forefront of articulating the need for a food policy for the people, for it was never part of the overall objective of the colonial or neo-colonial State to provide a proper balanced diet for the people. The post-slavery consumption habits which relied heavily on imported food – especially cod fish and chicken back for the poor – guaranteed that the tastes and eating habits of the society integrated Jamaica into the North American agricultural/food complex.

The preference for using Canadian flour rather than cassava flour for dumpling was but one manifestation of a wider problem – a problem which was connected to the continued emphasis on exporting sugar, coffee, bananas and citrus. There has never been in Jamaican history a programme for the building of an integrated economy where the industrialisation of agriculture would bring new skills to the rural areas, while at the same time organising the kind of farming which effectively produced, utilised and preserved local food crops.

Report followed report in tragi-comic succession, outlining the levels of malnutrition among the poor; and it is significant that even the United States Army commissioned a study of the *Ecology of Malnutrition in the Caribbean.**

Despite the overwhelming evidence in these reports of how the fact of undernourishment and malnutrition affect the general health of the society, especially the working poor, there is still very poor knowledge of the nutritional value of local foodstuffs. Rastas embarked on a project to use the fruits, vegetables and plants of the countryside so that they could break the dependence on imported food. Yams, boiled bananas, plantains, callaloo, chocho and a wide range of local foodstuffs, which had been the food of the slaves, were prepared meticulously by the Rastas. They made use of the coconut, which could be used to make cooking oil or to provide the natural base for other food.

There is no major or dramatic difference between ital food and the food of the

*This report was atrocious in its analysis of the changes in Cuba in the area of food production. Its distortions showed just how possible it was to use statistics to confuse. This report did, however, quote a study comparing 204 Jamaican children who had died between the ages of 6 months and 3 years with living children. They established that 70 of the deaths had been caused by malnutrition and that malnutrition had been a contributory cause of death in 132 cases. See Jacques M. May and Donna L. McLellen, *The Ecology of Malnutrition in the Caribbean,* Hafner Press, N.Y., 1973. Apart from the US Army, the Rockefeller Foundation has sponsored studies and seminars on the problem of *Malnutrition.* It should not be a surprise that the US Army is interested in the food habits of the Caribbean people, for the US capitalists have given notice of using food as a weapon.(1)

poor rural farmer, except that many Rastas do not use salt, processed condiments, or chemically preserved canned food. Over the years many Rastas have become vegetarians, though some continue to eat fish, especially since before the redevelopment projects changed the landscape of the Kingston and Montego Bay seaside, many had made their livelihood as fishermen or fishmongers.

Whatever the differences between the vegetarians and the eaters of flesh, however, they all renounced the eating of pork. This renunciation of the pig had a tremendous impact on Jamaican society, such that pig farmers and the importers of ham and bacon witnessed a tremendous drop in sales.

This intervention in the discussion of a food programme could not be far-reaching enough to affect the rate of malnutrition, and the defects in diet still show in the deformed bodies of rural Jamaicans, though the tradition of ital food was becoming significant in the society. Yet, as in all aspects of Rasta culture, over-zealous supporters have been rigorous in their condemnation of the use of the pig, to the point where a level of intolerance developed.

This rigidity was especially noticeable when Rastafarians went to Cuba and were critical of the widespread eating of pork in this socialist island. No effort was made to distinguish pig rearing and pork preparation in a socialist society from the pig rearing which uses a large abundance of nitrates and nitrites in the factory farming of the advanced capitalist countries.[2]

Rastas live in a world where there are huge butter and wheat mountains, where capitalist rationale dictates that it is more economical to shoot cattle than to provide cheap meat, while there is no reorganisation of the priorities of the globe to stamp out world hunger. Ital food is only one rejection of the persistent attempt to get poor people to want to eat Kelloggs Cornflakes every morning, or to get them to support Kentucky Fried Chicken restaurants, McDonalds, and other fast food chains of the US which have sought to become established in Jamaica.

The preparation of food consistent with the resources of the society was only one other aspect of the overall thrust towards independence and self-reliance. In an effort to deepen their roots in the society, and the link with the rugged, defiant slave, the Rastas have built upon the foundations of the Jamaican language, resisting the traditions of the local whites, mulattoes and educated blacks which said that the language of the people was 'bad talk'.

Through the years of slavery and colonialism the language of Jamaica had developed out of the fusion of African and European languages which were spoken in the society.[3] This language incorporated a conceptual system in keeping with the retention of skills, the existence of a technical vocabulary, the prevalence of handicraft skills, a system of beliefs, entertainment and those cultural values which formed the world of the poor African Jamaican. The standard English of the schools and law courts was a second language to the sufferers.

Louise Bennett was among the ardent nationalists who took the language of the people to the whole society, such that her work precipitated a debate about the place of the Jamaican language: a healthy debate which still continues with a high level of research and publication on the potential for the use of the Jamaican language in schools.*

Nowadays the pride of Louise Bennett's defiance is still frowned upon by the State, for in Jamaica, English remains the language of commerce, education, State affairs and the radio. It is still the ambition of poor people to master the skill of using the English language, for the use of English is coterminous with the acquisition of higher education, and a much sought-after escape from poverty under neo-colonialism.

But in their search for this escape out of the ranks of the working class, many children of the poor who got this passport effected a level of alienation which was expressed in snobbishness, idle boastfulness, and oftimes an affected Oxbridge accent.

Rastafari understood the importance of education, but they aspired to the kind of education which would not alienate them from their communities. The first Rasta were avid readers, and they saw it as their duty to be informed on the politics, economics, geography and history of both Jamaica and Africa.

In their determined effort to break with the sophistry of the English culture of Jamaica, some even struggled to learn the Amharic language of Ethiopia. But this could never be a language of communication in Jamaica; so a slow process was started to develop expressions and to form a language which reflected their solidarity, self-reliance and Africanness.

This was a major task in the era of cultural imperialism when indigenous languages throughout the underdeveloped world were deteriorating as a result of the degradation of work and the dispossession of peasants, artisans, and skilled personnel by the transnational corporations. Rastas took up this challenge, and in their confrontation with the mystique of Hollywood they found it necessary to strengthen the Jamaican language with their own variant, 'Rasta talk'. This talk sought the deepest expression of racial memory, and the power of this memory was expressed in the lyrics of the Rasta song – reggae.

The Roots of Reggae

> *"Cultural poems spring from the history and experiences of the people who develop them, so are calypso and reggae products of the historical experiences of Africans in the Caribbean. But, while the medium of expression of protests and sentiments of the Africans in the Americas have taken varying forms, we find the content and spirit of Jazz and Blues in*

*The foundations of the work of Louise Bennett had been built upon F.G. Cassidy, *Jamaica Talk*, Macmillan, 1976, and F.G. Cassidy and R.B. LePage, *Dictionary of Jamaican English*, Cambridge University Press, 1976. These studies have now been supplemented by the work of Caribbean scholars who have participated in the lively debates on the question of language.

Afro-America, and the present Reggae in Jamaica reflect the same message – a reaction to the exploitation and oppression of the Africans in the New World."

Patrick Hylton, 1975

This quotation, from the study by Patrick Hylton on the politics of Caribbean music, encapsulates the essence of the role of cultural resistance and political assertion by the denigrated black souls of the West. Robbed of their language and forcibly tied to the institutions of capital, African peoples developed musical forms which were means of both communication and inspiration.[4] When the planters banned the nocturnal drummings, this African drumming survived the storms of prosecution and repression by taking refuge in the villages and in the spirit of those who kept the memory of Africa alive.

Like the seed which awaited conditions favourable to assure the survival of the species and its development, African culture in Jamaica took shelter in the religious expressions of Cumina, the Bongo Men, and the drumming of 'John Canoe', only to explode triumphantly out of the confines of the persecution in the form of reggae. But this had to await the period of decolonisation, when political independence had ushered in the need to emancipate the mind from mental slavery.

In Jamaica the planters and their allies had been relentless in their denigration of black cultural forms. Unlike the United States of America or Britain, where the capitalist class could boast their own bourgeois cultural values, the local planters aped the achievements of other white societies, but could not fashion a cultural apparatus of their own. Though they poured scorn on everything black, the ferocity with which they did this stemmed in part from their own insecurity and lack of creativity.

Those blacks who had internalised the ideas of Europe and felt that other black people had no culture joined whites and mulattoes in putting on second rate ventures; while the energetic blacks, like Louise Bennett and Ranny Williams, competed with those purveyors of Shakespeare who wanted to tell black people that their cultural link lay with the 16th century English countryside.[5]

The work songs of the banana loaders (e.g."Day O", which was popularised by Harry Belafonte) and the calypso of the villages were commercialised during and after World War II to the point where Jamaica mento and calypso were seen as products to lure tourists to the palm trees and sandy beaches, just as certain forms of black music were being used in the US to sell soap, deodorants and toothpaste.

As in the US, where the raw blues and jazz sought to distance themselves from this commercial product, so it was in Jamaica as the Rastafari continued a musical tradition of Africa – the call and response (lead and chorus) – as a mode of expression. The Rasta continued a vocal and instrumental form of black music which was as alive in Brazil, Cuba, Haiti and Memphis as it was in Trenchtown.

The similarities between the evolution of reggae and the blues may be explored in future research, but one fact remained constant, i.e. the power of the spirit. Leroi Jones, in tracing the social evolution of black American music, said:

> *"to go back in any historical (or emotional) line of Black music leads us inevitably to religion, i.e. the spirit worship. This phenomenon is always at the root of black art, the worship of the spirit – at least the summoning of or by such a force."*

Inside rural Jamaica this spirit spoke through the music and rituals of Cumina, Pocomania, and the Bongo Men. These spirits spoke through the drum, and the spiritual and secular forms of Jamaican music were fused together in what was to evolve as reggae. At the base of the secular and spiritual black music of Jamaica was the drum. Verena Reckford, in her introductory study of Rastafari music, identified the drums which were prominent in the Rasta drumming: they were the Fundeh, the Repeater and the Bass drum.[6]

The pride of the Rasta drums and the chants of the brethren coincided with a period when a new musical form was taking place in Jamaica – called ska. During the euphoria of political independence talented musicians like Don Drummond, Ernest Ranglin, Johnnie Moore, Roland Alphonso, Tommy McCook and Jackie Mittoo created a unique Jamaican jazz culture where the melody of horns was fused with the drums in a free form music which was mellifluous and rebellious.†

Rasta music and Jamaican black nationalism fused in the music of the *Skatalites*.* Because the radio stations of Jamaica continuously played the music of white America – Elvis Presley, Pat Boone, Doris Day and Neil Sedaka – the

†The process of change from ska to rock steady was imperceptible and undramatic. Ska was a musical form which combined the best traditions of black American jazz with black Jamaican music. It was a music which was primarily performed and not written down according to defined patterns. Some of the music of the Skatalites is now being studied, especially in Europe where there has been a conscious attempt to write the music of ska and study the early records. See two-part series on "Blue Beat and Ska" in the *Melody Maker*, May 12 and 19, 1979 London.

*Because of the pungent criticism of this music and clear working content of the lyrics, the music of the people did not get financial support: for the record companies exploited the singers and petty politicians sought to exploit the music for their own ends. The presence of a large community of working class Jamaicans in England, whose disposable income was more than that of those at home, meant that there was an outlet for the music beyond the petty prejudices of the radio stations and the Festival Committees which looked disparagingly at the musical forms forcing their way into the history of Jamaica and the Caribbean.

In this period young singers like Bob Andy, Jackie Opel, Ken Boothe, the Paragons and Bob Marley began to sing songs on the problems of the society, and the up-beat tempo of ska was replaced by the songs of the suffering.

people had to develop their own institutions, called *Sound Systems,* where the music of Jamaica and of black America could be played without restraint. These powerful sound systems were usually played in big yards with bamboo fences, where the songs of the Skatalites and the drumming of the Rastas would be heard.

The drumming of *O Carolina* heralded a new era of music, for the songs sung by the Rastafari which extolled Ethiopia and Africa were developed within the confines of the sound systems which vied with each other for supporters.[7] Socio-religious and political songs echoed and reverberated across the gullies from the sound systems, with *By The Rivers of Babylon, Let The Power Fall On I,* and the *Macabes Version* played along with the classic instrumental records called *Man in the Street, Schooling the Duke, Far East,* and other music of joy, consistent with the pride of achieving the status of political independence.

Those songs which had been sung at Warieka Hills, and at Rasta camps throughout the country, were now being released on record for all to hear. It was in this period that the Rasta began to influence the content of Jamaican music; and despite the component of idealism and deliverance, the songs were pregnant with criticism of the racial hierarchy of the society.

At this time young workers and unemployed youths who had not been part of the 1983 struggles were no longer ostracising the Rastafarians, but were joining in large numbers, though the State had done all it could to crush the nationalist tendency. The more astute politicians understood the full force of the social community embedded in rock steady, so that there was an effort to co-opt the Rastafarians by inviting Haile Selassie to Jamaica on a State visit, in April 1966.[8]

With the visit of His Imperial Majesty, the whites of the hills of St. Andrew were shocked to find that the Rastas were no mere fringe millenarian 'cult of outcasts' as they had been led to believe; for the political leaders had to take a back seat when Haile Selassie visited Jamaica. So massive was the outpouring of support for this African monarch that the State had to call upon Rastafarian leaders, such as Mortimer Planno, to participate in the official functions.

The profound feelings expressed by the black masses led the Jamaican ruling class to conclude that there had to be 'new modes of relationships with this respectable force'. The essence of this new relationship was to consist of the promotion of those studies which centralised the personality of Haile Selassie in the overall world view of the Rastafarians.

Young Rastas, who were not aware of the links between Rasta and the international struggle against fascism in 1935, began to speak of Haile Selassie in terms of the Christian concept of God. The Jamaican State encouraged this deification of Haile Selassie to the point where for the first time in the history of the society, the Ethiopian Orthodox Church was recognised as an authentic religious institution, along with the Anglican and Roman Catholic institutions.

The older Rastas, who felt that their church was within their body and that their religious belief should not be isolated to one-day expressions, but part of their overall world view, looked on as Rasta beliefs were institutionalised in order to be more effectively controlled.

The attempt to isolate the black nationalist thrust of Rasta by forcing it into a religious mould increased with the intrusion of anthropologists and sociologists, who referred to Rasta as members of a 'messianic cult', comparing the movement to cargo cults and calling Rasta escapists.[9] From the ideological spectrum of the cultural pluralists who called Rasta racists, and from the Marxists who termed Rasta 'false consciousness', the movement was denigrated until Walter Rodney brought new meaning and purpose to the understanding of the Rasta by his patient reasoning with the Brethren in sessions called *Groundings*.

Walter Rodney's Groundings With His Brothers

Walter Rodney, who was born in Guyana, spent three years as an undergraduate at the University of the West Indies in Jamaica, from 1960 to 1963. His interest in the *slave*, slavery, and the Atlantic slave trade led him to the School of Oriental and African Studies in London, where he concentrated his energies on vigorously recounting the history of the Upper Guinea Coast in West Africa.

In reconstructing the picture of the society before the European invasion, Rodney took pains to portray the relationships between classes and between ethnic groups, and to show how the influence of the slavers eventually led to the warfare and depopulation which strengthened the European merchants. He was however careful not to project a European framework onto the societies, and he avoided the pitfall of treating all Europeans as 'devils' and Africans as 'saints'. As it was explained in the first chapter, Rodney detailed how although African intermediaries facilitated the trade, it was Europe which ultimately benefited.

After a year of teaching in Africa he returned to Jamaica to teach at the university, and he took his history lessons to all sections of the society.

Rodney took his training as a historian and researcher to the Rastafari to share with them his view that African history should serve in the process of liberation. Rodney stated that:

> *"One of the major dilemmas inherent in the attempt by black people to break through the cultural aspects of white imperialism is posed by the use of historical knowledge as a weapon in our struggle...*
>
> *"The white man has already implanted numerous historical myths in the minds of black peoples; and those have to be uprooted, since they can act as a drag on revolutionary activity in the present epoch. Under these circumstances it is necessary to direct our historical activity in the light of two basic principles. Firstly the effort must be directed solely towards freeing and mobilising black minds. There must be no performances to impress whites, for those whites who find themselves beside us on the firing line will be there for reasons far more profound than their exposure to African history. Secondly, the acquired knowledge of African history must be seen as directly relevant but secondary to the concrete tactics and*

strategy which are necessary for our liberation."[10]

In Jamaica, Rodney perceived the Rastafari movement as a major force in the effort towards freeing and mobilising black minds; and he offered his knowledge and experience to the Rastas and all sections of the black population of Jamaica who wanted to break the myths of white imperialism. The history lessons on Africa which Rodney took to all sections of the communtiy brought uneasiness and fear to a pretentious leadership which never considered itself black, for Rodney stated simply that "being black was a powerful fact of the society".[11]

This assertion was not made out of intolerance, but out of an understanding that there should be no privileges for whites or mulattoes to exploit Africans. By bringing the combined power of African history and historical materialism to Jamaica, Walter Rodney was living out an experience in building the consciousness of the poor blacks in a way which had not been attempted since Garvey.

Rodney did not approach the Rastas in any populist manner; with his patience and tolerance he promoted the positive aspects of the movement, while painstakingly clarifying the misinformation on Ethiopian history and culture.

Unlike the Pan-Africans of the 1930's, and the Garveyites who extolled the African empires of the past with indiscriminate compliments, Rodney sought to break the preoccupation with the highly developed political States. Maintaining that the written history of the continent did not touch on the lives of millions of Africans who lived outside of States such as Egypt, Kush, Axum, Ghana and Benin, etc., he wrote:

> *"Even within those Kingdoms the historical accounts often concentrate narrowly on the behaviour of elite groups and dynasties; we need to portray the elements of African everyday life and to comprehend the culture of Africans irrespective of whether they were resident in the empire of Mali or an Ibo village. In reconstructing African civilisations, the concern is to indicate that African social life had meaning and value, and that the African past is one which the black man in the Americas can identify with pride. With the same criteria in mind, it is worth noting the following aspects of African social behaviour: hospitality, the role and treatment of the aged, law and public order and social tolerance."*[12]

Walter Rodney elaborated these themes in a society where the rut of neo-colonialism had engendered the growth of rude bwoys, armed thugs, and political leaders who exploited those tendencies. Rodney broke with the traditions of those intellectuals who confined their knowledge to the libraries and their social activities to the chit-chat of Senior Common Rooms. He brought a concrete understanding of the importance of Ethiopia without building up any of the mysticism which surrounded Haile Selassie.

Highlighting the positive contributions of Haile Selassie to the African liberation struggle, he said:

> *"His Imperial Majesty, the Emperor Haile Selassie, was the first African to realise the importance of the European invention of aircraft, and sought aeroplanes, not to be like Europeans but to protect Ethiopian culture by strengthening it with something new."*

He made an urgent appeal to the Rastas by declaring "*Africans (Especially Youths) Must Learn New Skills*".[13]

Rodney saw his experiences with the Rastas as a two-way process, for he understood that their insights were part of the tradition of oral history among the African peoples of Jamaica, asserting that:

> *"The collective knowledge of the African experience is the most authentic basis of the history of the colonial period. Unfortunately, much of the experience was not written down."*

This fact was to prove a major detriment in the development of working class ideas in the Caribbean, for the tradition among historians was not one which recognised the strength of the traditions of oral history, indeed African history. Consequently, those who sought to develop a materialist world view looked at the stages of development in European history in order to understand the historical path of black and non-white peoples.

Rodney recognised that the scheme for development charted by Marx could not adequately explain the richness of historical variety, and so in his work he sought to fill this gap, culminating in the major work – *How Europe Underdeveloped Africa*. He showed how capitalism in the form of colonialism, slavery and indentureship failed to perform, in Africa and the rest of the colonial world, the tasks it had performed in Europe in changing the social relations and liberating the forces of production.

Walter Rodney was conscious of how the idea of race had become part and parcel of the struggle for the liberation of blacks everywhere.

> *"Colour had become important because the white man found it convenient to use racialism to exploit the black peoples of the world. As Africans, we will use the question of race to unify ourselves, and to escape from the oppression of white men and their black lackeys. So long as there are people who deny our humanity as blacks then for so long must we proclaim our humanity as blacks."*[14]

Rodney perceived the Rastas as part of the proclamation of that humanity, for not only did they see the importance of the African cultural heritage, but they also wanted to live that culture so that it became a way of life. It is this perception which led Rodney to say that:

> *"In our epoch the Rastafari have represented the leading force of this expression of black consciousness"*.[15]

By the time Rodney was banned from Jamaica, some Rastas had understood his message to the point that they themselves began to question the emphasis on

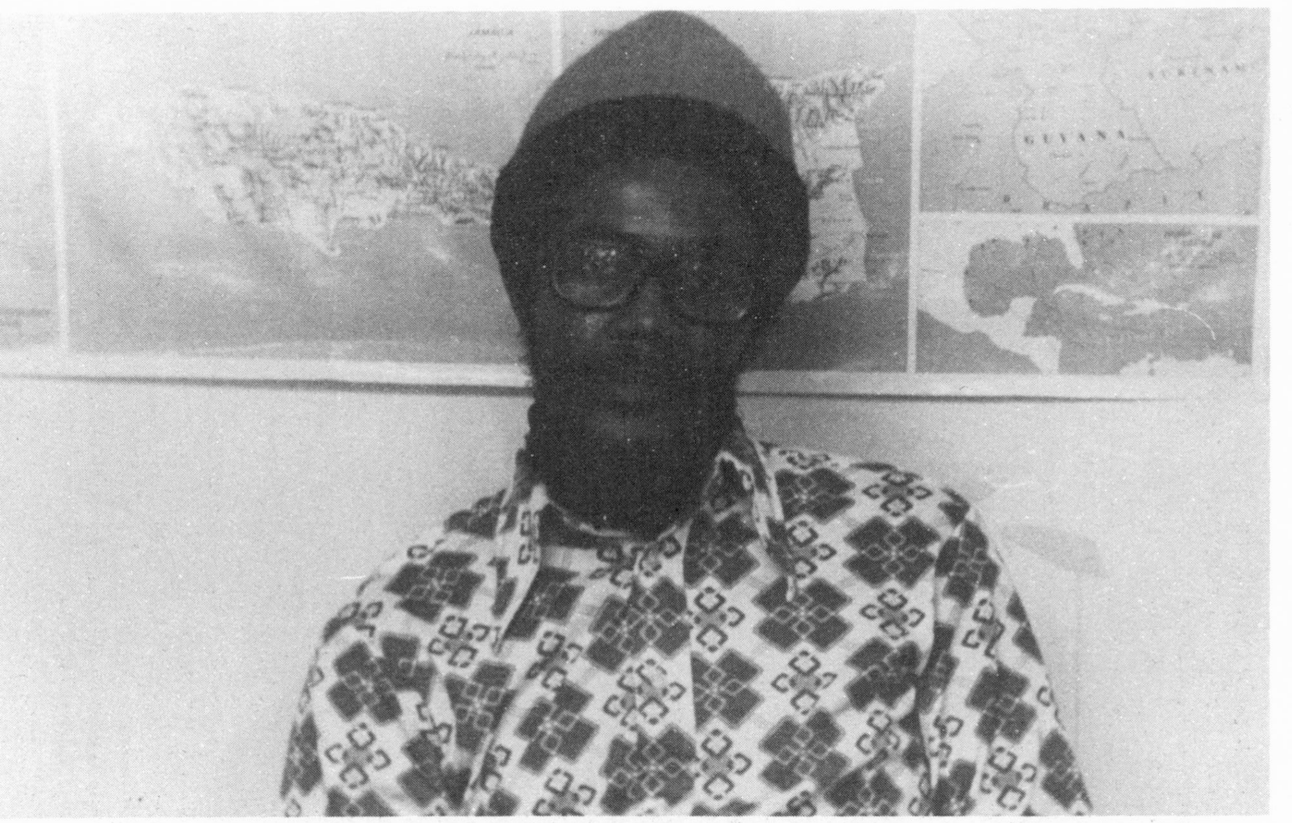

Walter Rodney positively identified with Rastafari in the Caribbean and sought to bring a materialist understanding to their interpretation of African history.

repatriation and Haile Selassie, and the more progressive were calling for a people's government in Jamaica and Ethiopia.[16]

The political activities of Walter Rodney, called *Groundings,* and the cultural expressions of Count Ossie, called *Groundations,* were too potent a force to be ignored by imperialism, so that the JLP regime of Hugh Shearer used the raw power of the State to prevent Rodney from continuing his work among the Rastafari and the working poor of Jamaica. He was barred from returning to his extended family after he attended the historic Black Writers' Conference in Montreal, Canada, in October 1968. The Minister of Home Affairs declared that:

> *"In my term of office, and in reading of the records of problems in this country, I never come across a man who offers a greater threat to the security of this land than does Walter Rodney."*[17]

Without the penetrating and materialist analysis, the State and their foreign supporters – who as a show of force had Canadian troops doing exercises in the country – hoped that the lessons of Rodney would be submerged by the anthropologists and sociologists who were intent on influencing the movement towards 'millenarianism'.

Although the government of Jamaica banned Rodney, they could not ban the demonstrative role of the need for the black intellectual to attach himself to the activity of the black masses. Rodney's conception of the role of race and class consciousness was taken seriously by a small Left within the University, which attempted to continue his work through a newspaper called *Abeng* (name used for the horn of the Maroon warriors, itself a reflection of the new sense of importance of the people's history).

But this small Left did not have the resources to match the jet set sociologists and anthropologists who exploited the friendship and hospitality of the Rastas in their pursuit of the project to confuse. Rodney's experience had shown many middle class youths that they need not be afraid to identify with Africa or the Rastas, and there was a new wave of identification with the movement among different sections of the society.

These two factors, the ideas reproduced by the sociologists and the emergence of the middle class Rasta, were to have an effect on the direction of the movement; and one of the new Rasta formations to emerge after this period was the 'Twelve Tribes of Israel'.

Robert Hill, one of those who sought to establish *Abeng*, described Twelve Tribes as middle class drop-outs who converted to Rastafari and formed a tight, closely knit sect under the leadership of a man called Gad.[18] The Twelve Tribes of Israel centralised the worship of Haile Selassie and repatriation as their beliefs, stressing the need to read the Bible. This organisation achieved notoriety and membership following the adherence to the Twelve Tribes' beliefs of prominent cultural reggae artists; and the Twelve Tribes was one group which took the promotion of reggae seriously.

Walter Rodney had broken the traditions of idealism in the society and in the process had begun to break the false antithesis between nationalism and communism, which had hindered the spread of scientific ideas since the time of Garvey. The two overt signposts of idealism in the society were the glorification of the European Queen and everything British on the one hand, and on the other hand the search for a link with Africa which led to identification with an African King.

At the level of the State this idealism was expressed in the dependence manifest in the interminable trips abroad for foreign aid. Rodney pointed to a direction for the society by linking himself to the most despised stratum, alerting them that they should link their struggles to the Africans of the villages, the mines and the plantations. Linking the Rastas to change in Africa was one way to assist their search for links with Africa, but he warned that:

> *"though Jamaican freedom fighters will read some African history in the course of preparing for hostilities; the struggle of the masses will not wait until the mass of black people reaches an advanced stage".*[19]

Rodney had perceived that the thrust towards African history would not in itself carry the working poor forward. What was needed was a level of theory and practice which built upon the foundations of racial and class consciousness, but in the search for a scientific outlook there were progressives who sought the answer to Jamaican history in the history of the Soviet Union or China to the point where the ideas of socialism were linked to the history of particular nation States.

This led to a new form of idealism, such that the old dichotomy between Garveyites and communists was replayed in the differences between Rastas and the organised Left movement. Such a rift allowed space for the *Gleaner* and the pseudo-Rastas to distort the legacy of Garvey, especially after *Burning Spear* unleashed new interest in Garvey with their album *Garvey's Ghost*. The self-expression which remained vibrant and powerful was *reggae*.

Dis Ya Reggae Music – Roots, Rock, Reggae

Walter Rodney's ban from the gullies of Kingston was one more indication of the lengths to which the State would go to stifle the development of ideas of race consciousness. This fear of the colour question was evident at the time of the formation of Millard Johnson's People's Political Party, when both the PNP and the JLP had sunk their differences to launch an attack on the PPP. The General Secretary of the PNP prepared a special paper on the dangers of the PPP, while the white overlords founded a movement for a 'Better Jamaica' and encouraged an interest in 'Moral Rearmament'.[20] Brother Sam Browne, one of the articulate leaders of the movement, had for a short while flirted with the idea of electoral politics, but this form of political participation and expression did not advance the cause of the poor, for they did not have the resources to compete with the capitalists.

The development of reggae music and its circulation was part of a deliberate effort by the Rastafarians to present their message to the wider Jamaican community and to the black world. The transition from rock steady to reggae was, like the transition from ska to rock steady, an imperceptible process which was both a response to and a reflection of the changing social conditions of the society. Where rock steady had the legacy of singing the sex and romance songs of Jackie Opel and Lord Creator, reggae laid emphasis on Africa, black deliverance and redemption.

This emphasis in the lyrics was combined with a bass line and drumming which harked back to the conditions of slavery. Count Ossie's ensemble, the Mystic Revelations of Rastafari, was at one end of a thrust of Rasta chants, while the bass guitar of Aston Barret and Robbie Shakespeare was at the other end of an evolving sound.

It was in the period of the development of reggae that the masses reasserted the strong influence of cultural values in the development of the confidence of the society.* Reggae opened possibilities at the cultural, political and technological level, and was an inexhaustible source of courage and moral support, such that reggae artists were able to enter the international arena and force onto the world an expression of oppressed peoples which had been considered culturally and artistically inferior.

Numerous studies have documented the struggles of reggae artists in the Jamaican society,[21] but in the course of the struggle they were able to draw inspiration from the people and in turn stirred the physical and psychic energies of the people, which enabled them to withstand the pressures of poverty, unemployment, gun men and ganja enforcers.

By the end of the sixties, the influence of the Rastafarian movement on the development of the popular culture was evident by the fact that most serious reggae artists adhered to some of the principles of the Rastafarian movement. Apart from the Mystic Revelation of Rastafari, which had always been prominent in the expression of their beliefs, 'Soul Rebels' such as Bob Marley and Toots and the Maytals (who sang "Do the Reggae")† were wearing their hair in locks and were not ashamed to shake their locks at their concerts.

Bob Marley and the Wailers, Dennis Brown, Burning Spear, Dillinger, Culture, Ras Michael and the Sons of Negus, the Mighty Diamonds, Third

*The period of the emergence of reggae also marked consolidation of other African art forms in Jamaica. One of the persistent Jamaican nationalists of the period, Professor Rex Nettleford, who started out as a youth in Montego Bay in the people's contests called Showboat, proceeded to establish the Jamaican National Dance Theatre Company. This company was but one of the authentic Jamaican institutions which was to gain international notoriety. By 1976 Jamaica could boast its own cultural complex, housing the National Schools of Dance, Drama, Music and Art. Despite the boast, however, that Jamaica is one of the major cultural centres of the developing world, the facilities of the cultural complex of Music, Dance, Art, Drama, are not yet open to poor people.

†The written record suggests that the word *reggae* derived from the words of Toots and the Maytals, who sang this song – "Do The Reggae" – in 1967. The reggae sound was slower than rock steady and the drumming to reggae music was slowed down to what was called the skank.

World, Bob Andy, and many other cultural leaders embraced Rastafari, and through their songs helped many other Jamaicans to discover their roots and the richness of their history. These artists, who were spearheading the development of a popular culture, were uncompromising in their identification with Africa, such that in 1969 both the ruling party and the opposition leader made pilgrimages to Africa and Ethiopia in an effort to keep abreast of this new pace.

These political leaders could go to Africa but they could not solve the underlying economic crisis, and the reggae artists did not wince in their critique of the capitalist system and its slavery antecedent. Bob Andy spoke of the hardships of the society by singing that:

"This couldn't be my home,
It must be somewhere else,
Can't get no clothes to wear,
Can't get no food to eat,
Can't get a job to get bread,
That's why I've got to go back home."

Bob Marley, who had the experience of a migrant worker both inside and outside Jamaica, told the people not to be ashamed of their roots; and the Wailers continuously wailed about the conditions of their neighbourhood – Trenchtown – while admonishing the youths not to be drawn into the competitiveness and viciousness of the society. One of the songs, "Man To Man", which was later reproduced as "Who The Cap Fits", warned:

"Man to man is so unjust,
You don't know who to trust,
Your worse enemy may be your best friend,
Your best friend your worse enemy,
Some will sit and drink with you,
Then behind dem soo soo pon you,
Only your best friend know your secret,
And only he can reveal it.
Who the cap fits, let him wear it."

This song protested against the competition within the society, using lines which were part of the folk culture for decades, at the same time breaking the tradition of dependence in music where Jamaican artists had simply put popular American songs to the reggae beat.

Reggae artists turned to the international audience because though the masses supported their music, the record companies exploited the singers and offered them bogus contracts – a situation graphically documented in the film, *The Harder They Come*, with Jimmy Cliff. Jimmy Cliff was among the first artists to leave the shores of Jamaica, while never forgetting his roots, and for a while he was the most popular Pan-African singer in Africa.

His song "Wonderful World, Beautiful People" could be heard in Egypt, and his forceful protest against the war in "Vietnam" linked reggae to the anti-imperialist movement. These songs were all linked to the deep spiritualism of Jamaican society, with the problems of wretchedness described as "Many Rivers To Cross".

Jimmy Cliff and the Wailers, in separate ventures, had mobilised the technology of Europe and North America to promote the music. For the Wailers this promotion took the shape of a partnership with Island Records which enabled them to prepare their music with electric keyboards, synthesisers and mixers.

But even this quest to use the most advanced technology did not stifle the content, for *Catch A Fire*, their first album with Island Records, went back to the horrors of slavery to bring a new form of Reggae:

"Slave Driver, the table is turning,
Catch a fire so you can get burn ...
Everytime I hear the crack of the whip
My blood runs cold,
I remember on the slave ship
How they brutalised my very soul.
They say that we are free
The only thing that change is poverty,
Good God I think illiteracy
Is only a machine to make money."

Not even the packaging which went into this album could detract from the way in which the lessons from *Groundings* and *Groundations* were now being circulated. The reasonings in Mortimer Planno's yard were now being put to song, such that the Wailers sang about "Concrete Jungle" and "Four Hundred Years" of the same philosophy.

While Jimmy Cliff and the Wailers were playing for the world of oppressed blacks, reggae singers led the protest to the Shearer regime by singing the songs of despair – "I an I Gwine Beat Down Babylon", and of hope – "Better Must Come". Michael Manley, the son of former Premier, Norman Manley, and cousin to the Prime Minister, Hugh Shearer, had by 1969 ascended to the leadership of the People's National Party. This party had in 1968 supported the ban of Walter Rodney from Jamaica but by 1969, after the riots, understood that the Rastafarian brethren were a force to be reckoned with.

Michael Manley found some legitimacy in the eyes of the young Dreads, for Claudius Henry, who by 1968 had been released from prison, supported the People's National Party and Michael Manley.[22] Not only did Manley utilise the songs of the people in the election campaign, but he trailed behind the masses and exploited their spiritual leanings, furthering the work of those US-trained public relations experts who projected Manley as the 'new messianic leader'.

In the process the PNP reinforced the negative aspects of leaderism and the cult of the personality in the political culture of Jamaica. Equating his rival,

Hugh Shearer, with the biblical figure Pharoah, Manley likened himself to the biblical Joshua; and to complete the mockery of the beliefs of the people and his image as their redeemer, he walked around with an African walking stick – which he called the 'Rod of Correction' – claiming that it was given to him by Haile Selassie. His party was able to mobilise considerable support, not only because of this symbolism, but because of the mass opposition to the anti-black and pro-imperialist position of the JLP administration. The PNP won the 1972 general election with an overwhelming mandate.[23]

The PNP's campaign reinforced the idealism and individualism of the society, for the PNP never went to the people with a coherent programme or platform to end unemployment and political violence. When the Rastas felt the full brunt of State coercion, consistent with the objectives of Operation Buccaneer and the anti-democratic Gun Court, the songs of relief and jubilation of 1972 were turned into warnings to the PNP. Max Romeo's stern warning to the PNP was in the song "No Joshua No":

"You took them out of bondage
And they thank you for it,
You sang them songs of love
And they tried to sing with it;
But now in the desert,
Tired, Battered and Bruised,
They think they are forsaken
They think they have been used.
Rasta is watching and blaming you,
Since you are my friend Joshua
I want you to forward and start anew."

This warning was taken seriously by sections of the PNP who wanted to ride on the wave of black consciousness to remove Manley from the leadership of the party. To keep abreast of the pressures in the society Manley declared for 'Democratic Socialism', invoking the 1940 platform of the party which had been placed in reserve during the struggle against the Left in the PNP in 1952.[24]

However, the reformist content of the programme did not affect the economic control of the clique of 21 families[25] who continued to live in opulence while unemployment and political thuggery remained the reality of the poor. This democratic socialism provided some scope for positive action for the Left in Jamaica. They could now publish and speak without fear of the anti-socialist hysteria of the capitalist class.

The political zigzags of Manley led the youths and Rastas to articulate their opposition to the social structure through reggae. Bob Marley and the Wailers articulated the statements of the poor in song, and made their claim as spokespersons for Rastafarian culture with the album *Burning*. The cover of the album showed the defiance of the anti-ganja drive, and they told the people "Get Up, Stand Up for Your Rights". This political rallying call by Marley and

Peter Tosh was backed up by the words "You can fool some people sometimes, but can't fool all the people all the time".

This album contained printed lyrics so that those who did not understand the Jamaican language could follow the themes of the songs. Already in the USA, the rhythm and blues singer Taj Mahal had made a reproduction of 'Slave Driver' in a blues version, as the culture of resistance took root in the Eastern Caribbean, the USA, Europe and Africa.

On the album *Burning*, the Wailers reproduced "I Shot The Sheriff", a song which had been written by Bob Marley but made famous by the rock star Eric Clapton. The content of this music found sympathetic audiences throughout the world, for the symbolism of defying the establishment endeared not only blacks, but white cultural artists such as Mick Jagger, John Lennon and the growing number of whites who identified with the counter culture.*

Rastafari as an all-class ideology was kept vibrant because of the pressures of the poor; consequently the metaphysical and mystical tendencies of those who wanted to look inwards could not become the dominant part of the movement. However, this did not stop the movement from suffering from some of the individualism and competition which was part of the political culture. Rastas were always struggling with the unity of opposites within their ranks, and, for a while after the Rodney intervention, those who spoke of the need for total liberation took the ascendancy, so that the Rastas were in the forefront of the international African Liberation Day celebrations.

These celebrations inspired a whole range of songs around the concept of armed struggle, and Count Ossie and the Mystic Revelations of Rastafari made a stirring tribute to the people of Mozambique when they became independent, with *Tales of Mozambique*. The Mystic Revelations of Rastafari not only took this message to the United States of America, but from their community centre in Wareika they preserved the strong African traditions of the society in making their music an integral part of the community.

It was in this community that the fusion of the instruments and the drum had led to the musical form called reggae. When the thrust towards reaching a wider audience led to the development of this kind of music, with the bass guitar taking the lead, another group emerged in Jamaica to carry on the traditions of Count Ossie† – Ras Michael and the Sons of Negus. This group used the

*From time to time comparisons have been made between the hippies and the Rasta movement in that both represented tendencies which were anti-capitalist. However, the historical record showed that while the hippie movement was a passing phenomenon of the '60s, the Rasta movement remains an expression of black consciousness and Pan-African liberation. There were some similarities in the ideological world view of the hippies and the Rastas, but it would be incorrect to dismiss reggae and Rasta (as some socialist States do) as mere reflections of capitalist decadence. Rasta culture is inextricably linked to the future of Africa.

†When Count Ossie died in a tragic accident in October 1976, the culture of Rastafari had already become Jamaican culture. At the funeral, the leaders of the PNP and the JLP jostled each other so that they could have their pictures taken carrying the casket of this cultural leader. Count Ossie always attempted to build unity in his community and among the Rastas.

foundation of the drum to chant the songs which said "Africa must be free, Black Man must be free, Rastafari".

The combined efforts of the Rastafarians and their leaders helped to place Jamaica in the anti-imperialist camp, so that by the time the South Africans invaded Angola in 1975, the Rasta movement and Jamaica consistently opposed the system of apartheid. Groups like Burning Spear, Bob Marley and the Wailers presented a variant of reggae music which centralised the question.

Burning Spear, taking their name from the Kenyan anti-colonial leadership, instilled a new interest in the work and philosophy of Marcus Garvey at a time when the State helped to make him a hero on the same plane as Norman Manley and Alexander Bustamante. The invocation of the coming to pass of Marcus Garvey's words and the inability to get food to eat and money to spend was added to the memory of slavery with "Do you remember the days of slavery?"

As a group, however, Burning Spear did not survive, for the collective spirit which was to be found in the Mystic Revelation of Rastafari crumbled in the face of international pressures towards individualism.

Bob Marley and the Wailers had already suffered this problem, for *Burning* was the last album to project the combined talents of Bob Marley, Peter Tosh and Bunny Wailer. The pressures of capitalist individualism, manifest in the efforts of the record companies and music magazines to project Bob Marley, led to the break-up of the Wailers, which had struggled for ten years to present the "Trenchtown Rock".

Fortunately, the talent and skill of Bunny Wailer and Peter Tosh did not suffer, for they went on to successful careers, making memorable albums. Peter Tosh's explicit political message came across on the albums *Equal Rights* and *Legalise It*. He had participated in demonstrations against apartheid by placing himself alongside those in the frontline of the struggle, singing "We must fight against apartheid". Meanwhile, Bunny Wailer exposed his reflective spirit in the album *Blackheart Man* when he reminded people that "they killed Lumumba for his own rights, but they can't keep the Rasta man down".

Space does not permit the full investigation of this vibrant expression of the Rastas, for alongside those artists mentioned above were groups such as Culture, which used the music to give history lessons – "The Arawaks Were There First" and to speak of Garvey's prophecy "When The Two Sevens Clash".

Simultaneous with the drive towards self-expression was the experimentation with *dub* and *rockers*, which presented a unique musical force. Dub was simply the genius of the engineer who mixed the music to emphasise particular instruments. This innovation demonstrated the technical sophistication which had been harnessed in the promotion of the culture of resistance, and the *dub* version was a non-verbal form of communication, reminiscent of the intense drumming of the slaves.

Rockers and dub* encapsulated a form of communication which said that the levels of 'downpression' were too dread to be spoken about. Sociologists and anthropologists could not understand the attraction for young people to go through the ritual of internalising one of the heaviest bass beats possible on the bass guitar, while standing silently and rocking till the wee hours of the morning.

Inside the black community of England the tradition of the sound men became important, and by the end of the seventies the police and local authorities began to learn of the influence of the neighbourhood sound systems so that in Birmingham the police and local councils undertook to support 'sounds' which were cooperative with the State. Imperialism hoped that if they could not stifle the music they may as well try to control it. Yet artists such as Bob Marley kept developing the music until it reached the freedom fighters of Zimbabwe.

Bob Marley and the Internationalisation of Reggae and Rasta

Unlike other artists who went in for the dub versions of their songs, Bob Marley never went in for this form of populism but remained consistent in using the power of the song to inspire and mobilise. Bob Marley's contribution to Rasta and Reggae was the way in which he brought a level of expertise and insight into the production of the music, in such a way that he could end the exploitation of black singers by multi-national record companies.

Robert Nesta Marley was born in the parish of St. Ann in Jamaica after the second world war, and his adolescent years, spent in the urban areas of Kingston, taught him to fully appreciate the problems of police brutality, poverty and harassment of Rastafari.

Marley's father was an Englishman and his mother an African-Jamaican, but unlike many other Jamaicans of mixed parentage, Marley clung to the society's roots of African heritage and turned his back on the deformities of the society which turned mulattoes into ambivalent citizens torn between Europe and Africa.

Marley's career as a singer and writer spanned 20 years, from 1961 to 1981, and during that period he distinguished himself as a spokesperson for the Rastas and other oppressed peoples in a manner which had not been attempted since the time of Garvey.

*The innovation which was called dub was essentially the work of an engineer. Sebastian Clark described dub in the following way:

> *"The dub would entail adding tape echo fed into the mixing board by a revox two track machine at a speed of three and three quarter i.p.s. The engineer could then move the dub button from its upward position downwards, and this sudden cutting of the guitar from the tape would create a spiralling reverberating effect. The engineer could also feed the tape echo into the phaser, which was then fed into the mixing board to create other effects ..."*

It was the sound men who in their efforts to create new excitement attempted to modernise their sets. These sound men were not always Rastas, for one of the more renowned dub mixers, King Tubby, was not a Rasta, though this did not prevent the police from continually harassing him.[27]

Despite the break-up of the Wailers, Marley's example of the defiant Rastaman gave courage to thousands of Dreads who could shake their locks as he shook his locks on stage and sang *Dread Natty Dread*. With the departure of Peter Tosh and Bunny Wailer, Bob Marley was backed up by the *I Threes* – Judy Mowatt, Rita Marley and Marcia Griffiths – Rasta women who were gifted artists in their own right. Dressed in long African gowns, and with their heads wrapped, they toured Europe and North America with Bob Marley, always on stage with a picture of the young Haile Selassie and Marcus Garvey in the background.

Bob Marley's music transcended the contradictions implicit in the attitudes of Rasta men, especially Twelve Tribes, towards their women; and this transcendence was epitomised in *No Woman No Cry*. The images of burning logwood, of the tenement yards of Western Kingston, of the food of the poor – cornmeal porridge – and the hopes for the future, were expressed with such humility that this song became one of Marley's must successful singles. Throughout his career Marley continued to sing songs of love and tenderness, for, like Che Guevara, he understood that one could not aspire towards changing the world unless one were guided by the principles of love.

The aspiration to change the world was central to the themes of Bob Marley, and in his music he helped to shift the movement away from mysticism and idealism. As early as 1974, when the politicians spoke of 'democratic socialism', Bob Marley told the Rastas and working people "Never trust a politician to grant you a favour, they will always want to control you forever" in his call for *Revolution*. The State could not countenance the overt call of the Rastas and reggae for social change, so the political careerists banned this music from the airwaves.

Remaining close to the tensions of the urban poverty from which he came, Marley translated the grimace of the poor into song, singing "I seem to wear a permanent screw". Marley complemented his call for "Revolution" in *Talking Blues* as he sang:

> *"I've been down on the rock for so long*
> *I seem to wear a permanent screw.*
> *But I'm gonna stare in the sun,*
> *Let the rays shine in my eyes,*
> *I'm gonna take a just one more step more,*
> *Cause I feel like bombing a church*
> *Now that I know the preacher is lying.*
> *So who's gonna stay at home*
> *When the freedom fighters are fighting?"*

The fear of the local politicians of this kind of reggae was replicated in the metropolitan countries as the State saw before their own eyes the creation of a strong popular movement based on the principles of African liberation. Marley had consciously sought to break the bonds of Jamaican chauvinism to progressively lend his music to all oppressed peoples, following the tradition of Howell and the first Rastas who had broken the petty distinctions between rural and urban people.

Under the labels of 'Jamaican Independence' and 'Black Nationalism', Millard Johnson had opposed the Pan-Caribbean idea of the West Indian Federation such that, despite the small size of Jamaica, the people derisively referred to the other peoples of the English-speaking Caribbean as "Small Islanders". Rastafari and reggae broke this tradition to the point where young Dreads in the Eastern Caribbean were assisting in breaking the historic intolerance between the island societies, and at the cultural level unleashed a new tradition of tolerance so that the stirring calypso critiques of Chalkdust and Lord Short Shirt were played along with reggae.

Rastafarianism as a force exploded in the Eastern Caribbean, projected by the image of Bob Marley and the sounds of Jimmy Cliff and Burning Spear. These Rastas, who showed that dread culture did not have to glorify Ethiopia, were inspired by the album *Rastaman Vibrations,* and in many ways the lyrics of this album were made household words in the region.

One of the most favoured of Marley's songs, "War", was the reflection of popular support for the African Liberation struggle at the time when Henry Kissinger, the then American Scretary of State, attempted to dictate to the Caribbean people who to support in Angola. The words of this song were from a speech delivered by Haile Selassie in the United States in 1964:

"Until the philosophy which hold one race
superior and another inferior
Is finally and permanently discredited
and abandoned;
Until there are no longer
First class and second class citizens of any nation;
Until the basic human rights are equally
guaranteed to all without regard to race;
Until that day, the dream of lasting peace,
world citizenship and the rule of international
morality will remain a fleeting illusion
To be pursued but never attained;
And until the ignoble and unhappy regimes
that hold our brothers in Angola, in
Mozambique, and in South Africa
in sub-human bondage, have been toppled
and destroyed;
Until that day the African continent will
not know peace;
We Africans will fight, if necessary,
And we know that we shall win
as we are confident in the victory of

good over evil."[28]

At a time when the confidence of the Rasta movement was shaken by the revelations of the 1975 revolution in Ethiopia, Marley was astute enough to promote the positive contributions of Haile Selassie on the anti-colonial front, while singing a single called "Jah Lives" to reassert the fact that Rasta had a life beyond Haile Selassie, saying that "Dread shall be dread and dread again". This single, which was one of Marley's most popular singles inside Jamaica, was never reproduced on a long-playing album, while he was alive.

Just as the slaves of the Americas had invoked the will of God in their deliverance, Rastafari was looking to a black land and a black God which would help to free them from neo-colonialism. The Jah which Marley and other Rastas sang about was one who had to be willing to join the struggle of black people, and bore little resemblance to the autocratic monarch which Haile Selassie turned out to be.

Rastaman Vibrations coincided with this affirmation of the future life of Rastafari as a movement, and Marley was consciously assisting in pushing the movement along with the dynamism of the struggles of the anti-imperialist movement. The complete album was a classic, with a song about African Liberation, a song on the plight of the workers – "Night Shift" – another song of praise for the music – "Roots, Rock, Reggae" – plus a castigation of the C.I.A. interference and political violence in Jamaica – "Rat Race". This song, written jointly with the soccer star Allan (Skill) Cole, showed that Marley was sensitive to the divisions which broke up the working class neighbourhoods of Western Kingston.

Neither Bob Marley nor the Rastafari movement could remain aloof from the political struggles which were taking place during the 1976 electoral struggles, when the ruling party spoke of a CIA campaign of *destabilisation*. Counter-revolutionary violence was organised in the society to create confusion, instability and fear among the working people.[29]

Similar to the popular support for change expressed in songs, during the 1972 election campaign reggae artists sang songs supporting the link between Jamaica and Cuba, though some limited their expressions to the partisan theme of 'Heavy Manners'. Bob Marley had intervened in the discussion with a People's Concert supported by the Manley administration. Three days before the concert, Marley was shot by gunmen who kicked down the door of his house. Marley escaped death in 1976 only to succumb to cancer in 1981, when he was only 36 years old.

Marley used his music as a vehicle of mobilisation. Some of the lyrics were linked to the Rasta formation to which he was closest, the Twelve Tribes of Israel; for the album – *Exodus Movement of Jah People* – was linked to a project of repatriation. Twelve Tribes, however, found out concretely the problems of translating a dream into a reality and Bob Marley saw some of the shortcomings of the scheme to settle in Ethiopia when he visited Shashamane, Ethiopia, in November 1978. From 1976 to 1977 the shock of the attack by gunmen forced

Marley into a temporary exile, and the content of his music suffered a temporary decline – as manifest in the album *Kaya*.

Marley's return to Jamaica after this period demonstrated that as a cultural artist he was at his best when he was close to the struggles and aspirations of the people. This became apparent from his last two albums – *Survival* and *Uprising*. In *Survival* he returned to the message of Walter Rodney, who spoke of how millions survived the system of slavery. Rodney's last words in *Groundings* were:

> *"Now we have gone through a historical experience through which by all accounts we should have been wiped out. We have been subjected to genocidal practices. Millions raped from the West African continent, a system of slavery which was designed to kill people . . .*
>
> *"Now not only have we survived as a people, but the black brothers in Kingston, Jamaica in particular, are brothers who up to now are everyday performing a miracle. They live and are physically fit, they have a vitality of mind, they have a tremendous sense of humour, they live in depth."*[30]

Marley joined this concept of *survival* with the quest to survive the proliferation of nuclear weapons in the world. *Survival* spoke of Marley's personal "Ambush in the Night", but he called upon the people to "Wake Up and Live", pressing for "Unity of Africa" with "So Much Trouble" in this "Babylon System". Quoting from Marcus Garvey that "A people without the knowledge of past history, origin and country is like a tree without roots", this musical expression linked Rastafari to the advanced struggles for liberation at the frontline of racism and imperialism in the moving tribute "Africans A Liberate Zimbabwe". African guerillas who were in the bush fighting Ian Smith heard this reggae song and claimed it as their own.

The Wailers were in the process of developing their self-expression to lift Rastas beyond the confusion unleashed by the coptics and bring them back to the original concept of African Liberation. Countless reggae singers had linked the struggles of the African peoples to their own plight, but Marley's song actually intervened in an ongoing struggle of technological inhumanity, atomic misphilosophy, "we are the survivors".[33]

In 1933, when Leonard Howell had begun to preach about the ideas of Rasta, it was an anti-colonial idea which took shape when Haile Selassie was part of the struggle of the Ethiopian people against fascism. Like this struggle against fascism, Marley had (in song) centralised the idea of armed struggle as his view of Rastafari. Marley then went on to participate in the independence celebrations in Zimbabwe. The following lengthy description has been recorded before but is worth repeating.

Marley in Zimbabwe

This author shared the joy and enthusiasm in Zimbabwe in April 1980, when it was announced that Bob Marley would perform at the official celebrations. It was

The power of art that Bob Marley's music represents has done more to popularise the real issues of African liberation movement than several decades of backbreaking work of Pan-Africanists and international revolutionaries.

an important tribute to the Rastafari, for in the limited four-hour programme of that historic evening on April 17, 1980, the African leaders gave Marley a billing at the celebrations at Rufaro Stadium in Harare Township. At 10.14pm Bob Marley arrived on stage, after the technicians had spent the previous two hours setting up the forty tons of speaker boxes, tweeters, mixers, lights and other technological components that had been harnessed for the circulation of reggae.

Shouting "Viva Zimbabwe" as he came on stage, Marley lifted the spirits of the audience as he moved straight into "Rastaman Vibrations", following with the appropriate reminder of the inequalities "Them Belly Full But We Hungry". Rastafari culture beamed out to the delegates and Presidents from 104 States who had gathered to witness the lowering of the last British flag in Africa.

As Bob Marley moved into "I Shot The Sheriff", there was bedlam in the stadium, everything seemed out of control. The policemen were running on the field, followed by the press. The band had stopped. The white Rhodesian police had dispersed teargas on the throngs of African workers outside the stadium who were pulled by the rhythms of "Family Man" Aston Barrett, the bass guitarist. The whole stadium was covered with teargas. Order was only restored when guerillas of Zimbabwe African National Liberation Army (ZANLA) marched through the stadium with raised clenched fists, reassuring the people that the Rhodesian police could not stop the celebrations.

Marley returned to stage, after this fifteen-minute disruption, and shouted *Freedom*. A crisp English voice at the other end of the stadium said "Bob Marley you have exactly two minutes left". In defiance Marley sang "War". *O povo* (the people) jumped and chanted with Marley that "there will be war until South Africa is free". This exhileration was the response of a people who were lifted out of the fear that the celebrations would be sabotaged by the racists who had said that black people in Zimbabwe would not achieve independence before the year 2035.

The hard drumming bass of the band reverberated across the African sky as the band put everything into the music, and Marley wailed "We Don't Need No More Trouble". All the energy, force, history and power of reggae filled the air as Neville Garrick, the dreadlocks engineer, frantically mixed the music so that the sounds from the 40 feet high boxes beamed out to all the poor people who could not get into the stadium.

After 15 minutes of the supposed two minutes, the Wailers sang "Africans A Liberate Zimbabwe". In one section of the stadium the whole gathering stood and joined in chanting this song of freedom, saying that they did not want to be fooled by mercenaries. It was an experience filled with emotion, and Bob Marley responded with the slogans of Pan-African unity which were an essential part of his outlook as a Rastafari.[32]

The whole energising experience was repeated the following night, for on that occasion Marley gave a free concert for the 40,000 workers and unemployed who were not able to get into the stadium the previous evening. That evening

Marley told the audience that the next time they performed in Africa they hoped it would be in a free Azania. During the whole week they were in Zimbabwe, Marley and the Wailers operated as Rastafari ambassadors to Africa, whether in the form of organising friendly football matches, attending a formal reception with the President – Canaan Banana – or in discussion with the guerillas in the camps.

Back in the Caribbean, Marley, who by then must have known that he had terminal cancer, worked at the pace of a lion and sought to build up the newspaper of Tuff Gong (his recording studio), *Survival,* in a conscious effort to stop the confusion of the *Coptic Times*. Despite the concept of mysticism and the talk about the 'teachings of His Majesty', Marley's paper was an effort to reach the youths. The masthead of the paper queried:

> *"Are the youths tomorrow's leaders*
> *Or are they tomorrow's shame,*
> *You must not be their impeders*
> *Less on you they'll put the blame.*
> *Train the youths while they are tender*
> *For what things you want them to be,*
> *When old they will remember*
> *Lessons taught to them by thee."*[33]

Such a dedication to the youths was augmented by Marley's lasting testament to Rastafari:

> *"I and I made our contribution to the Freedom of Zimbabwe. When we say Natty going to dub it up in a Zimbabwe, that's exactly what we mean 'give the people of Zimbabwe what they want'. Now they got what they want do we want more? 'Yes', the Freedom of South Africa. So Africa unite, unite, unite. You're so right and let's do it."*[34]

And Rita Marley added her voice, declaring:

> *"I and I firmly believe that music going to teach the world a lesson. Black women stand firm and keep the faith for your reward shall be great. Zimbabwe now, South Africa next. When all Africa free, all black people free."*

Bob Marley and Rita Marley raised their voices and their pens to the push for full liberation of the continent of Africa, for they had understood the teachings of Walter Rodney that full dignity would never be achieved by blacks until there was an end to white rule in Africa and social justice.

Bob Marley, Rasta and Uprising

> *"History has given to mankind outstanding individuals who have made significant contributions to society and who, in fact, are significant because of their contribution. It is the task of the chroniclers of history to*

make a proper analysis of the role of these individuals." Eusi Kwayana.

Because of the history of individualism and messianism in the population it would be incorrect to venerate Bob Marley in the way in which the State wanted to venerate him on his death in May 1981, even though they had banned his music while he was alive.

As an outstanding individual Bob Marley earned a special place in world history, in spite of the clear contradictions of his relationship with women and his belief in Haile Selassie. He went as far as the Far East, New Zealand and Australia to proclaim the view that people should "Get up and stand up" for their rights and not give up the fight. He found time for the Peace Concerts of Jamaica, which hoped to end the political violence; and jammed at the reggae sessions called Reggae Sunsplash,[35] always promoting the ideas of liberation and struggle.

The last album which he produced reminded the people that they must fight for their rights, and it was appropriately called *Uprising*. So aware was Marley of the struggles in the world that when the South Africans exploded a nuclear device in September 1979 to intimidate the freedom fighters, Marley sang "Have no fear for atomic energy for none a dem can stop de time." This song – "Redemption Song" – exposed the versatility of Marley, for he returned to strumming the guitar like the blues singers, so that the bass and drum would not hide his words as he simply asked "How long shall they kill our prophets while we stand aside and look?" These prophetic words were written a few weeks before the assassination of Walter Rodney in Guyana.

Marley, like Rodney, called upon the people to "Emancipate yourself from mental slavery, none but ourselves can free our minds." It was a pity that Gregory Smith, the agent who planted the bomb on Walter Rodney, did not hear Marley's words, for in the midst of the violence and terror in the Caribbean Marley asked the youths:

> *"Would you make the system make you kill your brotherman – No Dread No."*

Bob Marley spoke out for the oppressed, in the end speaking for a constituency which was larger than Jamaica, and then larger than Rasta, while never forgetting that it was the rhythm of Rasta and the struggles of the people which projected him to become an international figure.

Cultural Resistance and Political Change

Culture is the total production and reproduction of men and women in society, and as such the full expression of the social relations of production and exploitation that operate in the society. Consequently, the cultural resistance of Rasta inscribed in reggae, while profound, could not change the social basis of the society. Inbuilt in the Rasta philosophy was a form of bourgeois ideology which tolerated the individualism of the Western capitalist system. Rastafari ideology remains a complex phenomenon, for while it rails against the commodity fetishism of late capitalism and the cultural project to turn humans into the zombies of Orwell's 1984, Rasta ideology has not been able to settle the problem of the relations between classes.

The self-expression called reggae, which transcended sexist songs like "Hey Fatty Bum Bum", has not yet transcended the individualism of capitalism. For example, Peter Tosh, who has been one of the most uncompromising in his opposition to hypocritical political leaders, unwittingly repeated a central tenet of individualism when he sang the psalm "I am that I am, that I am."

These words were an affirmation of the dignity and humanity of black people, and had been asserted in the Civil Rights movement in the US when black leadership found it necessary to say "I am somebody." At the base of these statements, however, are the assertions of bourgeois philosophy, for at the dawn of capitalism René Descartes had proclaimed "I think, therefore I am."

These philosophical assertions from Rasta stem from the way in which race remains important to black people. However, this very fact has had its contradictory effect, as evidenced in the operations of the Ethiopian Zion Coptic Church. The other example of this manipulation of the racial question was in Haiti where Duvalier used the race question to exploit the mystical and spiritual tendencies of the people to perpetuate the most horrific dictatorship in the Caribbean.

René Depestre, one of the sons of this society and an important black philosopher, called out for total cultural change in the Caribbean, the kind of social change which would link the relationship between thought and social being. He said:

> *"Making revolution is the foremost historical evidence and the foremost cultural value which involves us in a new postulate of reason: I make revolution, therefore I am, therefore we are."*[36]

In his appeal, which pointed to the revolutionary possibilities of the black intellectual, Depestre challenged black people and Rasta with a philosophy which rose above individualism to collective action. Such a philosophy is needed among the Rastas, for imperialism has entered the movement to ensure that the negative aspects of the ideology are linked to the new capitalist ideology of science, technology and organisation. This science, technology and organisation formula is stamped on the international operations of the Ethiopian Zion Coptic Church, and their project to confuse has accelerated since the Grenadian Revolution.

Walter Rodney, the Caribbean philosopher and Marxist, called for a new kind of organisation and technology, one which was mobilised on the side of the working people in the process of transformation. For Rodney, this transformation must be in the direction of *socialism*.[37] Imperialism has done its ultimate to cut off the Rastas from the ideas of black thinkers such as Walter Rodney and René Depestre, to the point where younger Rastas claim that "I man no involved in a politics."

The essence of this disclaimer is terrible in areas such as England and North America, where young Rastas express an antipathy to scientific ideas even to the point of declaring most ideas as "white man's ideas." This hostility to white man's ideas is a manifestation of their own resistance to the cultural and ideological assault which they face at the centre of the Babylonian system. The cultural resistance from the hills of Jamaica and the symbols of defiance become their form of resistance as they attempt to create their own autonomous cultural institutions.

The crisis of imperialism dictates a certain urgency to the Rasta movement. Despite the power and clarity of reggae as epitomised by Bob Marley, this thrust of cultural resistance has not affected the basic institutions of Caribbean and Jamaican society. Rasta culture must be linked to an ideology of change, one which recognises the need for *cultural liberation* in its most dynamic sense, that is, when the working class controls the means of production and reproduction.

Imperialism understands this, hence the Coptics and the anti-communist Rasta formations which declare Rastafari as a religion. The local political leadership in Jamaica fears the power of Rasta, so despite the verbal adherence to social change, there was never an attempt to dismantle the structures of education and communication which were inherited from the colonial State.

Rastafari culture remains an inspiration. The gains of the movement forced back the racists to find new rationalisations for their moribund theories. Rasta culture shows the potential of the people once the social structure is changed, so that theirs is a full release of the people's creativity.

This is why imperialism decided to attempt to use Rasta as part of the project of destabilisation in Grenada. These challenges are compounded by the changes in Ethiopia where the mass of Ethiopian people call on Rastafari to come to grips with the Revolution which swept the Emperor from his throne in 1974. It is to this question which we now turn.

FOOTNOTES

1. In 1976 the Secretary of Agriculture of the United States declared that the use of food as a weapon was "a powerful tool in our negotiating kit." The CIA at the same time announced that increased grain shortages could give "Washington... virtual life and death power over the fate of the multitude of the needy." See Susan George, *How The Other Half Dies*, Penguin Books, London, 1976, p.16.
2. This impatience is even more overt in the United States where the eating of the pig is such an important part of black American cultural habits. For an examination of how the pig is processed in capitalist Europe see the *Ecologist*, April 1977. For a useful critique of the capitalist nature of food production and packaging see *Time Out*, 17 October, 1980. This piece has some useful references for those who would like to look closer into this question.
3. Frederick Cassidy, *Jamaica Talk*, McMillan and Co., 1961. The Jamaican language, sometimes called patois or creole, is very different from the French-based patois of Guadeloupe, Martinique and St. Lucia.
4. *Blues People* by Leroi Jones traced the history of Afro-American music in the US.
5. During the 19th century when the Jamaican Jews were struggling against the petty discrimination of the English, they formed their own theatre. See J. Andrade, *A Record of the Jews in Jamaica from the English Conquest to the Present Time, 1940*. Though a new radical theatre group, the Theatre Group for National Liberation, now flourishes, it remains an urban phenomenon. For a critical analysis of the cultural struggle see Rex Nettleford, *Caribbean Cultural Identity:* The Case of Jamaica, Institute of Jamaica, 1978.
6. "Rastafari Music – An Introductory Study" by Verena Reckford, *Jamaica Journal*, Vol 4, No 1 & 2, 1977.

Verena Reckford, in her study of the Rasta drums, stated that the slave masters allowed Burru drums and permitted Burru bands to play music in the fields: this buoyed up the spirit of the slaves and made them work faster, thus speeding up production.

See tribute to the drumming of Count Ossie by Oku Onuoru, "Beat Yu Drums" in *Echo*, Sangsters, Kingston, 1977.

7. Patrick Hylton "The Politics of Caribbean Music" *Black Scholar, May 1975.*
   There have been a number of books and articles on the development of early Jamaican music in North America and Europe. This study of Jamaican music is now being undertaken in Jamaica by G. White. For an analysis of this see *Jah Music* by Sebastian Clarke, Heineman Books, London, 1980.
   See also *Reggae Bloodlines* by Stephen Davis and Peter Simon, Anchor Books, N.Y., 1977.
8. For press reports of the impact of the visit on the white rulers and the politicians see *Daily Gleaner*, April 19-24, 1960. See also *Mirror Mirror* by Rex Nettleford, 1970.
9. See especially Vittorio Lanternari, *The Religions of the Oppressed*, MacGibbon and Kee, London, 1963.
   I. Owens makes a useful critique of these studies in his article "Literature on the Rastafari 1955 – 1974", *New Community* 1977/78. For an analysis of the use of anthropology by imperialism see (1) *Reasons for Anger*, by Roger Griffault and Kathleen Gould, and (2) *Anthropology, Child of Imperialism.*
10. "African History in the Service of Black Revolution" in *Groundings With My Brothers*, by Walter Rodney, Bogle-L' Ouverture, London, 1969, p. 51.
11. Rodney, op. cit., p. 31.
12. ibid., p. 53.
13. ibid., p. 40.
14. ibid., p. 39.
15. ibid., p. 61.
16. The Rastafari Movement Association in Jamaica were in the forefront of this tendency. They were the only group in the society which consistently called for the state to lift the ban off Rodney. Through the pages of their paper, *Rasta Voice,* they linked the social situation in Jamaica to the struggles in Southern Africa.
17. "The Rodney Affair And Its Aftermath," Ralph Gonsalves, *Caribbean Quarterly*, 1978, p.2.
18. Arvli Ward, "Bob Marley and the Brethren of Rastafari," *Nommo*, Feb. 1980, University of California, pp 8 and 9.
    The Twelve Tribes of Israel turned to reading the bible and were the most religion-steeped of the Rastafari groups of this period. For a list of the Rastafari organisations see *Mirror Mirror*, op.cit., *p.75*.
19. Rodney, op. cit., p. 52.
20. For the response of the whites see John C. Gannon, *The Origin and Development of Jamaica's Two Party System 1930-1975*, PhD Thesis, Washington University, 1976. See especially chapter on "Race and Class."
21. (a) Sebastian Clarke, *Jah Music*, The Evolution of the Popular Jamaican Song, op. cit.
    (b) *Reggae Bloodlines*, op. cit.
    (c) *Bob Marley, Music, Myth and the Rastas*, Henderson Dalrymple, Carib-Arawak Publishing, 1976.
    (d) "The Politics of Caribbean Music," Patrick Hylton, op. cit.
22. In 1969 Claudius Henry distributed a pamphlet supporting Michael Manley, at a time when there was serious bitterness in the party at the seeming nepotism in the choice of Michael Manley as leader of the party to succeed his father, Norman Manley. For an analysis of the role of Henry see A. Barrington Chevannes, *Claudius Henry and Jamaican Society*, paper, The Library Research Institute, University of the West Indies.
23. Michael Manley's support did not only come from the popular masses. There is evidence that he met and had discussions with the US representatives in Jamaica about the future of transnational capital. When this information was revealed in the US Senate, Manley declared the US Ambassador persona non grata. See J. Anthony Lukas, *Nightmare:The Underside of the Nixon Years*, Viking Press, N.Y., 1975, p. 136.
24. In 1952 the Left in the PNP were purged by Norman Manley who brought in his son from abroad to take over the trade union movement. For an analysis of this period see Louis Lindsay, *The Myth of Independence: Middle Class Politics and Non-Mobilisation in Jamaica*, ISER, Jamaica, 1975.
25. C. Stone and Aggrey Brown, *Essays on Power and Change*, Jamaica Publishing House, 1976. See chapter 2 "An Introductory Approach to the Concentration of Power in the Jamaican Corporate Economy and Notes on its Origin," by Stanley Reid.
26. In 1976 *Culture* became famous with the song "When The Two Sevens Clash," a song which reminded the people of the importance of Garvey.
    In 1977 Rupert Lewis perceived how reactionaries were manipulating the memory of Garvey for their own purposes, and he has consistently tried to differentiate between "Myth and Reality in Garvey," see *Jamaica Daily News*, May 12, 1977, p.8.
27. Sebastian Clarke, *Jah Music*, op. cit., p. 131. The dub mixers came from the long tradition of sound systems. By 1970 deejays began to talk over the record giving sounds of encouragement to the dancers, with U Roy, I Roy, Big Youth among the more prominent of this genre of reggae toasters.
28. Speech by Haile Selassie, "What Life Has Taught Me," delivered in California, Tuesday, 26 April, 1964.

These words were reproduced on the record "War," on the album *Rastaman Vibration*, Island Records, 1976.

29. "Caribbean Conflict: Jamaica and the U.S.," *NACLA Report of the Americas*, Vol XII No 3, May-June 1978.
30. Rodney, op. cit., p. 68.
31. This concept of *Survival* was also the theme of a pamphlet by E.P. Thompson, in *Protest and Survive*, published by the Campaign for Nuclear Disarmament and the Bertrand Russell Foundation, Spokesman Pamphlet No 71, 1980.
32. For a full account of the situation in Zimbabwe at that time see "The Night The British Flag Was Lowered in Rhodesia" by Horace Campbell, *Westindian Digest*, June 1980, pp 64-66.
    See also *Caribbean Contact*, July 1980, for a previous tribute to Bob Marley by this author.
33. *Survival*, Vol 2, June 1980, p.1. This poem was part of Marley's support to the Hunger Project. Page three of the paper said: "Bob Marley has given his support in both moral and material forms. He has donated two songs to the cause...."
34. *Survival*, p. 8.
35. For an analysis of the full range of reggae talent at Reggae Sunsplash 1979 see "After the Flood," *Melody Maker*, July 14, 1979.
36. René Depestre "The Intellectual Revolutionary and His Responsibility Towards the Third World," speech to the *Tricontinental Congress* in Havana, 1968.
37. In the last year of his life Rodney dedicated his energies to the working class organisation of the Guyanese people, the Working People's Alliance. The Principles and Programmes of the WPA outline the path *Towards A Revolutionary Socialist Guyana*, Georgetown, Guyana, 1979.

Chapter Six

THE RASTAFARIANS IN THE EASTERN CARIBBEAN

Introduction

When Walter Rodney was banned from grounding with his brethren and sistren in Jamaica in October 1968, there was a groundswell of popular resentment in the whole Caribbean. As a regional centre, the University campus at Mona was the focus of the circulation and reproduction of ideas, and those ideas relating to black dignity and respect were prominent in the discussions taking place at that time.

From the University emerged a core of students who sought to spread the ideas of black power, and they figured prominently in the protests against the British invasion of Anguilla and the protests against racism in Canada, particularly after the arrest of Caribbean students at Sir George Williams University in Montreal.*

The significance of this political tendency, which was anti-capitalist and anti-racist, was exposed to the world when the youths and the unemployed precipitated a rebellion against the neo-colonial misrule in Trinidad in 1970. Spontaneous protests taking the form of massive black power demonstrations paralysed the State; but the workers and unemployed of Trinago escaped the blood-letting which had become so prevalent in the developing world, because the soldiers mutinied instead of shooting the demonstrators.

The limitations of the philosophy of black power emerged when the leaders of this popular movement failed to link the spontaneous protest to the organised activities of the working class and farmers. In Trinago, the leaders of NJAC attempted to make concrete links with the trade union movements; but as long as the question of race lay at the core of their ideology, without an understanding of the question of class and the specific conditions of Indian and African workers, black power as an ideology could not have a future.

This was particularly so when some of the leaders expressed open hostility to scientific ideas while the State moved to arrest, murder and harass the youths, while using the pacification programme – called 'Special Works' – to demobilise and disorganise the unemployed section of the movement. The experiences of

* In 1969 black students at Sir George Williams University in Montreal violently opposed Canadian racism in the educational system. See Dennis Forsyte, *Let The Niggers Burn*, Our Generation Press, Montreal, Canada, 1971.

the National Joint Action Committee and the National Union of Freedom Fighters led to a re-examination of the all-class notion of race, and new political groupings emerged or gathered strength as they sought clarification and answers to the pressing problems of the people.

Moko, New Beginning Movement, Union of Revolutionary Organisations, and others emerged in Trinidad; the Forum Groups in the Windward Islands; the Afro-Caribbean Liberation Movement in Antigua; Amadala in Belize; and Ratoon in Guyana. The rise of these popular and democratic organisations marked a new turning point, but the failure of some of these groups to root their movement in their own historical specificity with the distorted and uneven development of the proletarianised masses led to the growth of the Rasta movement among the youths.

The islands of the Caribbean face the social scourge of high unemployment. It is usual to speak in terms of 30% to 40%, and even 50% unemployment. This section of the unemployed were the raw material for the development of a lumpen proletariat, but the youths spurned the idea of chasing the trinkets of capitalism. They had learned from the depressing experience of Jamaican lumpens how the politicians and the State could distort the lives of youths by dangling 'carrots' and arming lumpens who terrorised the society.

It is significant that the 'Dreads' mushroomed in the underbelly of imperialism, where the struggle to master the natural environment took precedence over the acquisition of commodities (the modern trinkets of capitalism). The youths who call themselves Rastafari have taken the culture of resistance to the beaches, the craggy hills, the shanties, and to the villages of the Eastern Caribbean, while in Grenada giving notice to the world that henceforth Rasta was to be part of the progressive movement in the Caribbean and not to be fooled by mercenaries. Through the medium of reggae, the drum and a more politically tinged calypso, they have declared themselves, à la Stalin, the Caribbean man.

The Nationalist Forebears of the Rasta

The English-speaking islands of the Caribbean stretch for 2,000 miles, from Trinidad in the South-East, including Guyana in South America and Belize in Central America, to Jamaica in the North. These islands have been bound together for three centuries through the British Colonial Office and the rivalry between French and British capitalism; and their specific identities have been moulded by the experiences of slavery, indentureship, colonialism and white racism.

The white slave masters were aware of the positive impact of the Haitian Revolution on the consciousness of the black masses; so they tried their best to present Africa as a continent of barbarous sub-humans so that the ex-slaves, whose forefathers had continually rebelled, would be afraid to admit that they were Africans. In this anti-African environment, where the possessing classes promoted the stereotype of the lazy Quashie, African culture went underground to appear in the form of shango or calypso.

It was to this part of the Caribbean that King Ja Ja of Opobo was exiled in 1887; and during his period of forced exile in St. Vincent he spoke to the people about Africa. The masses made calypsos on the martial and marital exploits of this African king, and the more literate section of the community took an active interest in the European partition of Africa. Some members of the budding African middle class were determined to return to their roots in order to contribute to the progress of their land of origin.

Edward Wylmot Blyden, who migrated from the Eastern Caribbean to Liberia towards the end of the 19th century, was one of the early nationalists. His ideas on black dignity and affirmation of the African personality had a considerable ideological and political impact on a generation of Africans both inside and outside the African continent.

Henry Sylvester Williams, from Trinidad, called the first Pan-African Congress of this century in London in 1900. The significance of this conference was that for the first time a group of Africans, motivated by the common experience of colonialism and driven forward by the commitment to end white plunder of Africa, had come together. Williams was part of a generation of educated blacks who found that their scope for self-expression and political mobility was blocked by the whites; so they looked to the liberation of Africa as a source of the liberation of black people.

George Padmore and C.L.R. James emerged in a later generation to join the growing international movement for African redemption. Yet both these spokespersons of Pan-Africanism faced the crucial question of penetrating the nationalist form of this Pan-Africanism to appreciate its class content. Because George Padmore, in particular, could not identify the working class as the leading force in the Pan-African struggle, he lost his sense of direction and wallowed in bourgeois theory and practice to the point where he propagated a false antithesis between Pan-Africanism and communism.

Significantly, Padmore's practical politics suffered a considerable decline – in spite of the fact that he once stood high in the ranks of the international working class movement. While Padmore was equivocal on the role of the working class movement in the Pan-African struggle, the Caribbean workers developed their own brand of support for the struggles in Africa, while struggling to better their own living standards.

Black workers in the Caribbean were in the forefront of the opposition to the Italian invasion of Abyssinia in 1935. In Jamaica the poor had opposed the invasion by 'blooding' the King of England, and had deepened their identification with the Ethiopian monarch. Throughout the Caribbean the poor blacks declared that they should be allowed to go and fight on the side of their brothers and sisters in Ethiopia.

At a forthright meeting at Clark's Theatre in St. Lucia on October 10, 1935, the 'International Friends of Ethiopia' denounced the Foreign Enlistment Act, which provided for penalties against British subjects serving in the armies of nations at war with which Great Britain was at peace. They passed a resolution that

> *"in view of the provoked aggression of Italy against unarmed Ethiopia, the penal clause of the above act be waived in so far as it applies to West Indians, to permit St. Lucians who may desire to do so volunteering to go to Ethiopia."*[1]

Similar resolutions were passed in Dominica, Barbados, Jamaica, Trinidad and Antigua. So concerned were the colonialists that the British circulated the criticism being made of the British role in Abyssinia to British Governors in thirteen African colonies, warning them to look out for similar protests in Africa. A section of this circular read:–

> *"In certain West Indian dependencies a very considerable degree of interest, amounting at times to undesirable excitement, has been invoked among the local population by the Italian Abyssinian war... While I have no doubt that, at any rate among the more advanced sections of native opinion in certain African dependencies, the present Italian Abyssinian war is followed with much interest, I have received no reports indicating that the war has aroused in any African dependency the same degree of excitement as it has in certain West Indian dependencies."*

Warning the Governors of what to look out for in Africa, the Colonial Secretary added:–

> *"Throughout the West Indies at present there is a large measure of unemployment and economic distress, that is the background of any unrest which may exist in the Caribbean waters today, and coupled with such economic difficulties, there is undoubtedly a widespread feeling of resentment to the Italo-Ethiopian conflict. The unfortunate incidents which recently occurred in St. Vincent and British Guiana bear witness that the advantage is being taken of this state of affairs by communist agitators and by rabid animosities at a time when the fundamental interests of the community demand that the difference of class and colour should be buried."*[2]

To counteract the criticisms of Britain, the Colonial Office went on a two-pronged response, one at the level of propaganda and the other at the level of coercion. To checkmate the protest against the prevention of Caribbean blacks fighting in Africa, it was suggested that the 'superlative' efforts to end the war being made by the British government should be highlighted.

In Jamaica, the Kingston and St. Andrew Councillors (elected on a limited franchise) passed a resolution praising the efforts of Britain to procure peace. This was printed in the planters' voice, the *Gleaner*, and similar resolutions were passed in the Eastern Caribbean, and circulated in the local papers.

At the same time the police intensified their vetting of the protest meetings, and in Trinidad Governor Hollis took away the people's right to assembly after the intelligence report of Major Johnson on a meeting of the Citizens Committee of San Fernando. This meeting had been attended by working class leaders such as Rienzi, Butler, Evelyn and Sandford. These leaders, in particular Uriah Butler, were to emerge as champions of the revolt of the masses during the strikes of 1937.

Meanwhile, individual Africans from the region took their own action in support of Ethiopia. From Barbados, Arnold Ford, who formed a sect of black Jews in the USA and determined that the real Jews were the *Falashas* of Ethiopia, moved to settle in Ethiopia. His wife, also from Barbados, started the first co-educational secondary school in Ethiopia. Herbert Julian, from Trinidad, was the most enigmatic of the Caribbean blacks who migrated to Ethiopia. As an airman, he had volunteered his services to help to develop the Ethiopian airforce and served in the armed forces, rising to the rank of Colonel.*

Both Julian and Ford had gone to Ethiopia from the United States of America where there was a sizeable Westindian community. They had figured prominently in the nationalist thrust of the twenties, for in the US they could organise, raise funds, speak out and agitate in a way which was not possible in the islands.

Nationalists such as Cyril Briggs, from St. Kitts, formed the African Blood Brotherhood and were involved at all levels of the anti-racist movement, from the armed confrontations in 1919 to the massive organisation of Universal Negro Improvement Association (UNIA) branches. Briggs moved in and out of the Garvey movement, the dominant ideological force among the black masses at that time.

Throughout the Eastern Caribbean, where there were local branches of the UNIA, they were either proscribed by the British or put under intense surveillance. Colonial officials quaked at the content of the *Negro World*, Garvey's newspaper, and they banned its circulation in Trinidad. They also barred Garveyites from employment because they took a leading role in the struggle for better conditions.

The problems of discrimination and the degradation of the black person also called forth a religious response in the formation of the African Orthodox Church. This religious group was started by Bishop George Alexander McGuire of Antigua. His experiences in the Anglican Church had led him to the belief that the white Christian denominations were too infested with racism for the black person to have spiritual fulfilment in these institutions. He presented a picture of a black God and a black Christ to his congregations and the African Orthodox Church expanded rapidly in the African world, building upon the nationalist foundations of Ethiopianism.[3]

This religious form of nationalism and anti-colonialism was soon superseded by the massive outpourings of the broad masses in 1937 and 1938. Strikes, riots, and other forms of worker manifestations forced the granting of democratic rights and sped up the process of political independence.

The natural quest for freedom and liberty had taken root in the Caribbean

*Julian has recounted his experiences and ambivalence to the Ethiopian royal household in his autobiography, *The Black Sea* Jarrolds, London, 1964.

with the kind of regional unity reflected in the experiment of the Westindian Federation. But the ideas of Caribbean internationalists such as T. A. Marryshow were to founder on the rock of petty bourgeois nationalism as the 'States' struggled for a form of political independence which promoted the narrow island chauvinism that later led to the banning of progressive intellectuals and trade union leaders from freedom of movement throughout the islands.

The most significant set of internal and external socio-economic contradictions which shaped the post-independence era were those which derived from the consolidation of the petty bourgeoisie as a class around the State. Even in the islands where the level of autonomy took the form of 'Associate Statehood' this up-and-coming stratum – usually referred to in pluralist literature as the 'middle class' – used the resources of the State to build up their level of consumption relative to the more established commercial intermediaries of foreign capital. This politically careerist stratum had achieved such notoriety in its abusive and corrupt use of power that the people became immune to the scandals, and made songs about the more excessive cases.

The concentration of power in the hands of this stratum, the extension of political repression, and the institutionalisation of corruption, were the features of political retrogression.[4] The governments hardly bothered to legislate for social change, since they were so preoccupied with legislation against the people, trade unions and opposition elements, popular cultural groups, and progressive intellectuals; and with spending the scarce resources on the coercive apparatus.

This repression and authoritarianism took place even in the smaller islands, such as Dominica and Grenada, where the friendship and kinship ties might normally be expected to counter tendencies towards political thuggery and obscene brutality. Rastafari developed as the cultural opposition to this political retrogression.

The Dreads

The obscene consumption and imitative nature of the petty bourgeoisie provoked a cultural and anti-capitalist response from the youths who called themselves *Dreads* and who identified with the resistance of the Rastafari of Jamaica. These youths were rendered unproductive by the inability of the society to provide meaningful employment for them. Instead of chasing the American and Canadian embassies for visas to migrate from their communities, the Dreads linked their destiny to the future liberation of the region and to the liberation of Africa. Through the medium of reggae, the sounds of resistance were circulated and these youths identified with the force and energy of this movement, without the encumbrance of the deification of Haile Selassie.

By the time the Dreads appeared as a social force, the Ethiopian monarch had been deposed into history by the Ethiopian people. The Dreads sought to form agricultural communes in the rural areas and adopted the symbols of resistance which had become so well known in Jamaica – the locks; tam; lion; ites; green and gold; and the use of the herb for spiritual and social communication and inspiration.

Because the anti-capitalist stance of this force made itself felt in the community, the politicians in the Caribbean, who were the transmission belt for Euro-American cultural values, were horrified at the Dreads. They perceived Rasta and Dreads as repulsive and subversive, and responded by arresting the brethren and violently attempting to shave their locks.

Whereas in Jamaica the State had mobilised social scientists to penetrate the movement and promote their version of millenarianism, the political careerists of Dominica could only respond with brute force. Faced with the growing number of Dreads calling for an end to colonialism and neo-colonialism, the Dominican government of Patrick John passed a law giving every citizen the right to shoot, without fear of retribution, any individual suspected of being a Dread who entered the property of the said citizen.

The law, clearly drafted from the ferocious slave laws of an earlier style of coercion, gave the police the power to arrest any person who resembled a Rastafarian; and a Dread could be given eighteen months in gaol merely for wearing locks.

The effect of this law was to give the armed members of the petty bourgeoisie and the police the right to protect property at the expense of the lives of the youths. For two years the Patrick John government unleashed terror on the youths, murdering six and framing two on murder charges. Desmond Trotter (Ras Kabinda) was one of those framed;[5] the regime went all out to hang him, and would have but for the regional and international protests.

It was only after Patrick John was removed in 1979 that it was disclosed that Trotter was indeed innocent. Yet, after the removal of Patrick John, the laws proscribing the Dreads remained in force. Significantly, those who were in the forefront of trying to prosecute Ras Kabinda were the ones making deals with US capitalists to beat the UN boycott of the sale of war materials to South Africa.*

Rastas, Union Island and the Sea

Because the narrow vision of development was concentrated on organising recreation for the international bourgeoisie, in the form of tourism, it was necessary to reinforce the incredible stereotypes of islands in the sun and a happy-go-lucky people. Rastas who lived in the poverty and degradation hidden behind these stereotypes opposed the mendicant and shuffling image consistent with the romanticisation of poverty and malnutrition.

In the tourist isles, Dreads were arrested, shaved and killed. Faced with this terror in Antigua, St. Vincent and St. Lucia, the Dreads called forums of

*The British Broadcasting Corporation television programme Panorama in 1979 exposed the links between leaders of the Dominican government and South African companies.

solidarity – called Nyabingis. The St. Lucian Rastas linked themselves to the opposition Labour Party in their call to end police brutality. Their organisation – the Iyanola Rasta Improvement Association – spoke out, not only for the Rastas, but for the downpressed of St. Lucia. One of the spokespersons for the St. Lucian Rastas, Earl Bosquet, clearly showed the orientation of these Rastas when he said:

> *"Unlike Jamaican Rastas, the St. Lucian Rasta does not want repatriation to Africa. Most believe that wherever they are, Africa is. There is no link between the St. Lucian Rasta and the Ethiopian Orthodox Church or any other religion of African origin."*[6]

Their newspaper, *Calling Rastafari*, was instituting a style of radical journalism in the midst of petty bourgeois squabbles. No sooner had they helped the Labour Party to achieve electoral victory than the new leadership showed that the petty squabble as to who should be Prime Minister took precedence over the question of solving other people's problems. Rastas found that the police treated them no better than under the previous administration.

Rasta children were being discriminated against in schools, Rastas were being harassed in the press and their independent activities as farmers and fishermen were threatened. These brethren remained firm in their call for a new society and were in the forefront of the annual African Liberation Day marches, singing Bob Marley's *War* and Peter Tosh's *We Must Fight Against Apartheid*.

From Montserrat to Nevis and from St. Vincent to Anguilla the politicians attempted to coerce the Rastas, a group of young men and women who wanted to reclaim the freedom of the Caribbean Sea. This claim posed a direct threat to those who were in the process of selling off the islands of the Grenadines to private developers.

The Grenadines are a chain of small islands between the islands of St. Vincent and Grenada. The St. Vincent Grenadines extend from Bequia, Mustique, Canouan and Union Island. The advertisements for the sale of these islands in the *New York Times* and the antics of Princess Margaret at Jelliceaux Bay, Mustique, were the other side of the poverty of the servants who worked for the Queen's sister and her guests.

Young Rastas who followed the deliberations of the Organisation of African Unity had followed with interest the sale of Diego Garcia to the USA and the subsequent removal of its citizens to provide for a US naval station in the Indian Ocean.* Moreover, the livelihood of some of the islanders as fishermen was threatened as the political careerists reserved beaches for swimming and for yachts.

Rasta youths led the protest against this form of tourist development in Union Island in December 1979. This insurrection, which was an ambitious attempt at

*In 1976 the US concluded a deal with Britain to buy the island of Diego Garcia in the Indian Ocean. All of the inhabitants of the island were removed to Mauritius to make room for the building of one of the biggest US naval stations in the Indian Ocean. At present, the OAU is calling for the return of the island to Mauritius.

secession from St. Vincent, was the dramatic expression of opposition to the total disregard for the islanders. Union Island, with a population of 2,300, was typical of the poverty, having only one school and no proper medical facilities, houses, water supply or electricity, while the government built an air-strip to land tourists.

The revolt was short-lived, as the St. Vincent government responded by arresting 34 of the 50 Rastas and youths who had organised this protest. The Barbadian expeditionary force rushed to the scene to assure their imperial overlords that all was in order.

The speed with which Barbados responded emanated from the concern in Washington, London and Paris over the growing militancy and rise of popular organisations in the Caribbean. During 1978, while the Sandinistas were in the last stages of their battle against Somoza in Nicaragua, Western leaders met in Guadeloupe; and James Callaghan, then the British Prime Minister, stopped off in Barbados to discuss 'security in the region'.

This new offensive by the West stemmed from British and US unease over the pressures of the poor countries (called the Group of 77) for the United Nations Law of the Sea Conference to set up a system of governance for the sea and the use of its resources.

As the old mercantile powers who had the technology and naval power to exploit the rich manganese nodules under the sea, the US and Britain had become impatient with the deliberations on territorial waters, exclusive economic zones, the continental shelf and the high seas. Tiring of gun-boat diplomacy, of the era of piracy on the high seas and land, the poor nations wanted the former freedoms of the big powers on the sea curtailed, with the sea zoned into coastal waters, sea bed zones and high sea zones. Each of the various zones would have a different status under the international law and different types of maritime use.

Island States such as Fiji, Indonesia, the Philippines, Mauritius and Malaysia – called archipelagic States – whose life-blood depended on the sea pressed that the sea around their States gained the same status as internal waters. In the Caribbean, however, the existence of British, French, Dutch and US colonies prevented the development of a coherent position. Elementary efforts by Jamaica and Trinidad in formulating a new Law of the Sea were futile in the haste of the American companies to begin to move on the sea bed.[7] The mineral deposits, the offshore oil wells and the protein in the sea had given the Caribbean a new significance in both economic and environmental terms.

Before there could be any agreement at the UN Conference, the United States and Venezuela drew up their own treaty to divide the Caribbean Sea between themselves, irrespective of the legal rights of the Caribbean peoples.[8] The only objection which they countenanced was that of France, who wanted the demarcation lines redrawn for her 'départements' – Martinique, Guadeloupe and Cayenne.

Due to this anxiety over the sea, the international media and the International Institute of Strategic Studies paid attention to the uprising of 34 Rastas in Union

Island. For, after the revolution in Nicaragua and in Grenada, the United States had been more alert to the need for stemming the tide of peoples' struggles. The Grenadian Revolution of 1979, "a big revoultion in a small island" in the words of Fidel Castro, lead the US to set up a new military task force for the Caribbean – the Caribbean Contingency Joint Force – and a Caribbean Central American Action Committee.

Official thinking saw the Caribbean as a US lake, and perceived social change in the interest of the Caribbean people as a threat to US interests. In June 1980 a National Security broadsheet declared:–

> *"The Caribbean is a closed sea. The Bahamas, Virgin, Leeward and Windward Islands, along with Barbados, Trinidad and Tobago, encircle the eastern edge. North, Central and South America ring the rest. The centre of the circle is dominated by the Greater Antilles – Puerto Rico, Hispaniola, Jamaica and Cuba, which also form a barrier between North and South America. Only three channels, Mona, Windward and Yucatan, cut through the Antillian island chain which lies athwart the sea lines connecting the two continents. These waters also wash Mexico and Venezuela, two of the world's major oil exporting nations. Seventy-five percent of the oil imported into the U.S. – some 30% of total consumption – transits the Caribbean Sea, thus the Caribbean rim and basin is a petroleum focal point.*
>
> *"Through Caribbean channels, Antillian passages and the Panama Canal pulses the petroleum of the Middle East, Ecuador and Alaska. Super tankers sailing from the Persian Gulf around Africa do not dock directly in the U.S. Atlantic or Gulf ports. These vast vessels transfer their cargoes at the Bahamas, Virgin Islands, Trinidad or Aruba-Curacao into standard size tankers which then sail to the Eastern or Southern seaboards of the U.S. Venezuelan oil moves Northwards through the Mona, Windward and Yucatan channels. Not all of this is crude. Since the US has not completed a refinery in over seven years much of this improved petroleum is finished product having been processed in off-shore locations."*[9]

Commenting on the fact that Grenada was situated on the Northern edge of the Tobago passage, through which super tankers from Aruba and Africa move, this broadsheet called attention to the presence of Cuban construction workers in Grenada building an international airport. It was due to this kind of sabre rattling, after the National Security Council decided that a naval blockade would not succeed, that the external forces decided to try to mobilise the Rastafarians against the Provisional Revolutionary Government.

The Rastas and the Grenadian Revolution

Forty-nine years after the first Rastas appeared in the Caribbean, young Rasta brethren in Grenada showed that with ideology and organisation, the Rasta can be mobilised to participate in a revolution. More than 400 Rastas were involved in the People's Liberation Army which overthrew the Eric Gairy dictatorship on 13 March, 1979.

The Rastas had remained very close to the New Jewel Movement, and the Left in Grenada had championed the cause of the Rastas. Maurice Bishop had defended Ras Kabinda in Dominica and he had defended many other Rastas against ganja charges.

When Gairy ruled Grenada, the Mongoose Squad, the Grenadian equivalent of the Ton Ton Macoute of Haiti, took special pride in cutting the locks of the brethren; so that when the New Jewel Movement* moved to end the politics of retrogression, the Rastas responded positively and took up arms to defend the revolution.

That these Rastas were not wanting to go back to Africa, but were participating in the fall of 'Babylon' in the Caribbean, was not lost to those who were horrified at the sight of Dreadlocks with guns. An academic debate in Trinidad and Jamaica as to whether the change was a coup d'état or a revolution betrayed the anxiety of the Caribbean petty bourgeoisie who had bailed out Gairy when the civil servants went on strike in Grenada. Their own Commission of Inquiry – the Duffus Commission – had highlighted the levels of brutality, nepotism and terror, but they were so wedded to the idea of parliament and elections that they could not envisage the people making their own history.

The change in the direction of the Grenadian society offered new possibilities for the Rastafari Movement. Rastas were integrated into the armed forces, rising to responsible positions; and with the new trust and cooperation offered by the political leadership, the Rastas took their proper place in the community without fear of harassment. Young brethren from St. Lucia, St. Vincent and Dominica flocked to see this new society where Dreadlocks did not have to shave their locks.

The euphoria of change was high, and the Rastas held their weekly meetings – Nyabingis. Three different influences contended at these sessions: the influence of the IRIA of St. Lucia, the influence of the Dreads of Dominica and the more idealistic and metaphysical variant of those who wanted to centralise the personality of Haile Selassie. But the social reality of their need to deal with the present situation held sway. The scope for division was limited as long as they were disciplined in the course of carrying out their role in making Caribbean history. They smoked ganja at these sessions and the boundaries of their behaviour was set not by the State but by their relationship with their own communities.

They made their own songs of freedom, and one of the more popular ones was "Dreadlocks on the PRA" by the Magnificent Six:

*JEWEL is the Joint Endeavour Welfare Education and Liberation. The New Jewel Movement was formed in March 1973 and was in the forefront of popular demonstrations against Gairy in 1974 when the father of Maurice Bishop was killed. For an account of the revolution and the New Jewel Movement see *Grenada, The Road to Revolution by W. Richard and Ian Jocabs, Casa de las Americas, 1979.*

> *"Never before have the dreadlocks been so happy since they are in the Provisional Revolutionary Army (PRA) and serving the country and the people.*
> *"The dreadlocks have been kept down by the obeah dictator and now they are being given a chance to show they are fellow West Indians. Natty never been so gay."*

This gaiety and openness was soon exploited by those elements who were apprehensive at the experiment of Grenada. Despite external pressures the regime had organised the beginnings of efficient fishing, agricultural and tourism sectors. There was increased employment as the Provisional Government moved to increase agricultural output. Literacy and school meals programmes were started, and Cuban doctors assisted in providing free medical facilities in the most remote villages. Cuban construction workers were also building an international airport to break Grenada's dependence on Barbados for its airlink with the outside world.

In the year after the revolution the Barbadian State increased its purchase of American weapons by 500% to act as the new spearhead to counter the 'Cuban presence' in the region. This counter was being pushed by the US, which feared the positive example of a Marxist-Leninist State which could give assistance, not only to the Caribbean peoples, but also to the African liberation movement, for example in Angola.

Local intermediaries of foreign capital were caught with fright at the positive assistance given by Cuba. Schooled in the anti-communism of colonialism, but without the political or material resources to mount their own opposition to the Bishop administration, they turned to fomenting divisions in the ranks of the Rastas.

It was a strange twist of history that those who hounded the Rastas under Gairy as dirty and unwashed now championed the cause of two young brethren, and manipulated these young brethren into stirring up trouble leading to a demonstration. At the behest of their class allies in Trinidad and Barbados, the owners of the newspaper *Torchlight* took the guise of championing the cause of the Rastafarians while leading the call for elections and opposing the assistance of Cuba to the Grenadian people, saying that Bishop was a puppet of Cuba.

Torchlight spoke for the Caribbean ruling class who understood that the existence of a higher social order than that of capitalism in Cuba ensured the possibilities of other societies in the hemisphere breaking out of the misery of capitalist exploitation. The anti-communists therefore moved to exploit the idealist tendencies of the Rasta movement, pressing two youths to denounce the PRG and Cuba. The whole process was important and is worth recounting in some detail, for this exploitation of the Rasta continues.

On Wednesday October 10, 1979, *Torchlight* printed the emotive picture of the Rasta drawn by Ras Daniel Hartman of Jamaica on the front page of its newspaper, and below this picture launched its most forthright condemnation of the Grenadian revolution, saying:

> *"Rastafarians in Grenada are likely soon to take to the streets in massive numbers to protest the debarment of Rasta children from schools and the arrests and charges for ganja smoking. This was told to* Torchlight *by two spokesmen for the Twelve Tribes of Israel, Ras Nna and Ras Ersto Ja Ja, when they visited our office yesterday...*
>
> *"The Rastas according to these spokesmen would like to know why the PRG is holding on to power for so long and what has become of the election promises. Local Rastamen have been holding weekly Nyabingis over the past five weeks and it was at one of these gatherings at Gouyave Park last Saturday that they decided that the PRG was anti-Rasta."*

This long front page article, which distorted the deliberations of the Nyabingis with deliberate lies, went on to quote the spokesmen who said:-

> *"we are not supporters of Cuba and Russia, we see (these countries) as enemies of Rasta, since they do not acknowledge Rastafarian doctrine. The Twelve Tribes of Israel congratulate* Torchlight *for its brave stand in this time."*[10]

The call by the two Rastas and *Torchlight* for a mass demonstration was later revealed to be part of a wider effort to remove the regime, involving an armed invasion. These two Rastas were being used as a front for elements who planned to assassinate the leadership of the PRG after engineering anti-goverment demonstrations. Full details of the plot were revealed after the regime arrested twelve persons, among them a black social science professor from an American University. The two young brethren were also arrested when the leadership revealed pamphlets which had been printed that stated the 'factors leading to the eventful, bloody, ruthless overthrow of revengeful communist Bishop regime.'[11]

Rasta brethren and sistren did not wait until the regime exposed the plot before they organised their own demonstration against the attempt at setting Rasta against Rasta, and against the PRG. These Rastas reminded those who went to *Torchlight* that it was the same organ which had defended the outrages of Gairy and the dreaded Mongoose thugs. Under the heading "Rastas Against Torchlight" they wrote:-

> *"Brethren, Sisters*
>
> *"Us brethren in the region of La Digue ask in the name of Jah that in your paper I and I brethren would like you to publish this report for us please. Us see that Rastafari have made headline on the reactionary and backward* Torchlight *who early in the revolution call us brethren 'Zumbie in a PRG' and who had nothing to say during Gairyism Terrorism.*
>
> *"By reading this issue us brothers brought together views and opinions. By this we strongly criticise* Torchlight, *Ras Nna, Ras Ersto Ja Ja and any of I brethren who form reactionary group to assist Babylon (Euro-*

American) downpresser man to take away us freedom. Us brothers see Revolution Time. The Report states that at the Nyabingi at Gouyave the Brethren say that the PRG is anti-Rasta, that the PRG is holding on to power too long and are not checking the promised election, that us brethren are anti-Cuban-Russian.

"We are strongly against these sentences made by the Rastas who falling as victims to the opportunist Baldheads and Torchlight *who bring about bribery (Blood Money). Us rasta believe in revolution whether social or political and not no ballot Constitution (oppression) Babylonian.*

"From 13th March 1979, to the present there is freedom to move to and fro. No more discrimination, no more Gairyism-Americanism, CIAism, Babylon. No more police at our doors before sunrise and after sunset. We strongly and firmly support the PRG and all the socialist Powers in the world for it is Cuba and Russia who are assisting our 'Black struggles in Africa' where our brothers and sisters are slain hourly by Racist imperialist Baldheads.

"In the name of Jah Rastafari may our message meet the masses. Let Jah be praised. Let correction be necessary.

"Oneness Brethren Comrades.

Ras Kula
Ras Andran
Ras Lyon
Ras Umbre
Ras Pyta
Ras Alan

Roots and Herbs Ghetto.

La Digue."[12]

Rasta, Ganja and Capitalism

Despite the initiative by the Rastas, those forces which harangued Bishop on the question of elections but turned a blind eye to the bogus elections in Guyana still hoped to foment discontent from within. The elementary initiatives towards solving the needs of the working people were affected by the deteriorating security situation as the incidents of bombings and shootings increased, culminating in the June 19, 1980 bomb attack at Queens Park, St. George's. Prime Ministers and the officials of the State had gathered to celebrate Labour Day when the bomb exploded. But no-one on the platform was hurt; the force of the bomb killed three children and injured others.

Some of the elements involved in this bombing campaign were involved in the large-scale planting of ganja. This ganja was not for local consumption but for the international capitalist market and the big planters attempted to use the centrality of the weed in the lives of many youths as a leverage to move the Rastas after the previous attempt at demonstrations had failed.

Ganja and its use pose a serious problem throughout the Caribbean for the way in which the trade is now linked to international gangsterism. Those imported psychologists and doctors who describe ganja as a dangerous narcotic forget that the British State imported ganja into the Caribbean up until 1907 to sell to the Indian indentured workers. The use of ganja by youths in the sixties and seventies was a principal method of social control, and as soon as a youth was perceived by the state as rebellious the charge of possession of ganja was always a useful weapon in the hands of the coercive apparatus of the state.

When the PRG came to power the leaders tried to change the use of the charge of possession, but at the same time to break the tendency for large-scale ganja planters to clear forest lands for extending the acreage under ganja. These planters affected the ecological balance such that there was damage to food crops when the rains came. At the same time those who were involved in this international capitalist trade raided the provision grounds of other rural farmers.

The regime tried to make a distinction between those Rastas who planted enough weed for their own consumption and those who were dependent on external outlets for their crop. For the regime knew that they could not unilaterally legalise ganja but they could, and did, carry out an educational and police campaign against the big traders. Maurice Bishop and his cabinet were not unaware that the Mafia were using the islands of the Grenadines as half-way stops between Columbia and the USA. Even the *Wall Street Journal* drew attention to this trade and the livelihood of capitalist gangsters such as Robert Vesco.[13]

Already in the Caribbean the experience of Jamaica, where the trade had led to a corresponding increase in the importation and the use of the gun, lumpen elements taking on the physical appearance of the Rastas were linked to a wide network of dealers. The pseudo-Rasta formation called the Ethiopian Zion Coptic Church – the only Rasta organisation run by whites, operating from the

United States of America – were involved in this trade. This 'Rasta' group printed its own paper, a slick professional tabloid called *Coptic Times*, which was distributed throughout the world of ganja.

To avoid this development, the Chief of Police appealed to the Rasta to assist in the cutting down of large-scale ganja plantations: there had been a marked decline in food production since the ganja traders paid EC$1,000 per pound for the weed while the State paid only 6 cents per pound for bananas. The promise of a quick dollar appealed to the more materialist among the young.

So bold were the planters that in May 1980 they organised a demonstration in Grenville to show their opposition to the government's measures to stamp out large-scale plantation of ganja. Farmers and conscious youths countered with another demonstration calling for greater self-sufficiency in food production; and the planters began a quiet campaign saying that the stamping out of the big planters was the first step towards clamping down on smoking ganja.

Budding exploiters always seek to disguise their activities and seek to speak on behalf of the majority; but ultimately the progressive Rastas rallied behind the call for greater agricultural production in the year of education and production. The initiatives of the PRG towards self-sufficiency in food production were being mounted against the increased crisis in the capitalist world, and Grenada was particularly vulnerable. As an island the society exists without much of the usual trappings of national sovereignty. There is no central bank, it cannot boast its own monetary system (the economy is still tied to the Eastern Caribbean dollar, thus allowing for illegal export of funds by opposition elements), its own communication system or national market. In fact, the society could not generate, under colonialism or neo-colonialism, the general technical preconditions which were indispensable for economic production and autocentric development.

The New Jewel Movement moved cautiously in the areas of agricultural diversification, without nationalising the bulk of private plantations. This caution was necessitated by the way in which the Grenadian society had been integrated into the international capitalist economy. This integration continued, though it was the long-term effort of the PRG to slowly disengage from Western imperialism. It was in the process of disengagement that there were greater tests for the future path of development than simply fomenting divisions in the ranks of the Rastas.

The experience of the organised Left in the Caribbean territories should have alerted the leaders of the PRG that contrary to the purveyors of the non-capitalist theory, the consciousness of the working class was not the product of the consciousness of the intelligentsia. The task of harmonising the State with society must be a long and slow process. Cultural initiatives and social experiments, such as the Theatre Group National Youth Organisation, embarked on dramatic presentations in the hope of instilling a new social awareness. Cultural exchanges and calypso artists ensured that the harmony which had begun between the State and society from March 13, 1979, continued. Grenadian Rastas came out in the forefront as a new force of cultural resistance in the region – a force which linked liberation to their social reality.

Rastas in Trinidad

The explosion of Rasta culture in Antigua, Barbados, St. Thomas, St. Kitts and Trinidad has led to concern by the State officials, who spend their energies arguing the best methods to coerce this dynamic force. In the more homogeneous societies, the politicians have been taken aback by the positive example of the Grenadian Revolution. It is these societies which are in the forefront of the call for elections in Grenada, while in their own societies the police move to intimidate Rastas.

While the Barbadian government bulldozes the settlements of Rastas, young sisters like Janet Tafari of Barbados proclaim that the Rastas want to move to a higher stage of society than one of shameless imitation of Europe.[14] In Antigua the police battered a youth to near death then sent him to a mental institution, for in the consciousness of the defenders of Europe, Rastas must be mad.

The Rasta movement in Trinidad offers a glimpse of the complex challenge of the sort of nationalism which is sweeping the Eastern Caribbean. The emergence of the Rasta as a strong force in Trinidad poses serious contradictions, because of the complex of racial attitudes which emerged out of the history of slavery and indentureship.

Two characteristics impart a kind of specificity to race and racial problems in Trinidad and Guyana. First, the decisive racial contradiction is between two non-white peoples; and secondly, both are exploited by foreign capital and local compradors. These characteristics distinguish the Trinidad and the Guyana situations from the Jamaican one, where the population is more homogeneous. This racial contradiction existed in Trinidad and Guyana, but in the past had been exploited by aspiring political leaders of the African and Indian petty bourgeoisie, leading to bloodshed and violence in Guyana.

Racial identification, of which the Rastafarian movement is an essential manifestation, is a variant of black nationalism and contains the dialectic of positive and negative ideas. Rastas in Trinidad have, in the midst of the squalor and waste, demonstrated the potential of the movement as a movement of oppressed people, for in Trinidad it is not uncommon now to see Indian Rastas – an affirmation by Indian youths that they identify with the culture of resistance of the African youths.

These young people, who form the underbelly of the chaotic capitalist society, see before their very eyes the best example of the failure of capitalism. Trinidad, unlike those societies which claim that they need aid for development, or that they need foreign exchange, salts away US$3 billion of her surplus in Swiss banks, while all the major capitalist powers converge on Trinidad to recycle the petro-dollars.

The Williams Government and its successor proved unable to provide proper medical care for the people, toilets for school children, houses for the poor, food for the needy. In area after area of the social life of the Trinidad community, the rot is evident, while the economic infrastructure grinds to a halt in the rush to support a seemingly boom economy on an untransformed colonial economic infrastructure. Road services, public transportation, the water supply system, the electricity, sewage and drainage facilities all function spasmodically, while the petty bourgeoisie invest TT$24 million in an air-conditioned race track with swimming pools for the horses.

The Rastafarian movement comprises part of those youths who refuse to be condemned to a life of political opportunism and mediocrity through the Special Works Programme called DEWD (Development and Environmental Works Division). Their resistance forms part of the broader tradition of resistance which has been the history of the working class movement in Trinidad. This movement, which has struggled to defend the democratic right of freedom of assembly and the right to industrial action, has resisted the efforts by the different politicians to use coercion and racial manipulation to ensure the political domination of the petty bourgeoisie.

The history of revolts and working class activity in Trinago is only matched by the cultural outpourings of the workers in the form of calypso, a vehicle through which the political aspirations of the people are expressed. People's calypsonians, such as Chalkdust, the Mighty Stalin and Lord Valentino, sing songs of discontent, exposing the class nature of the society; beside them the calypsos of sex and infidelity pale into insignificance.

With the rise of the Rastas and the increasing identification with reggae music among the poor, some calypsonians have sought to merge new musical forms. At the forefront of this tendency is Lord Valentino, who proclaimed himself to be a Rasta and continues his shafts of critical commentary at the US domination of the society. The Mighty Stalin in 1979 dedicated his calypso to the Rasta, calling him the *Caribbean Man*, and saying that:

> "*De federation done dead*
> *And Carifta going to dead,*
> *But de call of the Rastafari*
> *Spreading through the Caribbean.*
> *It have Rasta now in Grenada,*
> *It have Rasta now in St. Lucia,*
> *But to run Carifta, yes you getting pressure.*
> *If the Rastafarian movement spreading*
> *and Carifta dying slow,*
> *Den is something dem Rasta done*
> *That dem politicians don't know.*
> *So dey pushing one common intention*
> *For a better life in de region*
> *For de women and de children,*
> *That must be the ambition of the*
> *Caribbean Man.*"

Those members of the Indian intelligentsia who feared the prospect of the kind of unity fostered by Rasta youths launched a series of critical articles on Stalin's conception of the Caribbean Man. Calling the calypso racist and sexist, they were exploiting the divisions which had been sown in the society by the colonialists – divisions based on race instead of between the oppressor and oppressed.

Essentially the intelligentsia were expressing their fear of the power of Rasta, for the State had seen the potential and was busy trying to ensure that the Rastas had nothing to do with the Left and organised working class movement. Most of the Rastas in Trinidad had been through the black power movement and were drawn to the Rasta movement through reggae music. The Rasta movement in Trinidad is poised between the example of Grenada and the ideas of deification of the former Ethiopian monarch. This latter tendency is linked to those activists from Jamaica who collaborated in staging a Jubilee celebration in Trinidad, one of the few areas outside Jamaica where young blacks still revere Haile Selassie.

Rastas, Guyana and The Left

That the cultural thrust of reggae poses a threat to petty bourgeois politicians in the region was best exposed in Guyana. Like the slave masters who banned the use of the drum, the Guyanese government banned reggae music from the airwaves of the society in July 1980.[15] Guyana provides the best example of the rise of pseudo-socialism and crude black nationalism. Pseudo-socialism was seen by the leaders of the People's National Congress (PNC), the ruling party, as a useful means of maintaining control over the working class.

At the same time, this regime perfected the mechanisms of oppression so that 'nationalisation' of foreign capital and support for African liberation have become dogma to disguise the real interests and motives of the petty bourgeoisie. The pseudo-socialist imagery offered real material advantages to the ruling party and its supporters in so far as it opened up the nationalised sector as a source for distributing political patronage.

The crisis of imperialism exposed the pseudo-socialist imagery of the regime as the International Monetary Fund (IMF) came in to oversee the reduction of the living standards of the society, especially of the working poor. The rise in unemployment, the impotence of old parties based on race, the political crisis which generated the violence leading to Jonestown, and the political activities of Rabbi Washington and the House of Israel demanded a new political force in the society. The consolidation of divisive racial alignments at the political level worked towards increasing the exploitation of the workers and the small farmers.

The Working People's Alliance (WPA) was formed as a political party to respond to this economic and political crisis in the society. Their "Principles and Programmes" outlined the theoretical basis for building a new society, while in practice this party went about the task of exposing racial insecurity as negative, and as working against the interests of the workers, showing concretely how racial and ethnic factors tended to overshadow the historical role of the working class.

The presence of Pan-Africanists and Marxists like Walter Rodney and Eusi Kwayana in the ranks of the Working People's Alliance meant that the statements towards black consciousness were directed in a conscious manner toward the emancipation of not only African, but also Indian workers. Africans in Guyana had been inculcated with ideas that they were the guardians of black dignity by the PNC, but the regime showed that this black consciousness was a sinister mythology which forced the people to live on their knees.

The scope for the spread of Rastafari was circumscribed by the nature of the racial conflict in the society and the conscious policy of the WPA to root itself in all sections of the working poor, those unemployed and those employed. The existence of cults such as the House of Israel and the People's Temple of Jonestown placed caution in the minds of youths.

Yet the Rasta movement developed among young Africans. It was prominent in the urban working class areas, and some Rastas petitioned the State for land to settle in the interior. However the State was not concerned about their potential for farming; the political leadership responded by using the mechanisms of the police and the law to harass the young brethren and sistren.

The main influence of the Rasta formation came from the Dreads, though a small minority wanted to centralise the person of Haile Selassie. But the leadership of the WPA always tried to pull out the most progressive aspects of the movement while through patient educational work they exposed the myths of Ethiopia and the Ethiopian monarch which were so entrenched in Jamaica.

The potential towards mobilising the unemployed and the Rastas was clear to Walter Rodney, who identified positively with this force in the Caribbean. In his last public address to the Guyanese people, he paid tribute to Edward Dublin, a member of the unemployed who died in the cause of the workers' movement. He opened by saying "As the brothers in the street would say, I man Irie, I man dread". This simply means that whatever pressures may be coming down upon one, one's will to struggle has in no way been lessened.

He spoke of the transformation of those members of the unemployed, those who were rendered unemployable by the nature of the system but who decided not to become lumpen and prey on the organised workers. Edward Dublin was a youth who in the process of working with the WPA became politicised, and thus a threat to the regime: he was killed on February 29, 1980.

Asserting the need to mobilise all sections of the masses Rodney maintained:

> "*What I am trying to say is simply this: The revolution is made by ordinary people, not by angels, made by people from all walks of life, and more particularly by the working class who are in the majority*. And it is a sign of the times, the sign of the power of revolutionary transformation, when a street force member is developed into a fighting cadre in a political movement." *(His emphasis)*[16]

Here Walter Rodney was leaving a lesson for the Caribbean Left, that the

Rastas, the unemployed youth, were part of the working class movement; that revolution is not made by saints, contrary to the assertions of those political movements which claim that their leaders were revolutionaries from birth. The simple statement he was making was that the movement of the people must harness the positive potential of the Rasta movement in the process of political struggle.

Walter Rodney did not live to continue his work among the working people of the Caribbean. He was assassinated by a young agent who was paid to gain his confidence. On his death, the Rastas declared that they would produce one thousand Rodneys.

Conclusion

The Rasta movement in the Caribbean today is the foremost Pan-African and Pan-Caribbean movement in the area. Despite the idealist and oftimes metaphysical tenets of the movement, it is decidedly a section of the oppressed peoples of the region and contains the history of their love for their African homeland.

The movement has broken down the big island/small island differences among the people and has spread to the French colonial territories of Martinique and Guadeloupe. In these islands the cultural forms of expression called Cadance proclaim that black people's ancestors were not from Gaul but from Africa.

While in Jamaica the struggle for influence over the Rastas intensified with the formation of the pseudo-Rastafarian Ethiopian Zion Coptic Church, the movement in Grenada pointed a new direction for Rastas throughout the world. Proclaiming that Rastas should never become pawns of capitalism, they called out:

> *"It is of great significance that the progressive movement included Rastas and have even placed brethren in key governmental positions in the security forces and other agencies and to show no prejudice to natty dread. It is with this in mind that we deliver this message to you as a reminder that the founding principles of the Rastafarian faith directed that we should at all costs serve the people in the truth and the right, so it behoves us to state emphatically and clearly the position of Rastafari on issues of temporal realities such as socialism, and communism which is opposed to capitalism, underdevelopment and imperialism. Rastafari must take their proper place in the Third World Revolution struggle against dictatorship and oppression. Rastas cannot and must not become the pawns of reactionary capitalists in their attempt to maintain imperialism."*[17]

FOOTNOTES:

1. FO 371/20154 in the English Public Records Office contains a full account of how serious the British considered these mass meetings throughout the Caribbean.
2. FO 371/20154, op. cit. Also see "British West Indian Reaction To The Italian-Ethiopian War: An Episode in

Pan-Africanism", *Caribbean Studies*, April, 1970.

3. *The African Orthodox Church*, Reverend A.C.T. Thompson, 1956. For a pluralist version of the religious proclivities of blacks in the Eastern Caribbean see G.E. Simpson, *Black Religion in the New World*, Colombia University Press, 1978.
4. Walter Rodney, "Contemporary Political Trends in the English Speaking Caribbean", *Black Scholar*, USA, September 1975.
5. See statements from the Desmond Trotter Defence Committee, Roseau, Dominica, 1976. Also see "Trotter's Message From Prison", *Caribbean Contact*, March 1976.
6. *Caribbean Contact*, April, 1976.
7. Richard Payne, "The Caribbean and the Law of the Sea", *Round Table*, July, 1980, p. 322.
8. See *Treaty of Limitation of Marine Frontiers Between the Republic of Venezuela and the United States of America*, March 1978.
9. *National Security Record*, Report on the Congress and National Security Affairs, Washington, June 1980.
10. *Torchlight*, October 10, 1979. It is significant that the Twelve Tribes Organisation in the region did not make a statement on the *Torchlight* allegations. The Twelve Tribes is an international Rasta group with its headquarters in Jamaica. It is the most hierarchical of the Rasta formations. They have settled about a dozen followers in Ethiopia and even there they defy the social reality by telling Rastas in the Caribbean that Haile Selassie is still alive.
11. *Free West Indian*, Grenada, November 3, 1979.
12. *Free West Indian*, October 20, 1979.
13. *Wall Street Journal*, November 19, 1980. Vesco was wanted in the US but is a fugitive in the Bahamas. He was very close to former US President Nixon. When Nixon set up the Super Drug Agency, the DEA, one of the stories which emerged was that "an investigation into a 200 kilo heroin smuggling deal was curtailed when the name of the billionaire Robert Vesco entered the enquiry; records were lost and a valuable informer was discredited and abandoned." It was also revealed that DEA agents electronically debugged Robert Vesco's home in New Jersey. See *High Times*, December-January, 1976/7, p. 79.
14. *The Nation*, Barbados, Wednesday, January 14, 1981. Interview with Janet Tafari.
15. CANA, July 9, 1980. The General Manager of Guyana Broadcasting Corporation sought to make a distinction between reggae and other forms of music, saying that "the ban was restricted to those records whose lyrics were inimical to the interests of the society ..."
16. From Rodney's last speech in Georgetown, Guyana, June 6, 1980, published in *Sign of the Times*, WPA Support Group (UK), London, June 1981.
17. *Free West Indian*, July 5, 1980.

Chapter Seven

THE RASTAFARI MOVEMENT IN THE METROPOLE

PART 1

Rastas and the Decline of the African Liberation Support Committee

The spread of the Rastafari movement, whether in the politicised form of the Dreads in the Eastern Caribbean or in the form of the mystical locksmen of Jamaica, had coincided with one of the periods of assertive identification with race and racial pride in the United States of America. A strident proclamation of 'Black Power', which came to the attention of the world through the Anglo-American media, was a manifestation of the black pride and self-assertion which was the continuation of the long struggle against racial discrimination and dehumanisation.

This Black Power Movement transformed a society where the economic basis of segregation had been eroded by the rapid industrialisation of the South, but where the backward ideas of racial superiority had put a brake on giving black people their rights as full citizens.

Segregated schools, segregated lunch counters, dilapidated houses, disenfranchisement, and contending with racists such as Bull O'Conncr were the lot of a working people who were being pushed off the land as sharecroppers into the low paying jobs in Birmingham (Alabama), Atlanta (Georgia) and Memphis (Tennessee). This working poor responded to the challenge by pushing the society beyond the vestiges of McCarthyism with a political movement which included sit-ins, occupations, and those long marches which rang through the deltas of the South with the refrain "We Shall Overcome".

Martin Luther King, Malcolm X, Angela Davis, George Jackson and Muhammed Ali emerged out of a violent struggle as leaders of a conscious generation of black people who struggled for Civil Rights and for basic human rights in a society which had the capacity to put a man on the moon, but where millions of people suffered from malnutrition and starvation.

These blacks had taken the lead in internationalising the struggles of oppressed peoples to the point where they identified the war in Vietnam as part of their struggle, and in the process unleashed a spirit of resistance among progressive young whites who took to the streets in those historic anti-war marches. Part of this internationalism in the black community included support for the African Liberation struggle. Leaders such as Malcolm X and Stokely Carmichael had consciously sought to mobilise black people in America to see their struggle as part of the African Liberation struggle.

Later, the Black Panthers took to carrying weapons for self-defence, for in the spirit of Malcolm X the fact that Africans had taken to arms in Southern Africa was being used to strengthen the Afro-American resolve to oppose police and State brutality in the years of sharp racial confrontation, between 1966 and 1974.

Jamaican support for African Liberation struggles dated back to the Italo-Abyssinian war, and had been linked to the internal struggles of the depression years, but took the additional spiritual form of identification with the Ethiopian monarch, replacing the European monarch at Buckingham Palace. Living in the great republic whose anthem glorified the fight against monarchy, black people in America were not burdened with this form of identification, but the deep spiritualism was embedded in the independent churches of black America.

One movement which arose in the USA with startling similarities to the Rastafari movement was that of the Black Muslims, called the Nation of Islam, under the leadership of Elijah Muhammed. Deriving their legitimacy from the nationalist and racial ideas of Garvey on the one hand and the Koran on the other, the Black Muslims developed as a strong religious-nationalist force in the urban centres of the USA, with a concept of solidarity and self-reliance which endeared them to wide sections of the black community.

Malcolm X received his early political education in the Nation of Islam, distancing himself when the open capitalist values of the organisation had cut off the Black Muslims from the struggles on the street.* Malcolm X had perceived that religious leaders could not be separated from the mass struggles, and it is significant that the solidarity of the black churches provided the base for the Civil Rights cause, bringing to the fore religious leaders such as Martin Luther King Jr., who combined his search for God with a passionate struggle for equality in the most unequal society of America.[1]

Caribbean nationals in the USA were part of the struggles for Civil Rights and during this period nationalist papers, such as *African Opinion*, carried out the Garvey tradition of appealing to a wider constituency than that of the blacks in the USA, in the attempt to rise above the petty tribalism between 'Westindians' and Afro-Americans. Caribbean nationals, such as Stokely Carmichael, had inspired the kind of Pan-Africanism which rose above these petty differences,

*One important distinction between the Rastas and the Black Muslims was that the Black Muslims preached that whites were 'devils' and manifested a level of intolerance which was never present in the Rasta movement. These Muslims had woven a curious historical account of slavery to legitimise their ideas, and though claiming some nationalist similarities with Garveyism, "it lacked the humanism which attracted great masses to Garveyism". See Theodore Vincent, *Black Power and the Garvey Movement*, Ramparts Press, 1976, p. 223. The philosophy of Islam proved quite attractive to some of those young Rastas who grew tired of the lack of organisation of some Rasta groups.

for there were thousands of Westindians who had made their home in the USA.*

The African Liberation Support Committee

During the sixties and seventies, the most active and articulate sections of the immigrant communities were linked to the US-based Black Power Movement and later the African Liberation Support Committee (ALSC). The ALSC had from its inception in 1971 aspired to embrace the whole Pan-African community in the West, from ASCRIA in Guyana (African Society for Cultural Relations with Independent Africa), to the Pan-African Congress Movement in the UK. At the core of this Pan-African Movement was the ALSC Secretariat in Washington DC, where the young blacks who had been the driving force behind the Student Non-Violent Coordinating Committee (SNCC) gradually shifted their emphasis from 'black' to 'African' in terms of political mobilisation.

The ALSC embraced a variety of classes and strata within the Afro-American community, and included not only organisations which were just beginning to understand the full implications of the struggle in Africa, but also older elements who had long and tenuous connections with the African continent. As a coalition of organisations, the energy of the young activists around Owusu Sadauki pulled together disparate class elements, from the organised workers of the Detroit motor industry to the fledgling black Representatives in the House of Congress.

During the years 1971-1974 Afro-American support for African liberation was the 'pivot' of an international black movement which ran the gamut of conventional solidarity actions, pinpointing particular multinationals – such as Gulf – for boycott, raising thousands of dollars in the black community and forwarding it to Africa, and persuading longshoremen to refuse to offload chrome from the illegal Ian Smith regime.[2]

The highlight of these campaigns was the observation of *African Liberation Day* on May 25 every year with marches. These marches in the USA coincided with marches in Europe and the Caribbean, and Rastafari positively identified with this movement, with the Rastafari Movement Association (RMA) in the forefront of the Jamaican celebrations.

Rastafari youths all over the world came out to support the African Liberation Day Marches. This form of political mobilisation was accompanied by a spate of published information,[3] which for a long time assisted in an effort to get beyond the mystification imposed by the established news media on questions concerning Africa.

As long as the ALSC survived, it promoted the cause of Africa with clarity for the Rastas, on the one hand, and furthered the radicalisation of Congressmen,

*From 1865 to 1952 the bulk of English-speaking Caribbean migration was to the USA, but this flow was effectively halted in 1952 when the racially inspired McCarran-Walter Immigration Act limited to 100 per year persons allowed to emigrate to the USA from each Caribbean territory. It was after this period that the bulk of Caribbean people turned to the UK in their rush to escape the unemployment and poverty of the island societies.

such as Charles Diggs, on the other. Diggs began to raise questions about the official ties between the USA and the settler regimes in Africa. Rastas in the Caribbean and Europe also benefitted from this information in that it helped to focus attention away from the narrow identification with the Ethiopian State and monarch.

However, as an all-class formation the ALSC could not indefinitely mask the disagreements which reflected the differing ideological positions of those who supported African liberation; and by the middle of 1974, the ideological differences within the ALSC had taken the form of extensive debates on the inter-relationships between race and class. This vigorous discussion, which began at ALSC meetings in Washington in May 1974, broke open at the Sixth Pan-African Congress in Dar-es-Salaam in June 1974.[4] Centralising the false dichotomy between nationalism and communism, which had begun at the time of Garvey, this discussion was pursued in the journal *Black Scholar,*[5] but on the streets was combined with the problems of individualism and a narrow, scientifically incorrect theory of two imperialisms.

The framework of the debate itself reflected the impoverishment of ideas in the USA, where the bourgeoisie had, through the resources available, sought to trivialise the idea of revolution and class struggle. This was part of the process of befuddling the white working class, who had been nurtured on an intense diet of anti-communism and white racism.

In the Caribbean, Pan-Africanists such as Walter Rodney and Eusi Kwayana had consciously sought to inform the black nationalist tendencies with the understanding that support for African liberation should be part of an anti-imperialist posture which must extend to South America, South East Asia and Europe itself. Their struggles against those leaders who opportunistically supported African Liberation Movements while suppressing genuine liberation movements in their society had led nationalists such as ASCRIA and the ACLM in Antigua to embrace a world view which was Marxist and anti-racist.

There was a similar quest in the USA by those who were not satisfied with couching their support for African liberation solely in terms of skin colour. These blacks sought to link the problems of the black struggle to the international socialist movement, and Angela Davis was one of those who identified with this thrust, though on the whole the history of the antagonisms between blacks and the Communist Party USA affected the quality of the debate. At the other side of the ideological divide within and outside the ALSC were those who thought that liberation should be based on ethnic identification, to the point where they denigrated the ideas of scientific socialism on the grounds that "Marx and Engels were white racists".[6]

Such glorification of ignorance was to find concrete manifestation in support for the United States of America and South Africa in Angola in 1975. The black nationalists who were stridently anti-communist supported the UNITA/FNLA front during the decisive Angolan War, for the front man of South Africa – Jonas Savimbi – used the same anti-communist rhetoric as the black nationalists of the USA and Europe.

The people of Cuba in the Caribbean decisively supported the forces of the MPLA to defeat the South African invasion to the amazement of the USA and her capitalist allies in Europe. The Americans, who had coordinated the South African/UNITA battle,[7] could not understand how a small nation that they had blockaded for many years, and which they had vowed would never survive as a socialist State, had not only survived, but had the capacity to aid a fighting African society to defeat the forces of Apartheid. So worried were the Pentagon strategists that the State Department intensified their anti-Cuban campaign, leading to acts of terror against anti-imperialist forces in the Caribbean, epitomised in the placing of a bomb on the Cubana Airlines plane in Barbados in 1976.

The vitriolic response of the capitalist States found a certain unity with those on the left who denounced the Cubans as agents of 'Soviet social imperialism'. This discussion had a profound impact on the whole project of support for African liberation, causing many young blacks in Canada and the UK, who had earlier marched under the banners of the support for black dignity and African freedom, to turn to the Rastafari, especially since they listened intently to the reggae songs of freedom.

A direct co-relation has been made in the United Kingdom between the decline of the Black Power Movement and the rise of Rastafari. Such a direct link is more difficult in North America, since the young Caribbean and Jamaican nationals who proclaimed the divinity of Haile Selassis were never a part of the ALSC. These Rastafarians were located on the eastern seaboard, primarily in New York and Connecticut, and they were so few in numbers that they did not take any clear organisational form.

By the middle of the seventies, the headquarters of the Ethiopian World Federation in New York had been relocated, for the organisational headquarters in Harlem had lost its significance after the removal of Haile Selassie from the Imperial Throne. The Ethiopian Orthodox Church (EOC) had a small following, and the liquidated heirs of Haile Selassie had hoped to use the EWF and the EOC as political bases of support; but the EWF had lost the vibrancy which it had elicited after the Italian invasion of Abyssinia.

Though small in number, the presence of the Rastafari was noticeable enough for the Chief of the Intelligence Unit of New York Police Force to prepare a report on the Rastafari. As usual, this report claimed that the Rastas had no regard for property, life or law, and the US Immigration Authorities declared that Rastas were "the most violent group in New York City".[8] Overlooking the violence of the Mafia and the organised looters of Wall Street, the police linked Rastas to the rise in ganja-related killings in the Bronx and Brooklyn between 1974 and 1975.

It was shortly after this period of the appearance of Rastas as a distinctive group in New York and the Cuban assistance to Angola that the pseudo-Rasta group, the Coptics, appeared as the major Rasta formation in the USA. Because everything in America is done on a grand scale, these pseudo-Rastas established themselves on Star Island, in Florida, and were so significant that the television news programme "Sixty Minutes" gave them national publicity in October 1979.[9]

Through their newspaper *Coptic Times* they expounded their anti-communist Rasta philosophy, eliciting the support of the State to use local radio stations to bind young blacks and whites to their 'misphilosophy'. During the period 1975-1980, the Coptics were able to develop a level of sophistication with respect to the campaign to 'legalise cannabis', so that they were able to gain widespread support from blacks and whites in North America, Europe and the Caribbean.

The Canadian Dimension

In Toronto and Montreal, Canada – where there was a larger proportion of Caribbean migrants – the Rastafari movement grew slowly during the sixties and seventies, but rapidly expanded after the closure of the Black Education Project in Toronto and the relocation of the Toronto branch of the Universal Negro Improvement Association. The struggle for Civil Rights in the USA had spread across to the Canadian blacks in the sixties, when local and immigrant blacks heightened their own campaign against racial discrimination, culminating in the violent confrontations of Sir George Williams University in Montreal, in 1969.[10]

For a brief period the Canadian arm of the AISC was a vibrant movement, but as in the USA, the Angolan War, coupled with the ideological struggles, had affected those organisations which were struggling for decent education, proper housing, jobs and against immigration witch-hunts. As a rich, vast and underpopulated land, Canada encouraged migrants from Europe, but hounded and harassed black immigrants. So it was not surprising that in 1975 the police and the immigration authorities launched an attack on the Rastas as a "Bizarre Cult which was responsible for violent Crimes in Toronto."[11]

Quoting extensively from the intelligence reports of the USA, the newspaper allegations exposed the extent to which the differing sections of the coercive apparatus of the Canadian State were monitoring the activities of the Rastas in Toronto. The Tacky Study Group (a small Caribbean group which derived its name from the leader of the slave revolt in Jamaica in 1760) perceived the media/police initiative not merely as an attack on the Rastas, but as a continuation of the attacks on the black community, and mobilised the progressive forces along with the Ethiopian Orthodox Church to refute the claims of the police that Rastas were violent murderers. A joint statement from Tacky, the UNIA (the Garvey organisation), and the Black Workers Alliance underlined the concern of the black community at the report, which blamed the Rastas for racism.[12]

Even at this point there were sharp differences between the Rastas. Those who were more steeped in religion claimed that it was the 'work of Jah,' while those who had participated in the general struggles of the black community saw the need to 'stand up and fight.' These two tendencies were to contend with the mystical faction, taking the ascendancy as the general black leadership dispersed and the community organisations were weakened by police infiltration and provocation.[13]

Rastas in North America continued the tradition of assertive identification with race and African origin, straddling the political/mystical divide. In the main, Rastas became a religious form in Canada: this phenomenon was linked to the general level of political development in the society. It was even more startling in Britain, where the Rastas formed the bulk of the black conscious youths.

Part II

Rasta, the Black Worker, and the British Crisis

The present Rastafari community in Britain is part of the large black population in the United Kingdom of more than 2 million.* Black settlement in the UK is not a new phenomenon, for hundreds of blacks have lived in England since the Elizabethan times. They have borne the brunt of the racism of a society which made immense profits from the buying and selling of human beings, and where for the white population the historical evidence of enslaving blacks forged the tie between racism and colour prejudice.

Racist philosophy produced not only a society of individual racists, but a society where white racism was so all-pervasive that it was not perceived for what it was, but over time permeated all institutions of the State and society. Anti-racist scholars have documented how the racism which spawned English literature and society laid the basis for the general European conception of black people; "for the Dutch, the French, and the Germans did not lag behind their English counterparts in providing the stereotypes and distortions which comprise racism".[14]

Black house servants had abounded in the society, consequent to the practice of Westindian planters of bringing large numbers of slaves to England with them; but the activities of the free blacks, such as Equiano, and the anti-slavery society led to the Lord Mansfield Decision, 1772, which outlawed slavery on British soil. Numerous black loyalists who fought on the side of the British during the American War for Independence sought their freedom, and on travelling to England they increased the already existing sectors of black unemployed.

Having a large degree of visibility, blacks were singled out as constituting a major social problem,which comprised destitution, crime and the threat of miscegenation; and the solution was that they should be deported from the

* A useful source on the statistical breakdown of the black population in 1980 is in *Britain's Black Population* by the Runnymede Trust and the Radical Statistics Race Group, Heinemann Educational Books, 1980. For the purposes of this section on Rastafari, black will refer to the black people of African origin.

realm. It would be quite instructive for the present Rasta campaign of repatriation to examine how a reactionary solution was combined with the humanitarian purpose of Granville Sharp in the wholesale deportation of blacks to Sierra Leone in 1786.

Many blacks feared that the dominant thrust behind the scheme was to dump them outside Britain without protection, so they eluded the armed search parties of the East End (London) streets, becoming the forebears of the black communities which settled in the seaport towns of London, Liverpool, Bristol and Cardiff.

At the end of World War II, this small community was augmented by over one million blacks from the Westindies, Africa and Asia, when Britain looked to its colonies to solve its post-war labour shortage. From the Westindies over a quarter of a million responded to the recruitment pressure of British capital.[15]

Similar to the exercise of Henry Ford after World War I in the American South, British capitalists took out advertisements encouraging black people to migrate to the factories of the Midlands, to the expanding health services, and most of all to operate the London transport system. But as outlined in a previous chapter, the pressures to leave the Caribbean were double-edged, with the case of the rural small farmers in Jamaica who were forced to sell their land being the best documented example of the pressures to migrate.

Black immigration to the urban centres was a reflection of the crisis of British imperialism, and was in itself one of the responses of the State to this economic and social crisis. British capitalism had been sheltered from innovation and rejuvenation by the promise of continuous exploitation of those colonies which were ruled under the British flag. These colonial possessions prevented Britain from taking part in the last great expansion of capitalism in the post-World War II era, when the Americans had initiated the Marshall Plan to prevent the general collapse of the system of capitalism.

Japan, Germany and France modernised their economies, utilising the resources of the globe, especially cheap energy, to usher in the third technological revolution – the era of petro-chemicals, atomic energy, sea bed technology, the conquest of space and micro-chip technology. Britain trailed behind these developments, limping later into the European Common Market, hoping to get protection for her ailing steel, shipbuilding and motor car industries.

The crisis of industrial production in Britain, to which the black worker migrated after 1948, was simultaneously a political and ideological crisis. Imperialist pillage of the 67 colonies had allowed the ruling class to grant concessions to its militant working class in the social democratic compromise. Social democracy embraced imperialism and chauvinism, with the Left justifying colonial domination as 'progressive', while the ideological organ of the State integrated the working class as a social partner and a consumer, thus subordinating the working people to the ideological domination of capital.

Social democracy became the material product of imperialism, while reformism became the ideological corollary of this capital/labour alliance.[16]

Wage improvements interconnected with the narrow political struggles of the trade union bureaucracy, led to the extension of the market, creating the conditions for the 'consumer society' and incessantly extending the scope of unproductive activities, and the domestication of progressive forces.

Black immigrants who came off the boats and planes to the foundries were thrown into the midst of the ideological and economic crisis which beset the British society when the conjunction of the extension of the socialist camp, the anti-colonial movement, and the massive competition had threatened the whole future of British industry. Capital benefitted from the presence of these immigrants, for not only did they have a cheap source of skilled labour, but they diverted the energies of the white workers from the problems of the workplace with hysterical stories that black people were taking away the jobs and houses of the whites.

Faced with this contradiction, the black worker also had to contend at the workplace with efforts by the State to tie the trade union to institutionalised procedures which ensured 'social harmony'. Countless black workers can tell their own story of their struggles in the trade union movement against the determined efforts of the bourgeoisie to reorganise industrial relations, not only to pit black against white workers, but also to consolidate the power of management over the shop floor.

By the end of the seventies, one of the main consequences of the institutionalisation of shop floor organisation was that unions lost their independence in the workplace. The setting up of common employer/union structures made spontaneous action less likely, and ensured that the shop stewards, whose job it was to defend the workers, were instead drawn into joint committees of peaceful industrial relations.[17]

Concentrated in the low-paying jobs where an effective working class organisation was most needed, but least available, the black workers made their contribution to the crisis-ridden British economy, while the State embarked on enacting legal statutes to reduce the black citizens to second-class citizens; and on the imposition of immigration controls which disrupted their families.

As building workers, carpenters, mechanics, nurses, orderlies and transport service employees, black workers toiled in unpleasant working environments and during unsocial hours, always struggling against the divide and rule tactics of the employers.[18] But however much the British capitalist class benefited from this influx of a vibrant, skilled labour force, the long-term problem of *transformation* could not be shelved. By the end of the sixties all the major sectors of the economy were in decline, for no amount of nationalisation could protect the British steel, British shipbuilding, or British automobile industries from more efficient producers. Black workers, even before they settled in their new communities, began to share the experience of blacks in the USA in being the last hired and the first fired.

Outside their place of work, the workers faced every major institution of the state and society, whether it was the courts, the iniquitous housing policies of the local authorities, the threats from uniformed and plainclothes racists in the streets or the thrust to dub their children *Educationally sub-normal* (ESN) in the school system. Racial discrimination confronted these workers everywhere, and they were forced from time to time to turn to armed resistance, as witnessed in the Notting Hill and Nottingham revolts of late 1958. The Notting Hill revolt foreshadowed the limitations of social democratic control over black workers.

Discriminated against at work, harassed at night by the coercive arm of the State, and denigrated by the media, the black workers and their families set about building social and welfare organisations for protection and solidarity.

Communal practices, such as the 'partner' scheme, provided a semblance of community banking, for the transnational banks and the building societies denied black customers the services offered to white citizens. In all spheres of social activity, a vibrant black community was in the making, with the beginnings of a black church movement,[19] black social clubs, black sporting clubs, a black press, in short a black way of life in Britain. All the British institutions had to adapt themselves in one form or another to the black presence, and this adaptation took very negative forms in the school system and in the coercive apparatus – courts, prisons and the police.

The Education System and the Growth of the Rastas

The one area where the voluntary black organisation could not effectively intervene with immediate results was in the training of their children in the educational system. Accustomed to placing supreme trust in the teachers in the Caribbean, black people eagerly sent their children into the school system that the politicians had spoken so highly of.

Within the consciousness of black workers, formal education had been identified with progress, a better way of life, and the ultimate escape from the factory. These black workers were bewildered as they saw their children grow up without the rudimentary skills of reading and writing. No amount of support through self-help institutions on Saturdays, called Supplementary Schools, could sufficiently heal the damage inflicted by teachers who deemed black children educationally sub-normal.

The disproportionate numbers of black children in the ESN schools clearly showed how the educational system was instrumental in perpetuating the sense of inferiority and lack of capability among black people. That the system was designed to produce failure was reinforced to those who were fortunate to go on to secondary and comprehensive schools, for the mentality of failure was inculcated to produce submission to the existing social order.

Blacks in Britain brought to the fore the weaknesses of the post-imperial system as they exposed the racist texts and the dead-end channelling of black children into the Certificate of Secondary Education (CSE) examinations. Black youths were bound to fail when they had to study required reference texts such as H.A.L. Fisher's *History of Europe*, which said that:

"To the conquest of nature through knowledge the contributions made by Asiatics have been negligible and by Africans (Egyptians excluded) non-existent. The printing press and telescope, the steam engine, and the aeroplane, the telegraph and the telephone, wireless broadcasting and the cinematograph, the gramophone and television, together with all the leading discoveries in psychology, the circulation of blood, the laws of respiration and the like, are all the result of researches carried out by white men in Europe."

When black parents and vigilant black teachers reveal the ideological basis of such books the liberal authorities fall back on the problem of 'public expenditure cuts' to justify the retention of this kind of material in the curriculum. For the non-white youth, the 'intentional' and 'unintentional' racism of teachers was decisive in shaping the kind of mind which could be geared to accept the status quo and not to challenge the system.

In the Caribbean, those youths who toiled uphill against the Eurocentric curriculum had their village communities or strong black neighbourhoods to act as a buffer against the psychological and cultural assaults; but in the UK the ideological assault was reinforced on the streets, on the playing fields, and in their homes through the media. Not even the old colonial tactic of calling Commissions of Inquiry could lull the outcry of the enraged Black Parents Associations who were learning that the struggle to change the educational system involved the struggle to change the class base of the society.

Faced with a militant and organised Black Parents' Movement, the State had hoped to siphon off criticism of the educational system with a promise of *multi-cultural studies*. However, the initiatives towards diversifying the content of education could not confront the fundamental problem of the rigid and elitist nature of British education. In practice, multi-cultural education introduced pockets of idyllic and romantic aspects of life in the Caribbean, Asia and Africa, and did not challenge the glorification of white supremacy.

Many young blacks rejected the ideology of the ruling class embodied in the curriculum, and at the end of the seventies the State had in their inquiry placed the stamp of 'under-achievers' on those who refused to acquiesce with the cultural assaults. A report called *The West Indian Child in Our Schools* confirmed what black families knew – that 98% of black children (in six local education authorities) received no A Level passes, and that less than 1% of the blacks born in Britain made it to university.[21]

So controlled and limited were the places in higher education for black and other working people that the State had dropped the myth of social mobility and equal opportunity by cutting back on expenditure so that only the highly capable and persevering black youths could make it into the universities.

Reformist solutions of multi-cultural education could not escape the fact that for blacks the school system was part of the whole system of social control, stretching from the 'disruptive units' in the schools to the SUS laws. Countless black youths were placed in 'disruptive units' when teachers could not cope with the assertion of their humanity, and from time to time students brought home stories which sounded very similar to the experiments of behaviour modification. It was not insignificant, therefore, that black students who were placed in disruptive units called it 'the slammer'. They perceived these units as one link in the chain of 'no go areas', remand centres, prisons and a life of harassment.

It was in the school system that many young blacks first became attracted to Rastafari, for the language of black dignity, coupled with the promise of black liberation, seemed a credible alternative to total submission to the Eurocentric and capitalist ideas of the system. Spurning the technological rationality, the materialism and the degenerate mass media promoting the celebration of commodity fetishism, Rastafari doctrine emerged as an alternative to the corrupt spirit of Europe.

While striving to rise above this corruption, the Rastafari could not but internalise a portion of the idealism and individualism of the society. More significantly, because many youths developed an antipathy not only to 'white man's ideas' but to all ideas, they were to open themselves up to manipulation by elements who took on the physical appearance of Rasta in order to further their own levels of materialism and consumption, especially through the ganja trade.

For the backward elements, it was easier to manipulate these youths who had not mastered the basic skills necessary to function in the society, and they had no interest in stressing or searching for alternative forms of education. The dictum of Cabral, which was repeated by the Rasta Movement Association in Jamaica in their newspaper, was needed in the Rasta communities:

> *"The Role of Education in the revolution is to create a new mentality free from superstition, subservience, and other forms of mental oppression – to develop among the masses a capacity to analyse, criticise and to carry forth revolution."*[22]

Thoughtful Rastas who had to go to the courts, prisons and other State institutions with the persecuted youths encouraged them with the Rodney admonition: *Africans (Especially Youths) Must Learn New Skills.*

In order to escape the cultural assault of the racism and ethnocentrism of the society, young black people searched for avenues of self-expression and development, and one of the most compulsive aspects was that of the Rastafari philosophy, which gave them a sense of pride in being black. Through the sound system, which was their primary source of identification and recreation, many were attracted to the lyrics of defiance and love for Africa, which were transmitted through reggae music.

This assertion of a love for Africa was passive, for unlike the early Rastas these youths did not go out to find out about contemporary struggles in Africa. For a while this assertion coincided with the organisational activities of a number of black groups which articulated their opposition to racial discrimination and harassment. Those organisations which in the fifties had been based on 'island politics' (consistent with the view that the migrants were going to return home) were in 1968 replaced by a number of groups which positively identified with the struggles in Black America and in Africa.

As early as 1964 Claudia Jones had questioned whether the welfare groups and umbrella organisations (such as the Standing Conference of West Indian Organisations) fully served the needs of the black populations in Britain, and she had undertaken a major effort to stimulate political and social thinking among the black population in the launching of the progressive news monthly, the *West Indian Gazette*.

During the sixties and early seventies this tradition of radical journalism flourished with a number of radical black newspapers accompanying the Black Power explosion. Among the newspapers and publications were: *Freedom News*, *Black Voice*, *Flambeau*, *Uhuru*, *Grassroots*, *Race Today*, and *West Indian World*, all papers which were linked to ideological tendencies; but by the end of 1975 only *Black Voice*, *Grassroots*, and *Race Today* remained as vibrant echoes of protest.

The ideological crisis which rocked the black movement in the USA had its local variant in the UK such that at the beginning of the seventies, the major force among young blacks was the *Rastafari movement*.

A few Rasta men and women were part of the wave of migration out of Jamaica, and even though small in numbers they had set up a branch of the Ethiopian World Federation – Local 33 – in Notting Hill. These Rastas were part of the outpouring of black resistance, and took their share of police harassment, brutality and distortion.

The numbers of Rastafarians in Britain increased sharply after the appearance of Bob Marley with locks, singing songs like "Dread Natty Dread". After 1975 the music of Marley and the Wailers had a dramatic impact on the youths, for the media complex was caught in the contradiction of selling reggae to a mass audience, but ending up with black youths who rejected the social injustice of capitalism.

At precisely the time when the State challenged the whole black community, culminating in the Mangrove Trials, the ideological crisis of the white Left, which deflected the energies of young people into non-revolutionary struggles, meant that the black people were on their own against the State. The Rastafari movement erupted as part of the overall black rejection of the 'Babylonian system', and acted as the fountain of spiritual renewal.

All over England there were small groups of blacks who had turned their backs on the schools, on the churches of their parents, and on the promise of unemployment, by their assertive identification with Africa. The newssheet of the Ethiopian World Federation, Local 33 – called *Rasta Cry* – voiced some of the sentiments of the growing movement when it sought to distance itself from the sectarian conflicts which blossomed after the Mangrove Trials. *Rasta Cry* declared:

"In this time Rasta doctrine is the only solution for black youths because it

> *is unique, it is collective and it is fundamental. It is not Marxism, Maoism nor Black Powerism. It is the only instrument that can destroy the yoke of imperialism and colonialism in the West Indies and Africa."*[23]

Local 33 of the international EWF, based in Portobello Road, Notting Hill (before it was dispersed and demolished) was, like the neighbourhood from which it emerged, political in orientation and did not promote the divinity of the Emperor of Ethiopia, saying:

> *"Selassie is the supreme defender of the faith of the Ethiopian Orthodox Church. He is not divine, indeed Selassie denied his divinity – but he is worshipped as the spiritual leader of the movement."*

Despite this disclaimer of Haile Selassie's divinity, the Rastafari as a group could not escape the powerful threat from imperialism to promote religious alienation and to cut off black youth from discussions about liberation in Africa and in Europe. The efforts of imperialism bore fruit, for the erroneous perception of Haile Selassie's divinity took root even after the massive information exercise on the excesses of the Emperor against the Ethiopian people.

Young Rastas refused to believe that the Emperor was so callous as to feed meat to his dogs while hundreds of thousands of Ethiopians died of famine. Not even the documented evidence of exploitation presented by Ethiopian students in their midst could shake the belief of some of the young Rastas. The more religiously orientated used the information on the revolution to say that the downfall of Haile Selassie was the 'fulfilment of prophecy', drawing comparisons between the overthrow and the sufferings of Christ.

The break-up of the African Liberation Support Committee in the same year and the absence of a reliable source of information meant that these religious Rastas held sway. A similar pattern had developed in Jamaica where, placed on the defensive by the dethronement, the movement developed theological explanations in order to survive and hold the support of its followers. The Rastafari youths, who could not analyse and interpret the events began to deepen their identification with Haile Selassie, in the process turning their backs on the struggles of the Ethiopian people.

The Twelve Tribes of Israel, the Rasta formation which had broken from the EWF in Jamaica, was most vigorous in its worship of Haile Selassie, and for the first time in the history of the movement suggested that the path to the doctrines of Rastafari lay more in the reading of a chapter of the Bible daily, than in the philosophy of Marcus Garvey.* By focussing on the narrow questions of *Haile Selassie, Ethiopia*, and the promise of *Repatriation* to *Shashamane*, the Rasta movement in England was to be influenced by the Twelve Tribes of Israel, an

*The Twelve Tribes of Israel claimed that they were the 'real Jews', the Israelites, without paying attention to the role of the present Israeli State in the Middle East, or of Zionists in South Africa.

organisation which helped to effect a level of confusion on the role of the State of Israel in African politics.

However, the hegemony of this group over less organised Rasta formations could not hold sway for long, for many Rastas objected to the introduction of whites into the 'organ'. Even if Rasta was religious, in the eyes of many Rastas it had to be black and anti-imperialist; so the divisions within the ranks of the movement led to the formation of Rasta International.

Rastas and the State: The Case of Birmingham

It is necessary to periodise this study of the UK movement as a relatively short phase, essentially 1975-1979. The ideas of the strict religious proclamation could not gain ground permanently as long as the Rasta movement, as part of the oppressed black nation in Europe, had to grapple with the State. Even the Headquarters of the Twelve Tribes of Israel, where the religious rituals were being fashioned, came under attack by the police, who feared all forms of black consciousness – even more so if that consciousness was shown in the physical form of Rasta.

Handsworth, Birmingham, provides a clear manifestation of the way in which the Rastafari youths were challenged to rise above idealism and mysticism. The police had recruited young hustlers, who wore their hair in locks and called themselves Rastas, to be part of a pacification project of 'community policing', and British society was forcing the movement to move to a higher level of interpreting the world in order to face the challenges placed before young Rastas.

Apart from the teachers, social workers and welfare officers who worked in the areas of large black settlements, such as the West Midlands and Manchester, the first images of the Rastas which were presented to the wider society were of criminals mugging innocent whites. A major scare was initiated between 1971 and 1973, when the media and the police embarked on a programme to depict all the black youths as muggers and criminals. Linking crime to race, and to the poverty of the inner cities, the newspapers, State intellectuals, and race experts pontificated on the problems of the black families which ensured a life of crime among the 'lost' youths.

In 1973 Handsworth, Birmingham, with over a quarter of its population black, became the focal point of national hysteria about Rasta muggers, covering up the unprecedented police assault on the whole black community. Using the case of two young blacks who were charged before the courts with mugging, the press quoted favourably from the statements of the Police Federation that mugging was a sport for young blacks. For good measure the well-known spokesperson for extreme racists, Enoch Powell, told the whole nation that "mugging was racial".

The case was publicised so much that it precipitated a major study by concerned progressive intellectuals on how the media helped to mould public opinion in using black people as scapegoats. Appropriately called *Policing The*

Crisis: Mugging, the State and Law and Order, this study showed the link between the economic decline of the West Midlands and the policing methods used against black people.[25]

The economic depression in the society had taken its toll in terms of higher unemployment among blacks, more redundancies – not to mention a higher incidence of high blood pressure amongst black people. The West Midlands, with one of the largest concentrations of blacks and Rastas, mirrored the decline of the society. Prior to the sharp decline of the old iron and steel-based industries, the whole area of the West Midlands, from Coventry to Wolverhampton, was covered with small workshops, and was the boom area of provincial Britain.

At the hub of this industrial boom was the motor car industry, employing over 400,000 workers, with the supporting factories providing component parts. Competition from the Germans, the Japanese and the French industrialists undermined British car sales such that foreign cars took a major share of the market, affecting the foundries, factories and steel works which supplied parts to the automobile industry in Britain.

Without the protection of her empire, the economic crisis affected every sector of British industry, with large-scale redundancies in the motor industry, shipbuilding, engineering and construction industries. Not even massive State subsidies of more than £1 million per day to the nationalised motor car and steel industries would stop the rapid de-industrialisation of the society. By 1980 the National Institute of Economic Review said:

> *"There was a greater fall in manufacturing output than that which occurred in the great depression between 1929 and 1931. Manufacturing output in one year fell by over 16% and the official figures of unemployment stood at 10% of the registered work force."*[26]

The West Midlands fared the worse, for the unemployment ranged between 12-14%, with unemployment in the black communities doubling and sometimes tripling the national averages. Black youths were growing up, not temporarily unemployed, but with the prospect of living their adult life without ever having a job, a phenomenon which their parents had sought to escape from in the Caribbean.

Throughout the period the only areas which seemed to attract new technological inputs were in the banking sector and in the repressive instruments of the military and the police. Successive administrations poured millions into the technological toys which strengthen the State over the working class and society. Through its computer systems, the police developed a comprehensive information system, collecting information on 22 million persons, having access to other data banks with health records, military records, tax returns, bank statements, telephone bills, thus enhancing the intelligence gathering facilities.

Without a national authority to monitor the use of this repressive technology, the State was in haste to codify its information on citizens, so that it could preempt major rebellious opposition in this rush towards authoritarianism. Working class institutions were integrated into the social democratic State through the Trade Union Congress, and the extra-parliamentary left remained a voice in the wilderness protesting 'Project 1984'.

The police forces had found the black workers and their families extremely difficult to programme, for the structure of the black and Asian communities did not easily lend itself to easy penetration, especially since the Rastas refused to be drawn into the mad commodity fetishism of the society. The police force in Birmingham intensified its campaign against the black community, and in particular against the Rastafarians, for to the counter-insurgency planners, the whole philosophy of Rastas represented a threat to the British way of life.

Hence, the major campaign for social control took the form of periodic attacks by the Special Patrol Group,* the vetting of the activities of black organisations by the Special Branch, and academic studies by sociologists to fill the gaps in the gathering of information.

From Shades of Grey To Cashmore's Rastaman

Policing-oriented research since 1975 has been centred in Birmingham, for race research replaced the historic centre for West African Studies as the main emphasis. The sociology of race relations *control* replaced colonial *control* as a major problem for the British State. Paul Gilroy, in his analysis of how Birmingham became the centre of sociological research, determined that:

> *"Race research had a new-found relevance for the institutions of social control demanded by the new historical conditions."*

Detailing the studies of the police in which black youths are seen to comprise a simultaneously criminal and political threat to the social order, Gilroy traced the convergence between the views of senior conservative politicians, senior police officers, sociologists, State intellectuals and the purveyors of racism in the media on the question of the black threat.[27] Through the sociological study of one State intellectual in Birmingham, the alleged threat was reduced to the Rastafari movement, and the 'Dread' replaced the mugger as the principal scapegoat for social disorder and black criminality.

The Shades of Grey Report

Continuous confrontations between black people and the police stimulated the need by the State for the John Brown Report on the Rastas, which was called

*The Special Patrol Group had gained particular notoriety in Britain for its violent attacks on the working class and the periodic invasion of black neighbourhoods. Because this force operated as a stormtrooper force and did not necessarily know the neighbourhood they were operating in, "a police computerised index of all streets and property numbers in the West Midlands was undertaken". The index gave the exact location of all 27,000 streets in the 429 'police beats' in Birmingham, Coventry, Dudley, Sandwell, Solihull, Walsall, and Wolverhampton. Also added to the index were details of house numbers, street junctions, telephone kiosks and other prominent local landmarks and features. *State Research Bulletin* No. 24, June-July 1981, p. 139.

Shades of Grey – subtitled "Police/West Indian Relations in Handsworth". Prepared as the ideological counterpart of the operations of the Special Branch and the para-military Special Patrol Group, Brown's report linked Rastafari to all the known crimes of a poor urban community.

Blaming the Westindian family (poor family relations), and poor educational attainment (Rampton's 'under-achievement') for the drift of 'idleness and crime', Brown provides the justification for police brutality by constructing the theory of the "criminalised dreadlock subculture of Handsworth". For those police officers who did not yet know how to identify the Rastafari, Brown told them to look for the red, gold and green, because:

> *"The majority of crimes involving violence were committed in a particular area of Handsworth, usually between dusk and the early hours of the morning and mainly by a particular group – some 200 youths of West Indian origin or descent who have taken on the appearance of followers of the Rastafarian faith by plaiting their hair in locks and wearing green, gold and red woollen hats."*[28]

To cement this image of the Rasta as a racial thug, the media publicised the Brown Report, warning the wider community of this 'crazed drug-smoking menace to British society'. Birmingham newspapers serialised stories of 'streets of terror', using the well-tried scare tactic of the Southern States of the USA – that the victims of hard criminals are 'defenceless white women'. Headlines of "Streets of Fear", "Violent Crime Is Mounting", "Terror Gangs Shock" warned whites of a structured and mobile group of Rastas which terrorised the whole community; and following the recommendation of Brown that "the first priority is to augment police strength", extra police were drafted into Handsworth to deal with the 'Rasta menace'.

Brown's report on the Dreadlocks was a pacemaker in that it set the agenda for subsequent discussion on the Rastas, and paved the way for efforts by the State to incorporate those Rasta elements who would cooperate with the state in experimental community policing. The project to control Rasta, which had been initiated with the 1960 Report in Jamaica and ritualised with the incorporation of the Ethiopian Orthodox Church as a State institution in Jamaica, was now being furthered in Britain as part of the overall plan to control black people. The clear resistance of black youth in Britain to the corrupt spirit of Babylonian culture had created a panic, and the only way to legitimise this panic was to put the stamp of criminality and terrorism on youths with woollen hats.

Brown's separation of the 'real Rasta' from the 'hardcore criminal Dread' was the key to a police experiment which needed 'real Rastas' on the side of the police in the community policing methods. These in turn were necessary to police a black force which was outside the social harmony parameters of trade union/management consultative committees. To provide further information to the police on how to identify the handbag-snatching Rastas from the 'real Rasta', a doctoral study of the Rastafarians in Birmingham was undertaken by Ernest Cashmore.

The resulting book, *Rastaman*, was a reader for the police on how to identify the religious elements, and it turned out later that the informants of Cashmore were in the forefront of the community policing work in Handsworth.

From the outset Ernest Cashmore revealed that his inspiration to study Rasta came from the police, in particular the Inspector of the Intelligence Bureau of the Metropolitan Police of Toronto[29], when the *Globe and Mail* attacked the Rastas in Toronto in 1975. Cashmore used the prestige of the university thesis to confirm the *Shades of Grey* image of criminals, and not even his claim to differ with John Brown could hide his overall effort to centralise the theme of Rasta criminality. He had added his own evidence by saying:

> *"Now whilst objecting to the rigid dichotomisation, I concede that a number of Rastafari adherents in the Handsworth area (and other areas of Birmingham) were prone to handbag snatching, pilfering and robberies of a more serious nature."*[30]

Invoking the worn-out ideas of bourgeois scholarship with obscurantist language of 'truculence', 'evasion', 'discrepancy', 'journey to Jah', and 'impositional concepts', Cashmore resorted to the standard preoccupation with locks, Selassie, ganja and the tam, to present his intervention in the discussion. Where Brown was content to blame the black family for their 'deprived and disadvantaged stations, and children who took out their idleness in crime', Cashmore told how the Rastafarians were potentially murderers, comparing the early settlement of Leonard Howell to the murderous Charles Manson cult in the USA. He compounded the historical distortions of the Pinnacle Commune with the following statement:

> *"After two years' imprisonment Howell decided to rigidify the Pinnacle Commune, installing guards and watchdogs and exercising his leadership almost tyrannically. The parallels with the family cult which emerged in the 1960's are irresistible. Its despotic leader, Charles Manson, was said to wield a strange mesmeric control over his followers, luring them with his apocalyptic vision of Helter Skelter, the ultimate confrontation between blacks and whites, and commanding them to murder figures of 'straight society'. Manson's cult used the hallucinogenic drug, LSD, Howell's used ganja, a marijuana cultivated on the estate, to which many Rastas were to attach religious significance. Both leaders gained inspiration from reluctant sources: in Howell's case, Garvey, and in Manson's, the Beatles, whom he claimed had sent him messages through their recordings."*[31]

From this characterisation of the Rastas as potential murderers Cashmore defined the Rastafari movement, and to ensure that the reader did not miss the continuities between the ganja smokers of Pinnacle and the purse-snatching Rastas he underlined the fact that the Rastas in Britain emerged from marauding street gangs. [32a] While claiming that his work was to clarify and develop understanding, Cashmore used the hospitality of the brethren and sistren to support the police in their work of harassing black youths. Later when the police undertook their own research, one police inspector linked reggae to terrorism, saying: "Music was always important at the Rastafarian meetings, the Nyabingi dance especially, having developed from the 'burra' which was used to welcome home criminals, which was an open commitment to terrorist violence". [32b]

At the time when the whole black community was sensitive to the increased police powers and the alarming numbers of black youths arrested under the 1824 Vagrancy Act on the charge of 'SUS',* Cashmore's study of the Rasta fuelled the drive towards increasing police powers and the deployment of the para-military Special Patrol Group. He repeated the falsehoods of John Brown that:

> *"Members of the Rastafarian movement were a threat to the order of the community, that they had scant respect for the law of the land and had no compunction for breaking it. Theft and robbery were their principal methods of gaining income, they preached peace and love yet practised violence and generally constituted a hazard to the community – and one which had to be checked."* [33]

Cashmore's work was one more piece of ammunition in the battle between the State and black workers in which the sociology of race relations proved to be an important weapon. However, the sociology was not needed to justify the police practices against black people, for the police had effected practices against black people which led to the arrest of many blacks, and not simply those who fell foul of the law. Numerous studies have outlined the consistent pattern of policing in relation to the black communities manifest in:

(a) police overmanning black events;
(b) police raids on black clubs and meeting places;
(c) police concentration in predominantly black localities, including:
 (i) the operation of special squads and
 (ii) the operations whose pretext is to apprehend a particular offender; and
(d) information gathering and surveillance. [34]

Police procedures for the arrest, detention and interrogation of black people were particularly notorious, and the stopping and searching of blacks in mainland Britain was complemented by trial runs of the Special Air Service (SAS) of how to seal off black communities. British policemen were learning from their South African counterparts in declaring certain areas 'no go areas' for black youths. They had to await the Nationality Bill for the British version of 'Pass Laws'.

* Under Section 4 of the 1824 Vagrancy Act, the police arrested a large number of black youths under the part referring to 'suspected persons loitering with intent to commit an offence'. People arrested under this Act could only be tried by a magistrate and all that was required for a conviction was the evidence of two police officers that the accused acted suspiciously on two separate occasions, which needed only be minutes apart. More than 40% of those arrested and imprisoned under this Act were black youths. See *Police Against Black People*, Race and Class Pamphlet No 6, 1979.

The combined efforts of the Special Branch, the Special Patrol Group and the Immigration Intelligence Unit kept up the idea that blacks and Rastas were criminals by going out and arresting large numbers of black people, reinforcing the idea that areas like Chapeltown (Leeds), Brixton (London) and Handsworth were areas of high crime rate. It is only in Brixton that the links between the police and the white sociologists can compare with the work done in Handsworth. Periodic SPG invasions and drug busts were usually followed up by press reports on the need to control crime, and then social commentaries on "Police and Thieves on the Streets of Brixton". [35] These sociologists support the para-military assaults against the black community and Rastafari, saying:

> *"For too many black adolescents growing up in the slums of Britain and the Caribbean, crime is about the only freedom they have left."*

D. Dodd pointed to the 'emergence of a black street sub-culture in working class slums' in British cities within which there is meaning in music, there is meaning in ganja and there is meaning in crime. [36] Like the police inspectors who declared that black music induced terrorism, the researchers linked reggae music to criminality. Scores of young students in the universities followed the lead of Cashmore and Brown in their studies of the Rasta, instead of researching the State institutions which oppress blacks and Rastas alike – institutions such as the prison system, the mental hospitals and the courts.

Blacks, Rastas and the Prisons

It was inevitable given the sociological police stamp of criminality that a high proportion of black youths and Rastafarians would end up behind bars. Britain, with the highest prison population in Europe, has followed the same path of racist repression as the United States of America and South Africa – both societies well-known for anti-black histories.

By the end of 1980 in Britain the "number of black people in prison was 17% of the overall prison population and over 36% of the young prisoners are blacks". [37] Because figures from the Home Office on the number of blacks are not publicly available it is only when the information is leaked to organisations like *Radical Alternatives to Prison* that the black community understand the alarming numbers of black males in prisons and remand centres. The *Abolitionist* of Spring 1981 commented that:

> *"given that the total black population in Britain makes up only 3-4 percent of the population, black people are almost 5 times as likely to be imprisoned as whites."*

Britain's record in 1980 was worse than the United States, for while blacks comprised more than 20% of the population in the USA and 60% of the prison population, in the UK blacks were 3% of the whole population but 17% of the prison population. Black youths wearing the symbols of Rastafari who were incarcerated suffered the additional problem of having their locks forcibly cut, with those who resisted being dubbed as 'schizophrenic' and placed in mental institutions.

Locked in the Victorian structures called prisons, the young blacks and Rastafari came face to face with one of the crudest arms of the State, the Prison Service; and as in the USA, many became politicised, through the Black Prisoners Liberation Front, as they confronted racist prison officers. Prison officers in the UK have not hidden their open allegiance to the proto-fascist organisations such as the National Front, and these officers took pleasure in cutting the locks of the Rastas, or refusing to acknowledge their demand for special dietary considerations consistent with their adherence to Rastafari beliefs.

Frequent protests from inmates brought the problem of incarcerated Rastas to the wider society, but the State refused to acknowledge that there should be any special considerations for Rastas. While John Brown was in the midst of carrying out his research in Handsworth, the British State consulted the Jamaican State in the form of the Jamaican High Commission in London on whether to accede to the Rastas' demands that they should not be fed pork. These diplomatic representatives, carrying the same anti-Rasta bias of the Jamaican ruling class, concurred with the Home Office that Rastas should not be given any special considerations under prison rules.

A throughly racist document prepared in consultation with the Jamaican High Commission emanated as "Circular Instructions To All Prison Departments – 6/1976" – informing prison officers that Rastafari could not be registered as a religion for the purposes of section 10 (5) of the Prison Act 1952, and rule 10 of the Prison Rules 1964. It instructed that:

> *"In support of a request to be allowed to wear hair long, an inmate may claim he belongs to the Ethiopian Orthodox Church. It has been confirmed with the resident priests of the church that long hair is not a requirement and governors may therefore require hair to be cut."*[38]

Rejecting the claims of the Rastafari because "there is no central organisation of religious authority", the prison officers forcibly cut the hair of the Rastafari brethren, and this practice was only halted after the incessant protests from the Black Prisoners Welfare Scheme (BPWS).

Some of the Rastafarians who objected to having their symbol of black pride forcibly shorn were placed in mental institutions. The well-publicised case of Steve Thompson in 1980 exposed how Rastas who were fully mentally alert were placed in the notorious mental institutions of Rampton, Broadmoor, Moss Side and Park Lane. Steve Thompson was committed under Section 72 of the Mental Health Act, and it was only the concerted action of the BPWS which led to his release.

That the weapon of psychiatry was being used increasingly against black youths and Rastafari was confirmed in 1981, when Dr. Aggrey Burke wrote in *Mind Out* magazine that:

> *"black working class people are in far greater danger of being compulsorily admitted to hospital under a special section of the Mental Health Act and*

sometimes repatriated."[40]

Perfectly normal blacks and Rastafarians have been diagnosed as schizophrenic by white psychiatrists, and the black community is not organised to challenge this effort to call Rastas mad. Learning from the Jamaican State, which first placed Leonard Howell in a mental asylum for his proclamation of black nationalism, the British State were now using the centres of brutality, such as Rampton, to coerce Rastafari. Even the organ of the bourgeoisie, *The Times* newspaper, attested to this effort when it acknowledged in 1981 that "some doctors regarded Rastafarianism as a sign of personality disorder".[41] The area of mental health remains the least developed area of modern medicine, and this stamp did indeed condemn some youths to a life of mental instability.

Rasta and the Challenge of the Crisis

The economic and social crisis of Britain confronts the black population at the level of the State, and has been most sharply expressed in the treatment of the Rastafari. Black people were being challenged by every institution of the society, the police, the prisons, the educational apparatus, the ideological apparatus, the judiciary and the trade union bureaucracy. What was clear was that no amount of local authority grants nor adjustment could change this situation, and that for the whole population the coercive apparatus of the social democratic State had to be replaced with a new set of institutions which reflected the racial composition of the society, while at the same time laying the basis for ending the long history of exploitation.

Such a task required the full mobilisation of working people in confrontation with the capitalist class, which had sought protection from the supra-national European Economic Community (EEC). However, with the organised working class tied to the consumer ideology, and the Left dogged by ideological differences, black people and the Rasta bore the brunt of the crisis.

Small groups of blacks – organised in political groups, women's groups, the prison welfare scheme, church groups and parents' associations – responded to the crisis with a holding action, exposing the police excesses carried out during the para-military invasions by the Special Patrol Group, campaigning against 'SUS' laws, and fighting the racists of the National Front, while spreading internationalism by identifying positively with the struggles in Southern Africa.

For the most politically aware Rastas, the struggles in Africa were followed eagerly, and they looked favourably at the transition of Bob Marley, who moved from singing *Exodus* to supporting the struggles of African Freedom Fighters in Zimbabwe. At all stages the State sought to coopt the more articulate sections of Rastafari and the larger black community, through which the race relations industry blossomed under the umbrella of the Commission for Racial Equality.

Efforts by the State to coopt those Rastas whom they did not imprison could be measured by the Rastafari groups which were allocated grants through the Inner City Partnerships or those schemes which aimed at pacification. It was in Handsworth, Birmingham, that some misguided Rastas sought to persuade other brethren to cooperate with the police, who promised assistance in repatriating them to Africa. The police, along with other race relations 'experts', organised meetings between the Rastas and Home Office. Hence, the majority of Rastas who did not cooperate with the policing methods were open to police frame-ups, being picked up on SUS, or being faced with general harassment.

Community policing and the ganja trade were the twin methods of control adopted by the State, subsequent to the rejection of the Brown/Cashmore portrayal of the 'criminalised Dreads'. Perceiving the confusion of those who insisted on speaking of Haile Selassie, the police in Handsworth invited Eldridge Cleaver to Birmingham in 1978, to promote another version of alienation called 'Born Again' Christianity.

A clear pattern developed in the society where the police and the State used their understanding of the strong sentiments of the Rasta movement to foment confusion among those young people who turned their backs on the society. Not to be exposed by those political activists who protested against the extensive police operation, the police began to promise finance to certain sound systems, adding this activity to their already wide range of seduction, which included organising discos, youth clubs, football matches, camping trips and an annual festival.[43]

Effective and organised opposition among the Rastas to this police tactic was circumscribed by those Rasta organs which insisted on directing the youths towards daily reading of the bible instead of towards the pressing question of State harassment; and those Rastafari who published their ideas compounded the general lack of awareness about Africa with the kind of mystification and idealism characteristic of the separation between ideals and practice.

While leaders of RAM in Birmingham met with the Home Office to discuss repatriation movements – rekindling the possibilities of the joint repatriation used to repatriate black people in 1786 – the widely circulated paper of the Rastafari Universal Zion (RUZ), *Voice of Rasta,* abounded with erroneous comments on African history, and called on black youths to turn their backs on the political struggle in England for the promise of *repatriation*. *Voice of Rasta,* the monthly organ of RUZ, focussed on the questions of the divinity of Selassie, of the sectarian doctrinal differences with the Twelve Tribes of Israel, and of support for Idi Amin in Uganda.[44]

Following the lead of the black nationalists, whose 'bible' was Chancellor Williams' unscientific *The Destruction of Black Civilisation, Voice of Rasta* created more confusion, while seducing youths with their own pacification schemes. The pages of this newspaper were devoid of concern for those Rastafari who were in prison, those who were being placed in mental hospitals, those youths who were being harassed on the streets by the police.

Instead, the paper tried to recast visions of old African empires, promoting black business and forgetting the innumerable struggles facing the black community. The theological questions which were debated in the pages of the newspaper were a general reflection of the crisis of the Rastafari movement in the UK, a crisis which was reflected even in the interpersonal relationships between Rasta men and women.

Rastafari Women

Some of the negative ideas of the Rastafari philosophy are most clearly expressed in their treatment of women. However, the problems of inequality between Rasta men and women reflect part of the wider problem of the inequality between the sexes in present capitalist societies and the triple oppression of sex, race and class faced by black women.

Although some Rasta men view the equality of women as important, many continue to treat their women with some of the shabby practices generated by the frustration and anxiety of exploitation. Inevitably, the biblical justification is used, as in the case of the separation of women from men during menstruation. Quoting Leviticus, some Rastas fall back on the social practices of pre-capitalist societies to justify their social relations with women.

It is those Rasta brethren in Jamaica who have striven to rise above the legacy of unequal divisions of labour in the family who have taken the lead in extolling those women such as Queen Nzinga, Sojourner Truth, Harriet Tubman, Amy Jaques Garvey, Josina Machel, and Angela Davis, and other black women who have exhibited attributes of discipline and courage in the liberation struggle. These brethren have denounced the Anglo-American culture which glorifies sex and violence and exposed the insecurity of those who have made sex a commodity.

Rasta women have had to cope with some of the frustrations and desolation caused not only by chauvinist men, but by the State's incarceration of an inordinate number of young Rasta men. While struggling to maintain a sense of dignity and decorum, Rasta women have had to grapple with mistreatment, at the same time ensuring that there was no deepening rift between Rasta men and women.

Though there were no overt signs of striving Rasta women in Britain in the early days, in other parts of the Rasta world some young women began to combat the negative ideas about women in reggae music. Recognising the importance of reggae music in communication between Rastas, researcher Makeda Silvera travelled to Jamaica to speak to those reggae artists who still sang degrading songs about women.[46]

Black women have developed organisations to address some of the problems of black women, but they have increasingly found it necessary to distance themselves from those feminists who reinforce racist myths about black men being rapists. Those who babble feminist slogans and generalise about the sexism of Rasta are a far cry from the courage and strength of Angela Davis, who combines her analysis of the exploitation of black women with the whole problem of racism, showing how the rape charge in the US was indiscriminately used against black men.[47]

Equally significant is the quest by Rasta women and black women to distance themselves from those women such as Viola Burnham, the wife of the President of Guyana, who speak on Women's Liberation at international meetings but who derive their legitimacy from the position of their man, thus reinforcing the notion of the inferiority of women.

To be sure, Rastamen need to be liberated from the myths about women and the vestiges of inequalities in the family, but in their day-to-day life they decry the impoverished condition of a Babylonian culture where sexual alienation and the pornography industry of the advanced capitalist countries have turned orgasms into a commodity. Rasta women are part of the resistance to the powerful tendencies of capitalism to shape women into mindless consumers, and while this resistance is in the main passive, other organised sections of the black women's movement in England have begun to struggle against those medical experiments which are carried out on black women.

The much publicised virginity tests carried out by the Home Office on Asian women is only one of the many tests being carried out on non-white women. In England, doctors have been experimenting on black women with the contraceptive injection Depo Provera, without telling them of the side-effects – of the risk of cancer in the cervix and the lining of the womb, and of the malformation of the foetus in women who are already pregnant when given the injection.[48] Conscious and organised black women have exposed the racism in the health service as part of the general struggles of the black masses.

Whither Rasta? From cultural resistance to organised resistance

Cabral's admonition on the need to condemn the regressive elements of a cultural force became urgent in England as the authoritarian State employed the carrot and the stick in their reaction to the social force called Rasta. But because the State could not plan class struggle or permanently impose those 'leaders' who competed for local authority grants, and acted as liaison officers, the cultural resistance embodied in reggae music acted as the main source of information and inspiration.

Like the neighbourhood sound systems of urban working class Jamaicans, in the principal black communities of England the sound system movement developed as a popular institution, usually under Rastafari leadership. So important were the sound men like Sir Coxsone, Jah Shaka, Fatman Hi Fi, Soprano B, Quaker City and others, that when the pacifiers in Birmingham attempted to control Rastas, they undertook to finance their own sound systems.

Coinciding with the development of the sound system, a unique reggae sound was developing in Britain, with bands such as Steel Pulse, Reggae Regulars, Misty, Matumbi, Aswad, Black Slate, Amba and the Cimarons. These bands carried the culture of resistance to their concerts and were prominent in the cultural presentations of the Anti-Nazi League. Reggae culture in the UK was part of the *embryo* of the diversified culture of a non-racial Britain.

No effort by the State to control Rasta could control reggae; so there was a direct plan by the police to break up blues dances by using the practice of measuring noise levels. A Conservative Member of Parliament gave public support to the police raids on black people's cultural events by declaring that 'black people's parties were a source of nuisance'. Seeking to create scapegoats for the rising unemployment and unabating economic crisis, the Prime Minister declared that British communities were 'being swamped by' black people.

These statements gave open support to the racists of the National Front and their supporters in the Special Patrol Group, who went on to kill the anti-racist demonstrator, Blair Peach.[49] Even though the State exonerated the murderers of Blair Peach, two separate inquiries exposed the racism of the police, especially the SPG. One of the officers of the SPG who was on duty when Blair Peach was killed had in his house:

> *"A leadweighted plaited leather-covered stick, Nazi regalia, bayonets, German awards and medals from World War I and II, daggers, whips, and swords. Weapons fascinated him and he collected stamps."*[50]

Armed racists in the SPG were supplemented by the armed racists of the British Movement, Column 88, and the right-wing movements who were determined to *Keep Britain White.* At the end of 1980 the tensions ignited by the State were fanned by the media, which complained of a noisy 10-day party held by black youths in Birmingham. The impression given by the police reports, the radio and the television was similar to the essays by the police inspector which said that reggae was an 'inspiration to terrorism'.

Reggae culture served as an antidote to the culture of domination which is embodied in the glossiness of the empty lives shown on Dallas and other such television programmes. Reggae culture was under attack as part of the wider assault on the non-white population, from the published recommendations of the Royal Commission on Criminal Procedure to the passing of the Nationality Act. This Act promises the spectre of another forced repatriation, by laying the basis for different categories of citizenship which would render two million non-whites stateless.

Those Rasta organs which were calling for repatriation now had to decide whether they were going to go to Africa by their own will, or give succour to those racists who wanted to repatriate all non-white peoples.* Those Rastas who were meeting the Home Office and calling for repatriation did not understand the full meaning of this Act to black people, nor did those who arranged the meeting tell them that already the Home Office was repatriating non-white peoples under Section 29 of the 1971 Immigration Act.

*Ernest Cashmore had perceived this in his study of the Rastafari, and his chapter on "The Spell of Africa" presented those sociological code words which could in future support a racist project of repatriation. Repatriation remained a strong sentiment among many black workers who were becoming of pensionable age, but once a group of blacks acquiesced to the racist schemes, there would be no way to distinguish who wanted to go and who wanted to stay. This was the case of the 1786 deportation when a perfectly humanitarian scheme by the anti-slavery leader, Granville Sharp, was taken over by racists.

The New Cross Massacre and Uprisings

This then was the political climate in which Rastas and the black working class were roused from their stupor by the New Cross Massacre, in January 1981. The death of 13 black children had taken place when they were having a party at their home at 439 New Cross Road, London. It took the tragedy of the massacre to stir the mass of black people to action in a massive protest march on March 2, 1981.[51]

The coalition of black people who formed the New Cross Action Committee carried the horrific story of the massacre and the police cover-up to all corners of the society, exposing the media/police project to blame the victims of the massacre for the fire. Police officers had by-passed the racists who had written letters declaring how happy they were to see the "niggers going up in flames". Some Rastas joined the march, playing the role of drumming and chanting during the eight-hour march of protest and confrontation.

The parallels between the early Rasta of Jamaica in 1938 and the Rasta movement in England at the end of 1980 are tempting, but while the society of Jamaica was stirred by a general mobilisation of the working class, in England the Left and the organised working class movement had remained silent on the racist murders of black people. Linton Kwesi Johnson, the reggae poet, in a way articulated the sentiments of black people when he spoke of the fact that it was black people who were riding the storm:

"mek dem gwaan
now it calm
but a wi who haffi really ride di staam

wat a cheek
dem t'ink wi meek
an' wi can't speak up fi wi self

wat a cheek
dem t'ink wi weak
an' wi can't stan up pan wi feet

but mek dem gwaan
now it calm
far in di en' is wi who haffi ride di staam

di SWP can't set wi free
di IMG can't dhu it fi wi
di Communist Pawty, cho, dem too awty-fawty
an' di laybahrites dem naw goh fite fi wi rites

so mek dem gwaan
now it calm
but a wi who haffi really ride di staam

di CRE can't set wi free
di TUC can't dhu it fi wi

di Liberal Pawty dem is nat very hawty
and di Tory Pawty a noh fi wi pawty

mek dem gwaan
now it calm
an' in di en' is wi who haffi ride di staam"*

Linton Kwesi Johnson, who had found it necessary to distance himself from those Rastas who insisted upon reading the bible, was in his poetry helping to instil the confidence in black people necessary to fight back. The Black People's Day of Action in March had stirred the black population to recognise the links between the murders in El Salvador and in Atlanta, and the South African bombings of Angola and Mozambique.

Cultural resistance, which had flowed from the Rasta movement, and served to strengthen the resolve of the youths, was being challenged, for the attacks on the black community called for the forging of concrete links between black political groups so that they could rise above the factionalism and sectarianism which had spread after the Mangrove trials. But the struggle in Britain was not waiting for the kind of organisation, discipline and ideology which was necessary, for as the crisis deepened, with three million unemployed, the police – with their terrorist invasions of black neighbourhoods – had precipitated a major uprising in Britain in 1981.

Uprising in 1981

Black youths made history in Britain in July 1981 when they confronted the agents of repression and took the lead in accelerating the class struggle in a way which had not been seen on this island since the revolution of the 17th century. For two weeks in July 1981 these youths fought battles which were described by one police chief as 'urban guerilla warfare', as the prolonged nocturnal confrontations on the streets exposed the pent-up anger of black people and their allies.

In the process of this rebellion, the youths took the lead in beating back the organised racists, and made a fundamental break with the century-old compromise of social democratic appeasement and bribery. At the same time they engendered a new multi-racial unity, showing that multi-racialism cannot be legislated for but must spring from the struggles of the Asian, black and white working people. The developments came from pure spontaneous revolt, and yet the labour movement remained silent as the State responded with CS gas, water cannons, rubber bullets and the opening up of military camps for the black freedom fighters.

* Taken from "Independent Intavenshan," poem by Linton Kwesi Johnson, *Inglan is a Bitch*, Linton Kwesi Johnson, Race Today Publications, 1980.

Brixton, in South London, had led the way for the resolve of 'Come What May We're Here To Stay'; and 'Blood A Go Run If Justice No Come', which had been the cry of the Black People's Day of Action, was turned into action in April when for three nights the people fought a police invasion called *Swamp 81*, an invasion which stopped and searched 1,000 persons in one week.[53]

The Brixton Uprising, coming a year after a major revolt in Bristol, had pointed the direction for other black youths who had assured their white neighbours that they were not racially intolerant, but that they would fight the police repression which was one indicator of the militarist ideology of the political leaders. Black youths had thwarted the national contingency plans of the militarists, who, after Bristol 1980, had drawn up a 'national' aid exercise to see how quickly police support units could come to the aid of the other forces.

These youths were leading the struggle against the monetarists/militarists who supported the deployment of the capitalist bomb, the neutron bomb, and would spend £6 million on Trident Nuclear missiles, while old people died of the cold and the social stock of the society deteriorated beyond repair.

Asian youths in Southall took their own stand against the invasion of their community by skinheads who were urged on to racist violence by the music of repression, which was the culture of the racists. Ignoring the police and sociological advice that they should be afraid of the Westindian robbers and muggers,[54] a new spirit of cooperation was founded between Asian and Westindian youths as they drove the racists out of their community.

This Westindian-Asian unity was a valid testament of the future unity of the working class in Britain, and this unity was even more valid because it was created in struggle. Meanwhile, the unity of the oppressors was exposed by the skinheads' use of police truncheons and riotshields when the police arrived to assist the invaders.

The battle of Southall on July 3, 1981 threw further panic into the operations of national contingency policing, for simultaneous and spontaneous revolts erupted that same evening in Liverpool, where the black poor defended their right to own means of transport and not to be suspected of stealing every article in their possession. Liverpool 8, called Toxteth – the concentration of blacks a stone's throw from the infamous Merseyside slave docks – stood out for its levels of substandard housing and for its level of unemployment – reaching 50% of the workforce.

It was in Liverpool that the black and white residents had come together in a new unity, which did not allow the media, the police, nor the right-wing room to whip up racist sentiments. Unity was amply demonstrated by the resolve of the youths to fight the police and to burn down the symbols of racial discrimination in their midst. When the police reinforcements from Manchester and other areas could not defeat the youths, the police resorted to using CS gas, water cannons and the failed technology of repression which had become commonplace on the streets of colonial Ireland.

Before the State could survey the damage and produce the water cannons, Manchester erupted, creating logistical problems for the police and military, whose forward planning scenario of 'Low Intensity Operations' had not foreseen that the *uprising* would be so national in scope. It was in Manchester that the SAS had carried out practice runs of how to seal off black neighbourhoods, for the black workers of Moss Side were concentrated in an architectural monstrosity designed for effective military control.

However, the scenario planners of community policing and the SAS, who were attempting to seal off communities,did not expect the levels of organisation and ingenuity from the black youths and their allies. The police were frightened by the frontal attack of the youths, who stormed the Moss Side police station to "set prisoners free". The frontal attack abated, again only after reinforcements were rushed in to support the brutal reaction of the Manchester police. Doctors who treated the injured in Manchester said that they had never before treated such injuries in peacetime.

Police brutality did not stop the black tide of resistance, for the whole society woke up every morning to the news that other centres of oppression had gone up in flames. Wolverhampton, Leeds, Birmingham, Leicester, Southampton, Newcastle, Hull, and different parts of London (Brixton, Wood Green, Battersea, Dalston and Notting Hill) all erupted, while white youths from Newcastle, who were just as tired of the emptiness of unemployment and the alienation of 'space invaders' machines, joined blacks in the ten days which shook the ruling class of Britain.

While the liberal establishment hoped to stir the Conservative leadership to revitalise the social democratic answer of more grants, instead of tackling the fundamental problem, the State responded to the uprising with the long experience of colonial terrorism. To augment the CS gas canisters and water cannons, the police were issued with armoured cars, and military camps were opened to facilitate the mass arrests which were being contemplated. The short-sighted leadership of the labour movement, steeped in the economism of wage increases, did not realise that the camps could in future be used against militant workers.

Black youths on the streets, though unorganised and facing daily repression, demonstrated amazing bravery and ingenuity. Numerous episodes could be recounted to show how the spirit of resistance of the slaves remains alive in the streets of England. The theoreticians of human subjugation could not understand the ferocity of those youths in Wolverhampton who stormed the magistrates courts to free the arrested youths; of those brave youths in Moss Side who seized the police stations; of those in Brixton who formed barricades and cut in on police radios to divert them so that they could make frontal attacks on the citadels of 'Babylon'. For these youths had the words of Marley ringing in their ears: "Let The Prisoners Free". It needed the lessons of the Paris Commune of 1871 for them to take the lead towards not just fire and looting, but storming and seizing the State. This had to await the stirring of the organised working class.

Even if the rebellion was short-lived, they created a new political situation. The police liaison project which integrated false Dreads and hustlers into the ganja/informer network crumbled in the black communities. Nowhere was this more evident than in Handsworth, Birmingham, where the police superintendent ally of the false Dreads was stoned. Not even a rearguard appeal for support in *Police Review*, 31 July 1981, orchestrated by his spokesperson, John Brown, could save his experiment.

The military planners had taken the upper hand, for colonial terrorism was about to come home to roost. The Home Office had invited the South African police to learn how to carry out similar projects in Soweto, but now it was the turn for the British police to learn from their South African brothers.

Overt and covert military cooperation between the British and the South African State were to show the Rastas very clearly that they could contribute to the African liberation struggle by fighting British imperialism in the streets and towns, helping to lift Europe out of its history of racism. The struggle in South Africa challenged humanity with the future of either socialism or barbarity.

Conclusion

As in 1938 in Jamaica, the ideological questions of Rasta took second place to the concrete struggles of the people. Rasta philosophy – which had been ritualised into a religious form in Britain – though giving some confidence to meet the cultural onslaught of the society, could not assist the struggles of the people. No longer was Ethiopia serving as a positive external reference point, for the early anti-fascist Haile Selassie had matured into a despotic monarch whom the people had had to remove from the Imperial Throne.

The Black People's Day of Action had carried forward the more progressive Rastafarians who joined the march and the ensuing uprisings. Rastas who marched under the slogans "Come What May We're Here to Stay" and "Blood A Go Run If Justice No Come" were affirming their rights to live and struggle in Britain for a non-racial society, free from exploitation.

It remained the right of Rastas or black people to repatriate to Africa or the Caribbean, but Rastas were being challenged to change their call to *liberation not repatriation* in the face of those racists who wanted to deport blacks wholesale. Moreover, the concrete example of the settlement at Shashamane, Ethiopia, demonstrated that those who laboured under negative ideas in Europe or the Caribbean would carry those ideas to Africa. This question is explored in the next chapter, along with the way in which the heightened struggles in Southern Africa were calling on the Rasta in Britain and Europe to consider the words of Peter Tosh: "We Must Fight Against Apartheid."

The uprisings had foreshadowed the need to illuminate the social realities of Europe and Africa with a perspective that was not only anti-racist but also anti-capitalist. Out of the spontaneous struggles, positive aspects of political life were emerging, for the repression pushed political groups to define strategies for collecting the various grievances that represent the interests of the mass of the exploited. In the long run, to define the major contradictions and to unite black and white workers around these contradictions, the Rastas were being called upon to join the struggle.

FOOTNOTES

1. *The Autobiography of Malcolm X* told of the impact that Africa had on his philosophy. For the role of black Americans in the war against Italy see William A. Scott, *A Study of Afro-American and Ethiopian Relations 1896-1941*, Ph.D. Princeton, 1971.
2. "Southern Africa and Liberation Support in Afro-America and the West Indies" by Walter Rodney, paper presented at *Conference on The Socio-Economic Trends and Policies in Southern Africa*, Dar-es-Salaam, November-December 1975.
3. One of the foremost publications of this period was the *African World* which sought to carry on the traditions of the *Negro World* of Marcus Garvey. This paper was published by the Malcolm X State University in Greensboro, North Carolina, 1969.
4. The statement of the chairperson of the ALSC, Owusu Sauduki, at the Sixth Pan-African Congress carried the class position that the black struggle should be against all forms of oppression. For the full text of his speech see Horace Campbell, ed., *Pan-Africanism: Struggle Against Neo-Colonialism and Imperialism*, documents and statements from the Sixth Pan-African Congress 1974, Afro-Carib Publications, Toronto, 1975, pp 103-113.
5. The debate became polarised around the persons of Haki Madhubuti and Amiri Baraka, who in the previous years were erstwhile nationalists. See the *Black Scholar* debates, especially *Black Scholar*, October 1974.
6. Carlos Moore, the black Cuban had published the provocative pamphlet *Were Marx and Engels White Racists?*, Institute of Positive Education, Chicago, 1971. He answered the question in the affirmative by using a selection of quotations. Moore also alleged that the Cuban revolution was a racist revolution and his views were widely circulated in the USA.
7. The operations of the USA were spelt out by the Head of the CIA in the Angolan War. John Stockwell, *In Search of Enemies*, Fontana Books, 1978, London. Roy Innis, the director of CORE, volunteered to provide black mercenaries to fight on the side of the South Africans and the forces of Jonas Savimbi, UNITA.
8. Reference to this report is to be found in *Globe and Mail*, Toronto, June 11, 1975, p.3. Copies of this report were sent to every major police force in Ontario, Canada.
9. Transcript of *C.B.S. Sixty Minutes*, Vol XII No 7, Sunday, October 28, 1979, USA.
10. Dennis Forsyte, *Let The Niggers Burn*, Our Generation Press, Montreal, 1971.
11. These allegations were made on the front page of the *Globe and Mail* on June 11, 1975. This detailed analysis by Peter Moon said that Rastafarians were responsible for violent crimes, including murder, armed robbery and drug trafficking.
12. Statement produced by the Tacky Study Group for a joint meeting held at the UNIA, Friday June 13, 1975.
13. The most celebrated case was that of the spy, Warren Hart, who was seconded from the FBI to the Royal Canadian Mounted Police to spy on the black community in Canada. His activities as an agent provocateur sent many young activists to prison, and his case came to light when he expanded his activities to spy on the Solicitor General of Canada. See details in *Today Magazine*, June 13, 1981, Toronto, Canada.
14. Walter Rodney, "Africa in Europe and the Americas", in *Cambridge History of Africa*, Richard Gray, ed., Cambridge, 1975. This piece traced the history of racism itself. See also James Walvin, *Black and White: The Negro and English Society 1555-1945*, Allan Lane, London, 1973.
15. Claudia Jones, "The Caribbean Community in Britain", *Black Liberator*, December, 1978, p.29. Claudia Jones was one of the foremost black activists in England in the post-war era. Her study was one of the early black statements on racism encountered by blacks on arrival in England.
16. V.I. Lenin, *British Labour and British Imperialism*, Lawrence and Wishart, London, 1969. See also Samir Amin, "Capitalism, State Collectivism and Socialism", *Monthly Review*, June, 1977.
17. There are, of course, major exceptions such as the militant mineworkers. For an analysis of this process see William Brown, ed., *The Changing Contours of British Industrial Relations*, Basil Blackwell, Oxford, 1981.
18. The black worker in the UK is strategically located in the transportation and health services of the economy. For an analysis of the skills brought to the society of blacks see Peter. L. Wright, *The Coloured Worker in British Industry*, Oxford University Press, 1968. This book contains a useful appendix on the location of black workers in the industries of the West Midlands.
19. See Clifford S. Hill, *West Indian Migrants in the British Churches*, OUP. There have been numerous accounts of the resilience of the Pentecostal churches in Britain. These churches continue to be the most organised and the strongest black institutions in the society.
20. Bernard Coard, *How The West Indian Child Is Made Educationally Subnormal in the British School System*, New Beacon Books, 1971.
21. *West Indian Children in Our Schools*, Report of the Committee of Inquiry into the Education of Children from Ethnic Minority Groups, chaired by Anthony Rampton, CMND, June, 1981.
22. *Rasta Voice*, No 87, Kingston, Jamaica. Research carried out by an undergraduate student at Sussex University on the *Rastafari Movement in Britain* showed that it was the 'bad experience' at school which led many youths to Rastafari. See Vernella Fuller, *The Rastafari Movement In Britain*, unpublished undergraduate thesis, Sussex University, 1977. This theme had been developed by Len Garrison in *Black*

Youth and Rastafarianism, ACER, London, 1979.

23. Quoted in *South London Press*, October 8, 1976. Past issues of *Rasta Cry* can be found in the Westminister Public Library, London.
24. Barry Chevannes, "The Impact of the Ehiopian Revolution on The Rastafari Movement", in *Socialism*, WLL, Kingston, Jamaica, 1975.
25. *Policing the Crisis, Mugging, the State and Law and Order*, Stuart Hall, et al. ed., McMillan Press, 1978.
26. *National Institute of Economic Review*, May 1981, p.4. For figures of the unemployment in the West Midlands see *Employment Gazette*, July 1981. So desperate were the British in maintaining a semblance of a motor car industry in 1980 that the *Economist*, Nov. 8, 1980, queried "If BL (British Leyland) did not exist, would Britain have to invent it?"
27. Paul Gilroy et al., "White Sociology, Black Struggle", paper presented to the British Sociology Association, Brighton, 1980.
28. *Shades of Grey*, Police/West Indian Relations in Handsworth, by John Brown, for Cranfield Police Studies, 1977, p.3.
29. *Rastaman, The Rastafari Movement in England*, Ernest Cashmore, George Allen & Unwin, London, 1979, p.2.
30. ibid., p.23.
31. ibid., p.26.
32. (a) ibid., pp 84-88. Like Brown he blamed the problems of black youth on the "exacerbating impact of familial fragmentation after migration to England".
(b) "Rastafari Is An Excuse Not A Religion", unpublished paper by Inspector M.V. Boast, West Midland Police, n/d, p.12.
33. Cashmore, op. cit., p.176.
34. *Police Against Black People*, Race and Class Pamphlet, No 6, 1979, p.5.
See also (i) Derek Humphrey, *Police Power and Black People*, Granada Publishing, London, 1972.
(ii) "Up Against the Police", *Race Today*, July/August 1976.
(iii) *Final Report of the Working Party into Community/Police Relations in Lambeth*, Borough of Lambeth, 1981.
(iv) "Criminal Procedure and the Black Masses in the United Kingdom", A.X. Cambridge, *Black Liberator*, December 1978.
35. D. Dodd, "Police and Thieves in the Streets of Brixton", *New Society*, March 16, 1978.
36. *New Society*, March 16, 1978, p.600. For an equivocal analysis of Dodd and standard sociology on the Rastafari see Robert Miles, "Between Two Cultures, The Case of Rastafarianism", *SSRC Working Papers on Ethnic Relations*, No 10, University of Bristol, 1978.
37. *Journal of Radical Alternatives To Prison*, No 8, Spring 1981.
38. Annex A to *Circular Instruction 60/1976*, Home Office. See also questions raised in Parliament on this question in *Hansard*, April 16, 1981. Further inquiries by this author at the Home Office led to the disclosure that a new circular instruction on Rastafari was prepared in July 1981.
39. *Guardian*, 15 January, 1981.
40. *Mind Out*, May 1981.
41. *Times*, 23 February, 1981.
42. See *Daily Star*, May 8, 1981, for picture of a 'Rasta' in a three-piece suit patrolling the streets of Handsworth with the Chief Inspector. This particular Rasta attempted to break up a number of political meetings in Birmingham in 1981. After the uprisings of 1981 he led his own demonstration of young misguided Rasta through the streets of Handsworth. See also *Guardian*, July 7, 1981, for an analysis of the efforts of the Police Superintendent towards community policing. In Brixton the police had recruited a leading sound systems man to act as a community liaison officer.
43. The energies invested by the police to mobilise the Rastas for the annual festival organised by the police can be gathered in the analysis of the 1981 event by John Brown in *Police Review*, 31 July, 1981. That this project is not limited to Birmingham can be seen from the elation of the *Times* at the Rasta celebration on the day of the Royal Wedding, in Brixton. See *Times* 30 July, 1981, "Brixton Rastas Dance For Peace", p.4. For a central analysis of the "Policing Methods in Handsworth" see *Caribbean Times*, July 24, 1981, p.2.
44. *Voice of Rasta*, Aug.-Sept. 1979. See "Nyerere: An African Enigma".
45. *Voice of Rasta*, Feb.-March 1980.
46. This project was undertaken by Makeda Patricia Silvera in Toronto at York University, where she had undertaken this research. In Toronto Makeda Silvera and Charmaine Montague had taken on the active leadership of the progressive Rastas in the Rasta Cultural Workshop. See interview in *Sunday Gleaner Magazine*, Feb. 10, 1980.
47. Angela Davis, "Rape, Racism and the Capitalist Setting", *Black Scholar*, April 1978, p.24. She shows how of the 445 men executed for rape between 1930 and 1967, 405 were black. See also Angela Davis – *Women, Race and Class*.
48. See *Speak Out*, No 1, 1980, by Black Women's Group in Brixton, London, England.
49. The studies showed that the police were responsible for this murder at the anti-racist rally in Southall in 1979.
(i) *Licence To Kill*, The Blair Peach Case, by David Ranson, published by the Friends of Blair Peach

Committee, London, 1980.
(ii) *Southall 23 April 1979*, Report of the unofficial Committee of Inquiry, published for the National Council For Civil Liberties, London, 1980.

50. *Licence To Kill*, op. cit., p.23. For a consistent account of the links between the police and the racists in England see issues of *Searchlight*.
51. Horace Campbell, "Blacks Marching Forward in England", *Caribbean Times*, March 13, 1981.
52. Linton Kwesi Johnson, "Independent Intavenshan" in *Inglan is a Bitch*, Race Today Publications, 1980.
53. "Uprising Inna Brixton", *Grassroots*, June-July 1981. For the role of the police see *State Research Bulletin* No 24, June-July, 1981.
54. Both the police and the State intellectuals had attempted to exploit the cultural differences between the Asian and Caribbean communities. In Handsworth the Chief Superintendent of the Police explained that the police were the only protection for Asians against Westindian robbers. See *Caribbean Times*, July 24, 1981, p.2. Ernest Cashmore, in his book *Rastaman*, had spoken of how Rastafari had caused concern to Indians and Pakistanis, see *Rastaman*, p.185.

CHAPTER EIGHT

Repatriation and Rastafari, the Ethiopian Revolution and the Settlement in Shashamane

Back to Africa

From the outset of capture in Africa, the African slaves were determined to go back to the land of their forefathers – a determination which was expressed in many manners, most overtly in songs of freedom. These songs were often the deepest expressions of memory – a racial memory. Racial consciousness became linked to the idea of Africa in differing forms, whether in the form of support for the cause of African liberation or the longing for Africa, which was translated by those who physically returned to reside in Africa.

Back To Africa as a philosophy among Africans in the West is as old an idea as slavery. The history of humiliation and dehumanisation in the West deepened the longing for a place in the world to which blacks could turn. The return to Africa – called *Repatriation* – meant that those who returned took the values that they had internalised in captivity with them to Africa, and nowhere was this better expressed than in Liberia, where some of those who escaped bondage in America and the Westindies in the 18th century imposed a conception of race consciousness which allowed room for racists in England to use the idea of repatriation to deport hundreds of blacks from England. The conception of repatriation proved compatible with the ideas of humanitarians, black nationalists and segregationists, and in 20th century England, with some Rastas and the British State.

The elements from the Rastafari movement in England who have met with the State, calling for repatriation, would do well to study the historical record; for in the consciousness of the British ruling class, the solution to the 'race problem' would be to repeat the 1786 scheme of rounding up black people and 'repatriating' them anywhere, as long as it was outside Britain. The lessons of the unity of positive and negative ideas in the history of repatriation becomes more urgent as the struggles in Ethiopia force Rastas in Shashamane (Ethiopia) to come to terms with the realities of the search for social change, or to continue to insult their neighbours by putting up pictures of Haile Selassie in their homes.

It remains the right of any black person to repatriate to Africa but this individual, or even collective, right should never be allowed to be used against the overwhelming majority of black people who want to struggle and change the society they live in, whether it is in Brazil, the USA, Jamaica, Grenada, the United Kingdom, or France. Moreover, the struggles in Africa should encourage Rastas to conceptualise the problems of Pan-Africanism as forging links with social groups, progressive groups, so that they can break the old preoccupation with kings, empires and dynasties.

Pan-Africanism, in the era of socialism and national liberation, must seek to develop an anti-capitalist and anti-imperialist perspective, one that speaks to the oppression of all people. If this is not pursued, then those Rastafari who go back to Africa will find themselves beach-heads for imperialism, as happened with the Liberian project. Three concrete experiences of repatriation will now be analysed in light of these considerations: (i) the Sierra Leone Experience, (ii) the Liberian Experience, and (iii) the Shashamane Experience.

The Slaves and the Concept of Repatriation

When the slaves saw the length of the journey across 'the great river' (the Atlantic Ocean), they realised the difficulties they would have in trying to escape and return to Africa; and many slaves unsuccessfully attempted to seize ships in mid-ocean to return to Africa. The successful seizure of the *Amistad,* leading to the legal struggles by slaves to reach Africa, is but one episode in the long history of the struggles of African peoples in the West. During the period of captivity, despite the brutality of the masters, the slave was never totally subdued, manifesting differing forms of resistance, whether individual acts of resistance – such as refusing to work; or collective acts – such as rebellions.

Frequent rebellions and revolts by the Africans led to a high death rate among the slaves, on the whole a courageous people who did not fear death. To considerable numbers of Africans, death was merely another phase in the life cycle, and the funeral arrangements were designed to assure a safe journey for the deceased back to the land of their forefathers.

Orlando Patterson, in his book on *Slavery in Jamaica,* quoted the records of slave masters who observed the funeral rites of slaves, noting the belief in "a return to Africa after death," claiming that:

> *"they took on death as a blessing.... are quite transported to think that their slavery is near an end, and that they shall revisit their old friends and acquaintances."*[1]

Funeral rites were accordingly a jovial and festive occasion, for the friends and family wished the deceased a safe journey to Africa. A meal was prepared for the departed and after the grave was filled up, "they placed a soup at the head and a bottle of rum at the feet." The slave master who observed the proceedings in the 17th century attested to the screams, which were not the "effect of Grief but of Joy; they beat their wooden Drums, and the women with their Rattles made a hideous noise." This drumming and noise was the joy expressed by those Africans who believed that on death they were joining their ancestors.*

As generations of Africans lived in Jamaica, the belief in the actual return to Africa subsided and the family plot became the symbol of the link with the ancestors; so much so that when slavery was abolished and the planters saw this important attachment to the burial plot, they attempted to tax the ancestral burial grounds in Jamaica in their efforts to keep the ex-slaves tied to the plantations. But some slaves never forgot their wish to return to Africa before reaching the spirit world, and the Maroons, who were sent to Nova Scotia after the Second Maroon War, literally fought their way back to Africa – the first Jamaicans to be *repatriated* to the continent of Africa.

The Sierra Leone Scheme

The first settlement of blacks from outside Africa in Sierra Leone, which the Maroons joined from Nova Scotia, were in the main black people who had been gathered up in England and 'dumped' in Sierra Leone in 1787. After the American War of Independence in 1783, the black community in England was increased after thousands of black soldiers and sailors, who had fought for the British in the American War of Independence, took up residence in Britain – primarily in London.

The British army, having found the blacks useful as frontline soldiers in their war, settled the blacks in London; but no sooner had they been demobilised than there was a public uproar over their presence. As noted in the last chapter, without jobs, proper housing or welfare, the black people joined the ranks of the London poor, eliciting hostile treatment from the ruling class.

Edward Long, a planter from Jamaica, wrote a pamphlet in 1772, prior to the demobilisation, saying that:

> *"the public good of this Kingdom requires that some restraints should be laid on the unnatural increase of blacks imported into it."*

With language similar to that of Enoch Powell in 1968, and of the newspapers of the British Movement in 1980, the pamphlet warned the population of the potential threat of miscegenation.[2]

Black people were blamed for every social evil visited upon England, leading to suggestions that black people should be 'dumped' outside of England, whether it was in the Bahamas, Gambia or Sierra Leone. *The Committee for the Black Poor,* the eighteenth century equivalent of the present-day Commission for Racial Equality, entertained plans by the Government to remove blacks, while they dispensed with the funds from the Treasury to maintain the ex-soldiers. The daily assembling at Mile End and Paddington for food was the instrument for the capture and forced expulsion of these blacks from England.

Granville Sharp, the anti-slavery activist, had considered the possibility of alleviating the problem of the misery of London blacks by supporting the

*Such a belief is still present today where urbanised Africans insist on being buried in their village so that they can rejoin their ancestors.

voluntary return of those who wanted to return to Africa. Sharp and his supporters, while embarking on a humanitarian scheme, intended that the settlement would show that free capitalist relations could replace capitalist slave relations on the West African Coast. Conceptualised as the alternative to slavery, where the trade in commodities was replaced by the trade in human flesh, the humanitarians found their scheme actively supported by the British Treasury – which saw that this scheme would rid London of the blacks. F. Shyllon, who documented the convergence of purpose between the State and the anti-slavery activists, said:

> *"the Government sanctioned the payment of public money for the repatriation of the black poor, and pending their deportation, payment of public funds for their maintenance. In all, the Government granted £40,562.10d 'for the maintenance, clothing and carrying of Free Blacks to Africa.' The Government's eagerness to get the blacks out of the country cut through Whitehall's red tape at every stage of the proceedings."*[3]

Rastafari in Britain who march in Birmingham for repatriation can learn a lot from Shyllon's documentation of how the British went through the streets of London, picking up black people to put on the boat to Africa, irrespective of whether they wanted to go to Africa or to remain in Britain. There were of course a number of Africans who were willing to go back to start a settlement, but the vast majority were unwilling to be 'dumped' in Africa without protection. Not that they did not want to go home, but slavery still raged on the West African Coast and they faced the prospect of recapture into the slave trade.

The slaving interests on the West Coast were opposed to settlement, but with the support of the British State, which was urged on by Wilberforce, a Royal Charter was granted to a company to oversee the interests of the settlers. *The Sierra Leone Company,* established in 1791, became the first of the nefarious trading companies which ushered in the transition from slavery to colonialism in West Africa. By the end of the 18th century, slavery stood in the path of further accumulation, so Sierra Leone became Africa's experimental station for the production of cotton, rice, sugar, tobacco, indigo and other cash crops.

A black dream of freedom had been turned into a nightmare for those forced to return, and the Sierra Leone settlement became an experimental colony of Britain, close to a hundred years before the partitioning of Africa. Subsequent to the abolition of the slave trade in 1807, the British Navy used Sierra Leone as the port for returning Africans captured at sea. There was in Sierra Leone a level of tranquillity compared to the slave hunts which continued in other parts of the West Coast of Africa, right up to the middle of the 19th century.

The Liberian Settlement

"The love of liberty brought us here." Slogan of Americo-Liberians

Liberian history since 1820 is one of the salient examples of the unity of positive and negative ideas embedded in the ideas of racial consciousness. The

Liberian colony was founded by blacks from the United States who wanted to escape the servitude of nascent US capitalists. Between 1820 and 1865 approximately 15,000 black Americans, the largest number of Africans from the West ever to return to Africa, settled in the area called Liberia, under the protection of the American State.

Leaving behind the values of slavery, the blacks who searched for freedom in emigration carried to Africa the values of competition, capitalist accumulation and individualism, and all the ideas they had internalised in the US. These emigrants received protection from the US State, because as early as 1817 the fathers of the American Revolution, agonising over the status of freed slaves who fought on their side during the American War of Independence, felt that the only solution was to 'dump' them in Africa. The American Colonisation Society was founded to exert pressure on the freed man to leave the country to settle in Africa, and the first settlers landed in Liberia in 1815.

The historical record does not show the same element of coercion as the British scheme of two decades before, but, as in Britain, the vast majority opted to stay. Some of the leaders of the free blacks in the North rejected the promise of freedom in Africa, emphasising:

> *"the determination to fight for the emancipation of those still enslaved rather than to become leaders, after emigration, in some black nation to be established overseas."*[4]

Many of those who migrated did so under duress, for pressures were placed upon the freedmen to emigrate, and an agreement to do so was sometimes the price of freedom (manumission). Among the emigrants were some of the most energetic and organised black leaders who took their education, skills and organisation to West Africa, establishing a colony closely modelled on the US State in all its symbolic manifestations. Declaring themselves to be an independent republic in 1847, the settlers of Liberia inscribed in their constitution the principle of repatriation, for Article V Section 13 of the first free black republic in Africa in the modern era declared that:

> *"the great object of forming these colonies being to provide a home for the dispersed and oppressed children of Africa and to regenerate and enlighten this benighted continent, none but Negroes or persons of colour shall be admitted to citizenship in this Republic."*

Unfortunately, these emigrants, while taking their skills, did not take their passion for freedom with them to Africa.

The African population which lived in the hinterland found out that the modelling of this republic on the US Republic bore similarities in more than just the symbolic nuances of flag, anthem, officers and monetary system. For though the settlers did not have the military might to do what the American pilgrim fathers did to the indigenous American Indian population, those who escaped slavery in America exploited the indigenous African population; and nowhere in the republican constitution was it stated whether the aboriginal population could be citizens.

These settlers used their ideas and skills to organise a system of production which compensated the penetration of capitalism into the African continent, organising a military force to collect taxes, to stamp out unrest; and it was expected that military detachments would live off the resources of the communities in which they operated.

These colonisers were not only from the USA, but also from Barbados; the Barbados Colonisation Society despatched 346 settlers who arrived in 1865. One Liberian historian, commenting on the significance of this input, said:

> *"This expedition was notable not only because it brought the first migration from the West Indies, but also because many of its members turned out to be among the most industrious and outstanding citizens of Liberia; including a family, the Barclays, which has produced two presidents of the republic and is still actively engaged in public affairs."*[5]

Whether from the Westindies or the US, the search for human dignity consistent with repatriation did not extend to the African people; and once in Africa the backward ideas of racial gradations, ranks and capitalist greed were to take its toll on the development of this republic. Despite the contradictions, throughout the 19th century Liberia was an important reference point for blacks in the West, and individuals made their way to settle there.

One of the most outstanding Pan-Africanists of the 19th century, Edward Blyden, made his home there, and for the rest of his life championed the cause of the people of the interior with as much passion as he championed the cause of the enslaved blacks in the US and the dehumanised blacks of the Caribbean and South America.* Blyden's work, while providing part of the inspiration of the Pan-African cry of the 20th century – 'African for the Africans' – could not alter the course of the established cooperation between the USA and Liberia. The United States Army approvingly looked on at relations in 1964, saying that:

> *"there have been American military advisers in the country since 1912....Liberia is the first and, up to 1964, the only African country which has concluded a defence pact with the United States".*[7]

This treaty was signed in 1942, "after some persuasion when the United States set up a major air base, communication and transportation facilities". Growing US economic penetration of the continent of Africa and the forward military planning of the USA were temporarily given a blow in 1980 when the Master Sergeant, Samuel Doe, broke the domination of the Americo-Liberians over the rest of the Africans in Liberia.

*Because of his opposition to and the way in which he criticised the small ruling class, Blyden came into constant conflict, leading to his temporary exile into Sierra Leone. He was the ambassador of the Liberian Republic to Europe, after a change of regime, and even though serving the State never relented in his opposition to the way the indigenous people were treated. As an ambassador, he defended the independent republic before Europeans, but among many blacks in America he blamed Liberians "for thinking like Americans, for trying to impose concepts of law and land tenure, and for trying to work the land in the gang system which we learned in America".[6]

Marcus Garvey, Liberia and Repatriation

Marcus Garvey and the UNIA regarded the Liberian Republic as an important staging ground for their concept of liberation, and from the outset the UNIA devised a comprehensive and well thought out programme of settlement, involving technicians, farmers, and craftsmen in Africa. Contrary to the historians and Marxists who have denigrated the UNIA and Garvey in simplistic 'back to Africa' terms, the Garveyites had a clear understanding of the long-term strategic significance of Africa.

> *"Garvey saw Africa essentially as the only place where black people could launch a successful bid for equality with other races and nations. Africa was the black man's ancestral home; he was still in a majority there; the continent was rich in natural resources, and with some technical help from black people in other areas a determined drive for equality could have the best chances of success there. And if the black man became powerful in Africa this would necessarily raise his status all over the world... As a means of consolidating its protection for the scattered members of the race, Garvey envisioned that such a strong African government should extend citizenship to black people everywhere."*[8]

This message was carried in the internationally popular voice of race consciousness, the *Negro World,* and the Garveyites backed up their ideas with concrete plans of action, firing the imagination of the *Line,* the shipping company which would speed up the trading, political and cultural links between Africa and her dispersed children in the West.

Marcus Garvey and the UNIA, in pursuit of their promise to the 400 million Africans of the world that they were in the forefront of redeeming the African continent, despatched a commissioner to Liberia to draw up plans for the settlement of those who wanted to contribute to the development of Africa. At the time the other parts of Africa were under colonial rule (except Abyssinia), so the Garveyites concentrated on attempts to set up a land base in Liberia. Garvey's embassy, sensitive to the suffering of the mass of black people in the West, quickly grasped the contradictions of the Liberian State; and in a secret report Eli Garcia, the Commissioner, categorised a long list of social ills and alerted Garvey to the fact that though endowed with natural resources Liberia was extremely poor due to the lack of enterprise of the ruling Americo-Liberians.

The Liberian leaders welcomed the proposals of Garvey for a settlement, for the popular mass organisation of the UNIA was a more powerful institution than the Liberian State, and they hoped that through their links with this organised movement, there would be an input of skills and capital into the society.

Imperialism, however, did not take too kindly to the prospect of an organised movement such as the UNIA having a foothold in Africa. They perceived correctly that if Garvey could carry out his promise of settling 14,000 skilled carpenters, masons, doctors, electricians, nurses and mechanics, not only would Liberia benefit, but in a short time the UNIA could use the land base in Liberia to support the embryonic anti-colonial movements elsewhere in Africa.

Britain, France and the USA undertook an elaborate campaign to sabotage the repatriation of Garveyites, a campaign launched in 1922 when the London-based imperialist journal *African World* published Eli Garcia's secret report to Garvey, clearly intending to embarrass Garvey and halt the negotiations which were then going on between the UNIA and the Liberian State. Tony Martin went through the many steps which Britain and France undertook to pressure the Liberian State, saying that:

> *"The leaking of the report, with its unfavourable comments on the Liberian society and its frank discussion of the UNIA aims in Liberia, in all likelihood put an end to Garvey's chances of success, even though he persisted in his efforts for two years more."*

The *Liberian News*, the newspaper of the Liberian ruling class, responding to the pressures of the imperialists, reported later that the documents *"gave a clear picture of the revolutionary purposes of the UNIA in Liberia"*.[9] When land earmarked for the UNIA was taken over by the Firestone Rubber Company, and the Liberians harassed individuals from the UNIA who were bent on reaching Africa, the British Governor of Sierra Leone lavished praised on the President King of Liberia, and the French made him a chevalier of the Legion of Honour.

Garveyism and Bilbo

At its prime, the UNIA was a formidable nationalist and anti-imperialist organisation, giving courage to the millions of black workers who were excluded from white trade unions and those in the colonies who were prevented from forming workers' associations. During this period, the mass base of the organisation ensured that the Garvey scheme of repatriation was a *positive idea*, linked to his overall concept of African redemption and liberation.

Racists in the US were always eager to deport blacks from the USA to Africa, seeking the moral support for this project from ex-Garveyites. In particular, the racist Senator Theodore Bilbo of Mississippi introduced a bill in the US Senate in 1939 – the Greater Liberia Bill – proposing to voluntarily repatriate Afro-Americans to West Africa with assistance from the US Government.

This proposal was invoked during the height of the depression, when Bilbo knew full well that with Garvey poor and isolated in England, the proposition of such a scheme would break the incipient gains of black workers in the US. When the mass of black workers saw the imprisonment of Garvey, they had redoubled their efforts to fight for a better life with independent black working class actions.

A few Garveyites had held on to the idea of repatriation, and some of the more vigorous among these were the members of the Peace Movement of Ethiopia. Led by Mrs. Mittie Gordon, a former UNIA member from Chicago, the Peace Movement of Ethiopia supported the Bilbo bill, when the majority of black organisations objected to the racist intentions of the bill. Bilbo envisaged the removal of 5-8 million black people over a period of 15-25 years.

> *"By concentrating on persons of productive age and young persons it was expected that those who remained would die out in the normal course of time."*

To avoid possible loopholes, Bilbo made provision for black aliens within the US to participate in the repatriation scheme.[10]

One of the most serious political errors of Garvey was to give public support for the Bilbo bill. At the 1938 UNIA Convention, the UNIA passed a resolution of support for Bilbo's bill, and Garveyites in the USA entered into correspondence with Bilbo. Such a bill could, however, never see the light of day, for not only was it against the long-term interests of American capital, which needed cheap black labour, but more importantly because the majority of black working people in the USA were committed to fighting the system.

Throughout the forties, the Garveyites called for repatriation, and though the impact of the UNIA remained significant, the power of the later Civil Rights Movement demonstrated the commitment by black people in the US to fight for their rights.

Again, during the euphoria of African Liberation, Stokely Carmichael led a small group which suggested that black people should abandon the struggle in the US and the Caribbean for Africa. The rhetoric of the All African Peoples Revolutionary Party spoke of the need for a 'land base in Africa, declaring that the future for black people in the West was in Africa.

This was clearly an impractical project, for the majority of black people would never be able to reach Africa. Commenting on the impracticability of calling for repatriation in the era of national liberation, Walter Rodney said:

> *"Some of us can get to Africa. The vast majority of our people will, in fact, not be able to go there, and struggle takes place where people live and work. That's the locus of struggle. And in that sense, it becomes self-defeating for someone in the Caribbean or in the United States to suggest that Africa is the sole, or even the main, vehicle of black struggle. Black struggle must be universalised where black people happen to be. But, there is a point suggesting that the struggle of black people in Africa has a certain strategic importance – a greater strategic importance for black people as a whole than say what's going on in the Caribbean. I feel that, to the extent that the African struggle advances and that continent is freed*

from the coils of capitalism and imperialism, to that extent the impact on the Caribbean and, particularly in the United States, on the black population will be decisive."[11]

Here Rodney was continuing the tradition of the Maroons, Garvey, Blyden and countless others who had longed to return to Africa. However, Rodney's analysis was informed with his experience of historical materialism and years of reflection on the positive and negative results of Garvey's contribution. He did not draw back from the centrality of Africa, he simply affirmed the decisiveness of the struggles on the continent:

"Yes, I would use as strong a term as decisive – because our history has been bedevilled by the fact that we, as a colonised people in the Western world, have never had a power to which we could turn and that our oppressors have never felt any sense of having to account to somebody else for the treatment which they accorded to us. I believe it is an important historical dimension and therefore, success of the struggle in Africa is likely to be critical with regard to creating new conditions and new awareness for struggle in what we call the new world."

Rodney's 20th century appeal rang out to the Rastafari who clung to the idea of repatriation to Africa. Those who listened to him carried out and joined their struggles where they lived, as in Grenada, while championing the cause of African liberation; others simply romanticised the concept of Africa, longing to return to Ethiopia.

Rastafari and Repatriation

Even the idea of repatriation to Ethiopia among the Rastas was an advance over the former efforts of Jamaican nationals to settle in Africa. Throughout the 19th century, individual Jamaicans made their way to settle and work in a quiet unpretentious manner. Many of those who returned to Africa did not seek to go to Liberia, for some of the nationalists who had gone to England realised the limitations of the Liberian settlement, and opted for settling in many parts of Africa.

Inside Jamaica, Garvey's *Negro World* had again invoked the spirits of Africa which dwell in Jamaican hills, leading to a tremendous upsurge of interest in Africa. As has been maintained, the racial history of Jamaica meant that the African identification was based primarily within the working class, expressing itself most overtly in the form of the Rastafari movement.

The African identification of the Rasta was rejected by the aspiring Jamaican leaders of the two-party structure, a rejection which was a 'statement of cultural preference as a consequence of cultural imperialism'. Because the Rastafari identification was also a reflection of the class struggle, the colonial State attempted to brutally suppress the movement. However, Rastafari would not be crushed by the repressive policies of the State, and the movement grew slowly until the fifties when the massive out-migration took place and the Rastas declared *Ethiopia yes, England No.*

It is important to perceive the emergence of the concept of repatriation as an active philosophy among the Rastafarians to help to correct the distortions that the Rastas were from the outset escapists. In Jamaica, the society had been exporting surplus labour – called 'unlimited supplies of labour' – since the end of the 19th century when waves of Jamaican workers provided cheap labour in the USA, Panama, Cuba, Costa Rica and other parts of Central America.

The first leaders of the Rastafari were among the migrant workers, and when Leonard Howell returned to Jamaica there was a genuine effort to work among the poor to attempt to deal with the problems of racism and unemployment, even if this implied the setting up of communes in Sligoville, St. Thomas and Clarendon. Throughout the thirties those who identified with Africa did not want to go to Liberia,* but to Ethiopia to fight against Italian fascism. Going back to Africa to fight was part of their philosophy, but the Rastas of Jamaica were not passive in the face of injustice: they joined the struggles of the people, incurring State violence and ridicule at the hands of the petty bourgeoisie.

The stress on *repatriation* as a central tenet in the philosophy of Rastafari emerged as the result of two factors:
(1) the land grant of 500 acres by His Imperial Majesty to Africans in the West, in the early fifties, and
(2) the massive removal of the rural population from Jamaica during the invasion of the countryside by the bauxite tractors and earthmovers.

Between 1950 and 1970 over 560,000 rural Jamaicans were uprooted from their village communities. This disruption of over one quarter of the total population had a tremendous impact on the consciousness of a working people who had just begun to emerge from a hundred years of bureaucratic colonialism. At precisely the period when the workers were to benefit from the 1938 battles, capitalism uprooted them, throwing some on the Dungle heaps of Kingston, while others were packed on the banana boats to be taken to face the racial discrimination of London, Derby, Nottingham, Birmingham and Manchester. *Ethiopia yes, England no,* became the cry of a mobile, alert and conscious Jamaican working poor who preferred to take chances in Ethiopia than to go to England.

Rastafarians found an alternative to the Liberian experience and the promise of racial discrimination, because as branch members of the Ethiopian World Federation they became eligible for a share of the land grant in Shashamane, which had been granted to Africans in the West.

*On July 21, 1984, B.B. Coke passed a resolution in the Jamaican House of Representatives to facilitate the repatriation of Jamaicans to Liberia. He moved: "Whereas there is a great desire on the part of many Jamaicans today migrate to Liberia...for economic and other reasons, and whereas great difficulties are experienced by these Jamaicans in obtaining the necessary funds so that they may travel and establish themselves in that country. Be it resolved that the government of Jamaica favourably consider the removal of all hindrances in the way of proferring full aid to those would be immigrants." [12]

Shashamane is in Shoa Province of Ethiopia, one hundred and sixty miles from the capital city of Addis Ababa, in beautiful rolling country, between the Malcoda and the Shashamane Rivers. The land grant of 500 acres was offered to the Ethiopian World Federation in New York after constant representations and the concrete examples of James Piper of the EWF, who, with his wife Helen, had migrated to Ethiopia in 1948.

James Piper, originally from Montserrat, taught carpentry in the technical school in Addis Ababa until 1952, when he returned to New York to finalise the arrangements. Returning to Ethiopia the Pipers, with a small group of Westindians and Afro-Americans, set out to make the EWF colony the mecca for those who had supported the Ethiopian monarch during the anti-fascist war. In pursuit of their efforts to develop this mecca, the Pipers, as administrators, sent out urgent appeals for settlers and for financial support for the settlement.

This is the background against which the spate of organisational activities by Rasta around the question of repatriation must be seen. Rastafari in Jamaica who objected to being forced off their land to go to England were not to know that those grouped around the *African Opinion* in the US favoured repatriation and had supported the Bilbo Bill, asking for Congress to aid the repatriation of black Americans to Africa.[13]

Rastafarians in Jamaica invested considerable energies in the efforts towards repatriation, leading up to the Nyabingi of 1959 which was violently dispersed by the police. Using language which reflected their determination, Rastas in Jamaica called repatriation a human right, posing the alternative as *Repatriation or rebellion.*[14] An ultimatum which was sent to the Chief Minister in 1959, and reprinted in the US-based *African Opinion*, said:

> *"We have never failed from declaring our Intention of repatriating to our homeland Africa, we do not seek political power and titles from the British. We are now demanding of you in a united voice to use your instrumentality to cut loose the bonds of serfdom, before it is too late. We have always resisted the British government and her colonial puppets passively. Yet now the hour has come, that we will not hesitate to raise the standard of Armed Rebellion, Guerilla Warfare and Arson in our determined bid for Freedom."*[15]

Signed under the seal of the order of Nyabingi the Rastafari called upon the State to open up negotiations; otherwise

> *"we shall give the order to our people for total war through Rebellion. We have reached the stage where our hands are on the trigger".*

Jamaica's first official mission went to the continent for six weeks in 1961, and in all five African States visited there was a "ready acceptance of the principle of repatriation of Africans living abroad to the ancestral land". Kwame Nkrumah, the former President of Ghana, noted the historic significance of the mission and said that he was:

> *"happy that there were forces at work in the Caribbean which were*

responsible for the present mission."

In obvious agreement with some of the principles of Rastafari,Nkrumah paid tribute to Marcus Garvey, who had been his inspiration:

> *"The back to Africa desire had to be realistically approached. The two peoples, West Indians and Africans, had developed separately over the intervening years when they were apart. There would have to be adjustments."*[16]

These sentiments were repeated in Ethiopia, Liberia, Sierra Leone, Nigeria and in every State to which the heads of government showed the importance they attached to developing relations with black people in the West. Young Rastafari today would do well to see the preparation and organisation which the Rastas in the mission placed in their diplomatic efforts. Preparing a minority report on the mission, these Rastas reported on the availability of land, on the transportation problems and on the prospects of Rastafari who wanted to return to Africa.

Whereas the African States were open to discussion and willing to make the 'adjustments' that Nkrumah referred to, there was no such concrete assistance given to Africans from Jamaica who wanted to return. When one compares the facilities made available to British capitalists for the recruitment of cheap labour from the Caribbean region, it would seem that the still-born initiative was as much a 'palliative' as the report on Rasta, 'designed to calm an explosive situation'. Capital in Jamaica, which was in any case primarily in the hands of whites, was not about to facilitate any large-scale emigration of cheap labour, for having skilled unemployed people in the society had proven an effective way to control the emergence of a powerful and independent working class.

Without the assistance of the State, a handful of Jamaican Rastas worked hard, saved their money, and repatriated to Ethiopia – to Shashamane. Significantly, in the USA, where there were far greater resources, the 'nationalists' who wanted Congress to implement the *Bilbo Bill* did not try to raise their own passage to Africa. Instead, they acted as cheerleaders when poor Rastas in Jamaica, such as Brother Clifford Baugh and family, left for Shashamane.[17]

One problem which is posed for the future transformation of Jamaica is why should a Jamaican worker or farmer put all of his or her energies into leaving the society for Africa? It is a problem which should concern serious people of the society, for the case of Noel Dyer illustrated the extent to which some Jamaican workers would go to escape the racial assaults of Jamaican society.

Noel Dyer hailed from the parish of Westmoreland, and was a promising cricketer who, like so many other Jamaicans, found the Rastafari doctrine to offer him the most in the early fifties. Caught in the wave of migration to England in 1960, he worked in London from 1960 to 1963, from where he decided to leave the 'pollution and smoke' for Ethiopia. Dyer set out on foot to

Ethiopia, a journey which took him one year, during which time he learned three languages – French, Spanish and Arabic – got lost in the desert, and was imprisoned for entering a country without a visa.

To listen to his stroy of how he crossed the English Channel and worked his way as a painter across France and Spain to Morocco; of his journey over land from Morocco through Algeria, Tunisia and Libya to Egypt; of his wanderings over the desert through Egypt, and his arrest in Sudan, one is amazed at the resilence of this black worker. * The story of Brother Dyer should one day be recounted to the young, as an example of what the racism of Jamaican society has forced some black people to resort to in order to escape discrimination and exploitation.

With his skills and knowledge, Dyer joined the ranks of the growing community of Rastas in Shashamane, supplementing his part-time jobs with subsistence farming. Living in Shashamane did not increase his standard of living over that of a Jamaican migrant worker; but one thing he was sure of was that he was at home in Africa.

The Shashamane Settlement and the Ethiopian Revolution

Rastafarians in Ethiopia were confronted with the contradictory position of their beliefs, when the Ethiopian people removed the monarchy in a popular revolution in 1974. This contradiction was posed for all Rastafari, but even more fundamentally for those who had settled in Shashamane, simply because their existence in Ethiopia was so closely linked with the whole dispensation of privilege by the Emperor.

Land, patronage and titles tied the regional landlords to the State and Church, so that the land grant to the Rastafarians was likened to the old practice of the monarch giving land to favoured retainers. And some of the settlers did act as favoured retainers for the administrators of the Shashamane settlement. They had access to tractors, seeds, fertilisers, and could sell their produce to the royal household, so that essentially the settlement was organically linked with the Royal Family, instead of with the people of the community where the settlement was based.

At its peak, towards the end of 1970, the settlement of Shashamane had between 40-50 Rastas and Afro-Americans, who had set up thir community with

* Noel Dyer lives in Shashamane, Ethiopia, which he has made his home since 1965. His story is a testament to the depth of feeling in the Jamaican countryside on the question of Africa. Walking through the streets of Addis Ababa in August 1979 and speaking with him, it was clear that the violence of the Ethiopian power struggles around Mengistu did not endear him to the principles of the regime. Brother Dyer left London in July 1964, hitching to Paris, and taking a train across North Africa. Taking a ship to Morocco, he learnt enough Arabic to get him by land across to Algeria to Tunisia, hitchhiking through Libya to Egypt. It took him three weeks from Cairo to Aswan, but he couldn't get a ship across the Aswan Dam. After spending three months in Egypt he told the police that he wanted to see the President, Nasser. It was then that he received assistance to cross the Aswan Dam. From there it was across the desert by foot to Sudan. Once in the Sudan he was arrested for trying to enter the country without a visa, but his insistence on his rights of passage to Ethiopia led to his deportation to Ethiopia. He reached Addis Ababa in July 1965, one year after leaving England.[18]

a pharmacy, a school, a small clinic – named after Dr. Malaku Bayen – a small store and a number of modest dwellings. There were no efforts towards collective farming, hence the problems of individualism, competition and envy plagued the settlers, who eked out an existence.

Petty differences between 'Jamaican' Rastas and Afro-Americans over the use of implements, and over access to the Royal household simmered. These simmerings continued with the advent of the Twelve Tribes of Israel, who had begun their own scheme of repatriation. Fortunately, size, limited resources, and the struggle for survival ensured that none of the petty problems could fester into the kind of armed confrontations which had taken place among the Liberian settlers in 1870-1873.

The Twelve Tribes of Israel was the only Rastafari organisation with financial resources to move Rastas en masse from Jamaica to Africa, and yet the members have remained very small in number. It is from the Twelve Tribes – called the 'organ' – that young Rasta who idealise Ethiopia could learn that even if there is a wish to return to Africa, there must be preparation.

Unlike the older Rastas, like Brothers Baugh and Dyer, who had the experience of urban and rural life, the first pioneers from the 'organ' were urban, thus not fully prepared for the rigours of rural life in Shashamane. One of the first settlers sent out by Twelve Tribes died because he failed to take the simple precaution of boiling the water before using it.

As an international unit with organisational hierarchy and a set of principles, the Twelve Tribes could have mobilised the resources necessary to conceive a different kind of settlement from the one administered by Piper. It would have been possible to develop a collective where young Jamaicans with skills and knowledge brought new farming methods to the area in a manner beneficial not only to the members of the organisation, but to the whole community in Shashamane.

To do this would have required that the settlers acquaint themselves with the soil, topography, rainfall and the range of possible agricultural crops which could be grown there. It would have required a level of study and understanding beyond the simple framework of reading a chapter of the bible everynight, and reaping a modest crop of the local cereal, teff, and vegetables.

It did not take any great skill to do the latter: any peasant in Africa or the Caribbean could simply scratch the soil for subsistence farming with the level of technology which had been used for centuries, the hoe. Romantic and idyllic yes, but not geared towards any long-term uplifting of the standard of living.

Yet even at this very low standard of living one could not but have admiration and some respect for all the Rastas who used their own efforts to reach the land of their forefathers. Unfortunately, this admiration had to be guided by the concrete problems which faced anyone contemplating repatriation.

Frustrations and disappointments were bound to set in when educated and trained young men were lured to the land of the 'father' to subsist in a scheme where they could not realise their full potential, commensurate with their skills and education. Moreover, petty bourgeois elements could not survive in the poverty and humility which life at Shashamane demanded. Such elements were able to use family ties and position to get some support from the Jamaican State for the settlers, although the small assistance offered could not improve the poverty which was the lot of the pioneers.

What was needed was a level of collective work, organisation and a spirit of co-operation to fully tax the brains of all the settlers. In the absence of these values, petty squabbles developed from time to time between the older brethren and the Twelve Tribes, including the leaders, because even as Rastas, the brethren and sistren could not easily rise above those negative values they had internalised in capitalist Jamaica.

Whatever the problems between the settlers and the administration, or among settlers, these problems were to pale into insignificance when the people of Shashamane expropriated the land from the Rastas in 1975, as their own expression of opposition to the monarchy. Following the lead of the Provisional Military Administrative Council, known as the Dergue, which had issued a land reform proclamation in March 1975 nationalising all rural land, abolishing tenancy, and setting up peasant associations, the poor of Shashamane seized all the tractors, land and assets of the Rastafari and the EWF settlers in Shashamane.

Fortunately for the settlers, there were elements in the Provisional Military Administrative Council who understood the sentiments of repatriation among Africans in the West; so after negotiations 44 hectares were returned to the Rastas who wanted to stay. It was inevitable that the elements who were closest to the Royal household from the administration of the settlement would leave, for the whole organisation of the previous form of capitalist intensive farming was broken down by the Ethiopian peasantry as part of the revolution.

The Unfolding of the Revolution

Space does not allow for a full elaboration of the complex forces in Ethiopia which led to the removal of the monarchy, but enough information has been published to inform those who want to understand the class struggle which violently erupted in 1974, leading to the deposing and detention of Haile Selassie on 12 September 1974. Haile Selassie died quietly in 1975.

The initiatives of the peasants in Shashamane to seize the land of those who they considered landlords was but one of the major changes which have taken place in Ehiopia, the land of diversity. John Makarkis has described the whole process as 'Garrison Socialism' in his attempt to grasp the essence of the radical and far-reaching changes, while at the same time penetrating the grave consequences of militarisation and commandism. Makarkis said of the changes:

> *"In 1974, Ethiopia was torn by class struggle which erupted suddenly, matured swiftly and generated a powerful momentum for a socialist solution to the manifold contradictions of a society just emerging from feudalism. The struggle began with a spontaneous popular uprising, which set off a set of events which defy facile interpretation. The uprising was followed by a coup d'état, carried out by a military force which had*

been radicalised and purged by social conflict. The military intervention provoked an internecine struggle within the revolutionary camp, a situation that invited counter-revolution, favoured secession, and encouraged a foreign invasion. Debilitated by an internal contest for power, the military regime was unable to cope with its foes, domestic or foreign. Timely, massive assistance provided by several socialist States and orchestrated by the Soviet Union preserved the territorial integrity of Ethiopia, and propped a government that seemed on the verge of collapse."[20]

The Dergue, which seized power after the overthrow of the Emperor, in a short time lost the opportunity to unleash the full potential of the people; so that internal struggles and militarism intensified to the point where the leadership degenerated to a militarist regime, and the vast masses were reduced to the limited role of a frightened audience in their own revolution. The 'campaign of terror' against those on the left who called for popular participation and civilian rule has only been surpassed by the bombings of the Eritrean people, who have since redoubled their call for self-determination and independence.[21]

Verbal declamations of socialism by the military regime in Ethiopia and military support from the socialist camp cannot conceal the fundamental *commandist* nature of the regime. Two factors graphically expose this commandism:

(1) the vicious repression carried out against the Eritrean people along with the intolerance to other oppressed nationalities, and
(2) the military command of the working poor which has led to military conscription, compulsory crops, forced labour and coercion.

Pan-Africanists and Rastafarians who yearned for the unity of the continent of Africa agonised over the struggles in Eritrea, with many taking the imperial and Dergue rationale for suppression, i.e., that the people of Eritrea were secessionists. The threatened disintegration of the old imperial borders in 1977, with the Somali invasion, generated some sympathy and support for the regime: support which was dramatic in the form of Soviet weapons and Cuban personnel.

The struggle in the Ogaden was not a popular struggle but the military thrust of the expansionist vision of a military regime in Somalia, which preferred to fight Ethiopia rather than put resources into feeding its people. Frightened by the far-reaching changes of the nationalisation process in Ethiopia, imperialism supported the Western Somali Liberation Front which thrust deep into Ethiopia. This attack was beaten back with the assistance of the socialist camp.

But in Eritrea, no amount of assistance could suppress the Eritrean struggle for self-determination. As long as the leadership of the Eritrean people sought to develop the kind of institutions and organisations among the people which aimed to break the capitalist relations – and at the same time break the legacies of religious intolerance, male supremacy and the differences between pastoralists and cultivators – no amount of Soviet weaponry could defeat such a people.

As early as 1916, V.I. Lenin had recognised the right of self-determination and independence for oppressed nationalities, a right which the supporters of the Dergue conveniently forgot. Inevitably, the prolonged liberation struggle in Eritrea had an incalculable impact on other oppressed nationalities, bringing to the fore the deformities of regional differentiation and cultural isolation which can now only be solved within the context of a socialist federation.

Pan-Africanists who support the right of the people of Eritrea to independence do so not because they want to see the further balkanisation of the continent, but because if the people of that region can effect a higher level of social organisation than that of the wretchedness of underdevelopment, there is no reason why they should be bombed into remaining a part of the old feudal empire.

An element of confusion has arisen among Rastas on the question of Eritrea and Ethiopia, not only because they supported the old empire, in all its forms, but also because the Left in Jamaica supports the Ethiopian regime and justifies the use of Soviet bombs against the Eritrean people.[22] Giving up their independence as socialists, this Left has attached itself to the foreign policy of the Soviet Union in such a way that the Rastafarians conceive of their support as part of the idealism of the old colonial order. At the same time, the more conservative Rastas who were open to American propaganda, emanating from such diverse sources as the *Gleaner*, the BBC or *Coptic Times*, condemned the military in Ethiopia as puppets of the Soviet Union.

This confusion called for the existence of a Marxist or socialist group in the Caribbean which could creatively interpret the events in the world without fear of great powers, an interpretation which could assist young Rastas. This creativity was made more urgent by the growing number of militarists and commandists who could call on Soviet or Chinese support when they deliberately distorted revolutionary concepts.

Commandist regimes, whether they be of the Forbes Burnham genre or the Mengistu genre, claim to be socialist but carry out repression in the name of socialism, for they know it is difficult to go to the people and say that they are ruling in the name of capitalism.

However, one litmus test of regimes who proclaim themselves socialist is their treatment of the working poor and working class institutions. In Ethiopia the working class, though small in size, played an important role in the revolution, but no sooner had the Dergue consolidated its power than it banned independent working class action.

> *"Throughout 1975, the labour movement lay dormant. Pending the appearance of a new labour code, all labour activities were banned, all collective agreements were suspended and a new one could not be negotiated, nor could the trade union movement organise workers in areas from which it had been excluded by the previous regime. A wage freeze lowered real wages in a time of continuous inflation, unemployment rose substantially, and the situation of the working class deteriorated progressively. Imprisonment and occasional shootings were the response to spontaneous worker protests."*[23]

When the regime did formulate a new labour code in December 1975 the rights and conditions of labour were defined according to 'conventional bourgeois standards'; the whole objective was to organise a mass organisation which promoted production and could mobilise workers to attend State functions. Similar degeneration took place in the 'kebeles' – the neighbourhood associations which were conceived as the embryo of popular participation and expression. Caught in the power struggles between differing tendencies and the military leadership, the 'kebeles' became militarised insitutions, bureaucratic and hierarchial, so that even positive efforts, such as the literacy campaigns, were carried out with coercion.

The Rastafari movement, though shaken by the events in Ethiopia, has since clung to its ideas in the absence of available information on the unfolding of the class struggle. The Rastafari settlers in Shashamane, like their counterparts in the Caribbean, went on the defensive, becoming passive bystanders in the whole process. Their continued support for the monarch placed them in opposition to the Ethiopian people.

Unfortunately some of them continued to attempt to defy reality by sending stories back to the Caribbean that Haile Selassie was still alive. Inside the country, they insulted their neighbours by insisting on putting up pictures of the deposed Emperor in their dwellings.

This act of displaying the picture of the Ethiopian monarch, which began as an act of protest in colonial Jamaica, became an act of reaction in revolutionary Ethiopia. For however much the popular masses speak derisively of the militarists, they enthusiastically supported the deposition of the monarchy and the onerous system of taxation of the feudal system.

Rastas cannot be against Babylon in the West and support reaction in Africa.

Rastas, Repatriation and Africa

For many Rastas, the continued struggles in Ethiopia demand proper analysis and explanation in order to transcend the romantic visions about the African continent. The hostility of the Caribbean petty bourgeoisie to the study of African history and towards African identification ensured that among the Rastafarians illusions took place of serious analysis of what actual struggles were occurring on the continent Africa.

The shattering experience of the expropriation of the land forced some of the Rastafarians in Shashamane to move on to other African societies; those who could not afford to do so have lingered on in Shashamane, surviving partially because of the positive image of Jamaica which developed in Africa during the Michael Manley administration.

But the disillusioning experience which stemmed from the removal of the emperor has not shaken the faith of the whole movement, for the movement had developed for a greater purpose than the personage of Haile Selassie. Rastafari had emerged as the outcome of the struggle against racism and cultural imperialism; Africa and Haile Selassie had become external references of support.

The removal of Haile Selassie is forcing the movement to come to terms with the realities of Africa. Moreover, the opportunism on the part of certain Caribbean governments on the question of identification with Africa has ensured that the African identification of the Rasta of the thirties is not a radical race conscious phenomenon in the 1980s. Regimes such as Forbes Burnham's have even gone further by giving aid to the liberation struggles in Africa to camouflage reactionary internal policies.

This opportunism has alerted Rastafarians and progressive Pan-Africanists to the fact that the link with Africa must be with social groups.

> *"The problem is to develop solidarity between the Caribbean people and the African peoples. It is not the same question as developing solidarity between African states and Caribbean states... We will have to be more selective in ensuring that our relations are nurtured with* particular *progressive governments*, particular *liberation movements, and* particular *social organisations – whether they be trade unions, women's movements, students' unions – various groups that develop a perspective on African struggle."* (24)

This formulation stared the Rasta movement in the face in the eighties, with the Rastafari in the Grenadian Revolution giving one answer: that their concrete support for African liberation could be measured by their support for the struggle against imperialism in the Caribbean. Throughout the region, sentiments towards repatriation have abated: however, many of the Rastas in the United Kingdom see the question of repatriation as the number one priority.

In a sense this priority stems from their unwilling sojourn in the 'heart of Babylon'. And yet, even though it is the right of any black person to repatriate (in this case to the Caribbean or Africa) the history of the forced deportations of 1786 should alert Rastas to the dangers of their call for repatriation. It is quite possible for the British State to mobilise opinion around the question of repatriation in order to deflect the energies of a stirring and vibrant black population. Rastas in the UK need to listen to the words of Walter Rodney, who said:

> *"We cannot romanticise the situation in Africa."*

Repatriation is the right of black people, but there should be no support for reactionary schemes such as the Bilbo-Greater Liberia Bill of 1939. Moreover, the struggles of Southern Africa are calling on Rastas to effect a level of organisation and perception of the struggles in Africa to help hasten the fall of 'Babylon'.

FOOTNOTES

1. H. Orlando Patterson, *The Sociology of Slavery*, McGibbon and Kee, 1967, p. 196.
2. Quoted in Richard West, *Back to Africa*, Jonathan Cape, London, 1970, pp 13-14.
3. Folarin Shyllon, *Black People in Britain 1555-1833*, Institute of Race Relations and Oxford University Press,

1977, p.130.

4. St. Clair Drake, "Negro Americans and the African Interest", *The American Negro Reference Book*, John P. Davis, ed., Prentice Hall, N.Y., 1966, p.667.
5. C.A. Cassell, *Liberia: History of the First African Republic*, Fountainhead Publishers, N.Y., 1970. One member of this family, Edwin Barclay, was Secretary of State at the time of the British and French opposition to the Garvey scheme to set up a base in Liberia.
6. *Back To Africa*, op. cit., p.250.
7. US Army Area Handbook for Liberia, US Dept. of the Army, Washington, 1964.
8. Tony Martin, *Race First*, Greenwood Press, Connecticut, 1976, p.113.
9. ibid., p.127. Imperialism also used the differences between the UNIA and the NAACP to sabotage the scheme. W.E.B. DuBois was appointed as a special representative by the US government to President King's second inauguration. See details, pp 135-136.
10. ibid., p.350.
11. Walter Rodney, Interview in *Black Scholar*, November 1974.
12. *African Opinion*, September 1964, p.9.
13. ibid., p.9.
14. *African Opinion*, March-April 1959. See details of the Nyabingi in Kingston in *The Report of The Rastafari Movement in Kingston, Jamaica*, M.G. Smith et al. 1966.
15. *African Opinion*, Sept.-Oct. 1959, p.9.
16. *Report of Mission To Africa*, Government Printer, Kingston, 1961.
17. See picture and story in African Opinion, May- June 1968
18. From discussions with Brother Noel Dyer in Addis Ababa, August 1979. Brother Dyer had moved to Addis Ababa from Shashamane temporarily in 1979. He was a skilled artisan who had been through many trials and tribulations in Ethiopia, but he was determined that he would never return to Jamaica.
19. Even the system of land tenure in Ethiopia was diverse: there was a system of large landowners in Southern Ethiopia of Northern origin, with their peasants and tenants of local origin. In contrast, the peasants of the North enjoyed security of tenure over their tiny plots. See *Ethiopia: Empire in Revolution*, Marina and David Ottaway, Africana Publishing Company, New York, pp 15-21. Also see John Markakis and Nega Ayele, *Class and Revolution in Ethiopia*, Spokesman Books, 1978.
20. John Markakis, "Garrison Socialism: The case of Ethiopia", Sussex University, IDS Socialist Conference Papers 1979. See also *Class and Revolution in Ethiopia*, op. cit.
21. The published material of the Eritrean Peoples Liberation Front gives some indication of the levels of organisation which have been effected to withstand the intensified attempt at forceful suppression by the militarists. In the process the EPLF has had to mobilise the people, rising above the narrow nationalist and religious appeal of the Eritrean Liberation Front. See *Vanguard*, Bulletin of the Eritrean Peoples Liberation Front, also *RAPE*, No. 19.
22. The Cubans lent to this confusion with the publication of the book by Valdes Vivo, *Ethiopia, The Unknown Revolution*. This book takes at face value the distortions of the regime that the Campaign of Red Terror against the Ethiopian People's Revolutionary Party was justified because they were reactionaries. In this whole analytic approach this book imported categories to justify the support of the Soviet Union for the Mengistu coup.

    For a critique see John Markakis, "Garrison Socialism: The Case of Ethiopia".
23. "Garrison Socialism . . .", p.16.
24. Walter Rodney, op. cit., p.14.

CONCLUSION

Rastafari: From Cultural Resistance to Cultural Liberation

The discussion of Rasta and Resistance began with the theoretical formulation of Cabral's dialectic of positive and negative influences. The centrality of race and race consciousness within the experience of the children of Africa lent a certain force to the Rastafari Movement, a force which made the Rastafari the foremost expression of Pan-Africanism in the era of political independence.

For many the movement is linked to the image of the late Emperor of Ethiopia, a link emphasised by the zeal and energy which lent to the celebration of the Golden Jubilee of the crowning of the Emperor. When this energy can be translated into the quest for social liberation, the societies of the Caribbean will have mobilised a major source of untapped energy.

This contradiction of black people in the Caribbean holding defensively onto their relationship with a deposed monarch can be understood within the context of seemingly independent States maintaining the feudal heritage of having a white Queen of an imperialist State as the nominal head of their country. Why should the Rasta not have their ritual and ceremony when the black Governor Generals seem to relish the pomp and emphasis of British tradition?

One short answer to this question is that thanks to the same doctrine of Rasta, the external reference point for the masses of black people is no longer Europe, but Africa. And if the people of Ethiopia and other parts of Africa call upon the Rasta to link themselves with the people of the villages and towns, instead of with empire builders, then those Rastafarians who have ears to hear will listen. Not even the social inequalities of the capitalist societies which are expressed in racial terms can save Rastas from turning into their opposites if they turn their backs on the African revolution.

Rastafari in the next fifty years face one challenge from the African villages, but in the Caribbean those who maintained that "I man no involved in a politics" are faced with the crisis of the societies. All around them the violence and thuggery of the economic depression call on them to be involved in change. Throughout the English-speaking Caribbean the working people battle against the deterioration of their living standards.

From Jamaica to Guyana the decay of the social stock of the society wreaks further hardships on the working poor. The decay can be seen in public buildings, private dwellings, the inability of the State to provide clean running water for the vast majority, the inability to maintain the semblance of a medical infrastructure, to organise garbage collection or to provide basic social services, such as transport, housing, cheap electrical power and food.

Everywhere the political leadership wallow in the idealism of seeking external solutions, looking for *aid,* but the concrete example of Trinidad and Tobago demonstrates that the problem is more than that of foreign exchange; it is one of a fundamental reconstruction of the society in the interest of those who produce the wealth of the society. In Jamaica the talk of democratic socialism was a manifestation that a section of the political leadership wanted to respond to the demand for change which issued from the tenement yards and the rural villages.

The discussion of democratic socialism was a failed attempt to keep abreast of the popular anti-imperialist culture, a failed attempt because this talk was not translated into the organisation of new institutions of popular power. Trapped in the history of 'jinnalship' along with the compromise between Europe and Africa, the political leadership could not break with the past in a way which could shake the foundations of the white power structure of the society.

Despite the limitations, there were external forces which did not even want question of socialism to be on the agenda. The prospect of the heightened consciousness of the masses and the beginnings of a serious materialist tradition, both in politics and ideology, created panic in the USA. Hence, the unprecedented terror campaign against the Jamaican people in the year of the fiftieth jubilee, 1980. The IMF programme of destabilisation, the campaign of psychological warfare and political violence were to be followed by the destruction of popular participation and expression in a coup d'état, if the Manley administration could not be removed by the ballot. To be certain of the campaign of confusion and subversion, imperialism also took on the cover of the popular movement in the form of the Ethiopian Zion Coptic Church.

The expanded activities of the Coptics in Jamaica, which are now being duplicated in other territories, and experimented on in the United Kingdom under the cover of 'community policing', led the far sighted Rastas to recognise that the all class appeal of Hailing Ja Rastafari, Selassie I must be transcended. It is no longer enough to call Rastas such as the Coptics 'false dreads'. Grenadian Rastafarians have given their answer to the attempt to call Rastas such as the Coptics 'false dreads'. Grenadian Rastafarians have given their answer to the attempt to exploit the mystical and spiritual reservoir of black people.

Grenadian Rastas identified with a force which wanted to change the old social order. With the positive assistance of the successful Cuban revolution, the Grenadian people were opening up the possibilities for a new politics in the English-speaking Caribbean. Along with Cuba, the Grenadian revolution was forming the embryo of a socialist Caribbean, a socialist Caribbean whose future was linked to a socialist American hemisphere.

Rastas in Grenada had joined with the oppressed peoples of the region to call for a new kind of Caribbean integration, beyond the failed experiments of island enclave economies. Starting in Jamaica, where the Rastas broke the petty prejudices between town and country, the Rastafari had assisted in breaking the big island/small island pettiness, giving notice that it would be part of the anti-colonial struggle in Cayenne, Guadeloupe and Martinique.

Reggae artists have already embarked on a programme of cultural change which seeks to release the full creative energies of the people. They have taken part in the struggle of the development of a *popular culture* as part of the struggle for full national independence.

It is apt to end with Cabral's call for a universal culture:

> "*In the framework of the conquest of national independence and in the perspective of developing the economic and social progress of the people, the objectives must be at least the following:* development of a popular culture *and of all positive indigenous cultural values;* development of a national culture *based upon the history and the achievements of the struggle itself; constant promotion of the* political and moral awareness of the people (of all social groups) as well as patriotism, *of the spirit of sacrifice and devotion to the cause of independence, of justice and progress; development of a technical, technological and scientific culture, compatible with the requirements for progress; development, on the basis of a critical assimilation of man's achivements in the domains of art, science, literature, etc., of a* universal culture *for perfect integration into the contemporary world, in the perspectives of its revolution; constant and generalised promotion of feelings of humanism, of solidarity, of respecct and disinterested devotion to human beings.*"[1]

This is the challenge of the Rastafari in the next epoch. Having survived fifty years of social and religious intolerance, discrimination and harassment, the Rastafari movement is poised between becoming a part of world history, contributing to a *universal culture,* and being a passing phenomenon of the 20th century.

Meanwhile the Rastaman vibration remains positive. In their own words, Rastaman vibration is positive:

> "*Rastaman vibration is positive, so positive in the man of the past, living in the present, stepping in the future. The mystic Rastaman is the same blackheart man, who after growing, gathering and learning has become the wise wonder of the whole wide world.*"[2]

FOOTNOTES

1. Amilcar Cabral, *Return To The Source,* Monthly Review Press, N.Y., 1973, p.55.
2. "Rastafari – The Coming of Black Power", *Daily News,* Jamaica, Sept. 14, 1980, p.9.